How to MARKET BOOKS

How to MARKET BOOKS

3rd edition

'The must read introductory guide to book marketing.'

Les Higgins,
Chief Operating Officer,
HarperCollins Publishers

Alison Baverstock

KOGAN PAGE

First published by Kogan Page Limited in 1990
Reprinted with revisions 1993
Second edition published 1997
Reprinted 1998
This edition published 2000
Reprinted 2003

120 Pentonville Road
London
N1 9JN
United Kingdom

22883 Quicksilver Drive
Sterling VA 20166-2012
USA

www.kogan-page.co.uk

British Library Cataloguing in Publication Data

A CIP record for this book is available from the British Library.

ISBN 0 7494 3105 9

Typeset by Jean Cussons Typesetting, Diss, Norfolk
Printed and bound in Great Britain by Clays Ltd, St Ives plc

Contents

Foreword

by *Alan Hill*
Formerly Managing Director, Heinemann Group of Publishers

This is a remarkable book. It was written for new entrants to publishing, but it could be read with great profit (and enjoyment) by all who work in publishing, in whatever capacity, from the Managing Director downwards. The title is in fact an understatement, for Alison Baverstock involves every stage of the publishing process in her discussion of 'Marketing'.

This breadth of view is especially valuable today, when the grouping of firms into big corporations, with resulting specialisation, denies new entrants the wide experience which many of my generation enjoyed. We worked in mainly small to middle-sized, independent, firms which encompassed all the publishing processes. I have therefore read Alison Baverstock's book in the light of direct personal experience of every aspect of the trade – from getting and publishing MSS to going out on the road to sell the finished product – and all this across a wide range of titles, from fiction and general to eductional books.

In the light of this experience, it is uncanny how accurately Alison Baverstock pin-points the sort of problems and opportunities, large and small, that I encountered over the years, together with many more that never came my way. Through extensive research she has concentrated into this one volume a range of detailed issues unequalled elsewhere.

It is equally impressive to read her sensible and practical advice on how to deal with this multifarious range of problems. Nothing is too small or too large for her agenda. Her judgements range from 'don't reverse text out; it is hard on the eyes' (page 108) to 'knowledge of export market seems to be an assured route to the top ... working overseas enables you to be the company's official face in what is often a large market and so gain confidence ... this brings maturity, while your colleagues back home have the chance to forget how young you are!' (page 32).

To appreciate the quality of this book, you need only turn to the opening paragraphs of Chapter 3 (page 57) for a characteristic sample.

The book is in fact a good 'read', quite apart from the value of its contents. In this respect it deserves to rank with Stanley Unwin's *The Truth About Publishing*, which was the 'locus classicus' of my generation. Unwin's book was first published in the 1920s, when the trade was far smaller, with only a fraction of today's £2 billion turnover and our current 20,000 workforce. It thereby catered for readers who were involved not only in the marketing, but the whole process from start to finish. Nevertheless, although the chapter on 'The Actual Selling' takes up only 15 per cent of the whole book, Unwin had the same emphasis as Baverstock, when in that chapter he declared 'Not until the book is produced does the chief work of publishing begin'.

Baverstock's book is based on the same priority, with the added dimension that, in today's far more highly developed and competitive book industry, marketing is not isolated but pervades the whole publishing process. This makes her book a text for those involved in all the other publishing functions, particularly as a refreshing basic realism is common to both authors. Thus, Unwin's assertion that 'A publisher cannot spend his time more profitably than in the company of booksellers' (page 162) is paralleled by Baverstock's 'Time (spent in book shops) is seldom wasted ... do at least acquire the habit of visiting book shops at regular intervals' (page 40). As with so much else in this book, this echoes something I always urged on my own staff. In fact I have learnt a great deal from this book, and my only regret is that it was not available many years earlier.

Additional foreword
by Bob Osborne
Managing Director, Heinemann Educational

When a book gets to its third edition, it has to be doing something right. This one, though, seems to me to be doing everything right. It has deservedly become the classic text for all involved in marketing in the book business.

What does it do that's right? It certainly covers all that you need to know for today's world in an accessible and practical fashion. It's full of imaginative ideas that you can put into action immediately. You'll see how to boost responses to mailings, unlock the potential of PR, and design campaigns that will energise and support the trade, educational or academic markets. And all the time the practicalities of production are painlessly addressed in a way that everyone can understand.

But what is particularly exciting about this new edition is its focus on the future. It takes an imaginative leap forward and looks at the whole world of Web marketing – a development that has the potential to completely transform our relationships with our customers. When Alan wrote his original foreword, he can have had only an inkling of what was to come in this area. But since Alan started a software publishing company immediately on his first 'retirement' in 1984 with the observation that 'you have to do something after breakfast', I know he would have been just as excited about and supportive of this aspect of the book as he was of the rest!

I still teach the in-house copywriting course to all our new publishing and marketing staff here at Reed Education. And I give everyone who comes on the course a copy of Alison's book. Perhaps more than anything, that says exactly how good a book I think it is.

Bob Osborne
Managing Director
Heinemann Educational

Acknowledgements

This is the third edition (fourth if you count a reprint with revisions in 1993) of a book designed to teach people how to market books and journals.

It was first started in 1989, as a marketing course handout. I kept writing and soon had a contents list and several chapters of a book, which Kogan Page promptly agreed to publish. I completed the manuscript four days before my daughter was born, and she has just had her ninth birthday.

My guiding principle has been to include everything I would like to have known when I started in the industry. My experience of the industry has been wide, but not exhaustive, so I have tried to set down a checklist of possible types of marketing activity that should be considered whatever the subject area of the list being promoted. Every chapter has been checked by those active in the area so hopefully we have missed nothing.

I am delighted this book continues to fill a need. Its updating has relied heavily on various friends and colleagues drummed into commenting on sections. I am particularly grateful to: Cathy Douglas, Dr Alex Gibson, Gill Cronin, June Lines, Bob Osborne and Alan Hill, who provided the introduction just before his death.

I would also like to thank: Wendy Allen; Veronica Angel; Florence Ascoli; Alberto Barraclough; Jacqui Bass; John Beale; Elaine Boorman; Susan Brent; Hugh Bulford; Rodney Burbeck; Jill Chapman; John Cheshire; Sheila Christie; Desmond Clarke; Dr Bill Crofts; Steve Bohme; Chris Chrystal; Mike Coleman; Tracey Cooke; John Davey; Roy Davey; John Davies; Simone Davies; John Downham; Margaret Drabble; Nancy Dull; David Dutton; Wendy Cope; Debbie Cox; Justine Crowe; James Ellor; Anne Fanning; Tim Farmiloe; Dr Frank Fishwick; Lindsay Fraser; Dave Golding; Leigh Goodman; Jo Henry; Jean Hindmarch; Caroline Hird; Steve Holland; Kerry Hood; Kelly Howe; Jo Howard-Brown; Robert Howells; Jeanette Hull; Matthew Huntley; John and Kate Hybert; Ian and Jan Jacobs; Liz James; Paula Johnson; Professor Emrys Jones;

Nicholas Jones; Louis Ingram; Irene Jordan; Louise Kaye; Barrie Kempthorne; Rob Langley; Clive Leatherdale; Tom Lee; Simon Littlewood; David Lindley; Tammy Livermore; Dot Lubianska; Finbarr McCabe; Sheila McGlassen; Miranda McKearney; Sally McKinnel; Alice Meadows; John Merriman; Peter and Jean Milford; Sue Miller; Roger Millington; Carol Monyios; Mary Lou Nash; Victoria Nash; Mary Nettlefold; Alice Noyes; Orna O'Brien; Pamela Oldfield; Chris Oliver; John Park; Dr James Parker; Dharm Patel; Janette Paterson; John Peacock; Jane Pembroke; Brian Perman; John Purefoy; Margaret Radbourne; Deborah Rea; Dr Kimberley Reynolds; Jennifer Rigby; Julian Rivers; Gerald Scott; Pippa Scoones; Allan Shanks; Barbara Singh; Alan Smith; Dag Smith; Clare Somerville; Jane Tatam; Ian Taylor; David Teale; Jonathan Tilston; Sara Tricker; Katherine Tozeland; Susan Turret; Mark Waite; John Walsh; David Walton; Andrew Welham; John Winkler; Mark Wray and Martin Wyn-Jones.

Finally thanks to Neil for managing the database and encouragement and patience throughout.

Introduction: Publishing in the New Millennium

Whether or not the new millennium has any real significance, it is a useful journalistic tool. It presents the opportunity for snapshot analysis; the isolation of a point in time from which we can look forwards and backwards. For me it marks 20 years in publishing.

I first entered the industry in 1980 after finishing my degree at St Andrews. And as I look back now, it seems to me that significant changes have taken place, most notably over the three years since I last produced an edition of this book.

Twenty years ago, much of publishing was still a cottage industry, characterised by individuals who ran eponymous publishing houses. My first job was as London rep for the academic list rental company IBIS and my clients were central London publishers. Each account had a card and around 200 cards sat in a box file on my desk.

One of the first things I did was to buy a copy of the London A–Z and plot the locations of these various firms. Had a large bomb hit the British Museum, most of them would have been wiped out. Today almost all of these once independent firms are now imprints within larger publishing organisations, and no more than 25 cards would be needed. For example, the Random House Group includes Secker & Warburg, Chatto & Windus, Vintage, Century, Ebury, Arrow, Cape and William Heinemann, all of which used to be separate companies.

The people have changed too. The individuals who ran their own houses loved to be different, and they were wonderfully good company. Helen Lefroy of Carcanet saw me in her own flat up several flights of stairs but rewarded me with a cooked breakfast. Marion Boyars dismissed my presentation on sticky labels as too commercial and grilled me about publishing. Once convinced I knew enough about the industry, she encouraged me to get a 'proper job'. When I eventually did get a job with Heinemann, one of my customers and henceforth competitors (Liz Newland, Publicity Director of Dent) rang me to congratulate me and assure me if I ever found myself in a tricky situation and didn't know what to do, I should call on her. And she really meant it. Alan Hill took the whole company hill-walking each Easter in the Lake District, long before the 'human resources' people had moved in to call it 'team-building'.

Today the key figures in the industry I knew then are dying off, and it's becoming commonplace to see in their obituaries that they were the last of the 'gentleman publisher' or 'the old school'. So what has changed?

The main change is one of consolidation of interests. Today five big firms dominate the UK publishing scene, and there are similar consolidations of interest in bookselling and wholesaling.

Terminology has changed too. 'Publishing' now needs to be taken in its broadest meaning, that of making public, rather than just referring to books. Each of the big publishing houses is in their own turn a subset of larger multimedia corporations which span television and film, video and theme parks; the entertainment dividends are spread as widely as possible.

The trend is to pursue commercial synergy: to develop a product that can simultaneously provide film, book, cartoon, T-shirt and merchandising opportunities, and which can be offered through retail outlets at the same time, world-wide. Opinions differ as to whether this leads to a bland culture as publishers fight over the latest 'soundbite' personality or juvenile sports star writing his autobiography, or whether we should rejoice that books are still chosen as a key medium of communication and that so much reading material is available in so many places at the same time.

The second major change is that British publishing is no longer UK-owned, or even dominated. Of the five biggest, Penguin and Hodder Headline are British owned, but Transworld and Random House both belong to Bertelsmann, and HarperCollins is part of the Murdoch empire. There are many influential international media groups operating former British companies (eg Holtzbrinck of Germany owns Macmillan, Dutch Elsevier owns Reed, French Hachette owns Orion). Judgements about what is being read in Britain may thus be made, or if not made, funded, outside the UK.

This is the result of a frenzied period of buying up which began in the 1980s, in an attempt firstly to profit from undervalued publishing companies and secondly to increase market share.

2

Publishing was left largely untroubled until the early 1980s; the city view was that book publishers were small, parochial and poorly managed. But then 'information' became the buzzword, value soared and books became hot property. Undercapitalised publishing houses were an attractive prospect to ambitious media groups, and the buying reached a frenzy at the end of 1980s when Jonathan Cape, Chatto & Windus and Associated Book Publishers were all bought by North American firms, and Rupert Murdoch's News International Group bought HarperCollins.

Since then further buying-up of smaller companies by larger ones has continued not because businesses are inefficient but because holding companies want greater market share, to remunerate share-holders and inflate the company price, whilst at the same time keeping overheads as low as possible. The search for companies to purchase has led to the same holding company owning several competing brands. For example, Pearson took over Simon and Schuster Educational to create the biggest educational publisher in the world and as a consequence now own several competing text-books. In personnel terms, today in publishing more employees are working for fewer organisations: 2 per cent of companies employ 62 per cent of the total workforce.

Does this matter? Britain no longer has an indigenous car-manufacturing industry either. It is out of date to lament the passing of a largely British-owned publishing industry?

The pessimistic view is that Britain is suffering a major cultural crisis. The writing of quality fiction is ignored by those funding the arts (curiously unlike independent poetry writing which does attract public support and sponsorship). There is a consequent loss of confi-dence amongst our writers. The argument continues that much of what does get published is predictable; the large corporations in the industry concentrating their efforts on looking for more of the same, and the industry's obsession with marketing means that too much type and packaging are masking what are in reality very ordinary products. Cultural pessimism has always affected disdain for the commercial. It continues to be the case that 80 per cent of the books in the bestseller lists never get any formal coverage in literary reviews sections.

As to the symbolic value of books to the national psyche, we seem to be on our own here; other countries who publish in English have a far more proactive approach to the maintenance of the literary community. Eire offers a lower rate of tax for artists, and includes writers in the definition of artists. Canada actively encourages writers from other countries to come and settle, and sees the maintenance (and subsidy) of a Canadian literature as a key element in keeping the national culture alive – and distinct from their immediate neighbour. New Zealand seems to feel the same. In Australia Peter Carey and Murray Bail are both published by university presses, supported by the state. British university presses seemingly take a completely different view of their responsibility. When asked about dropping poetry from their list, Keith Thomas, Chairman of OUP's finance committee, commented that: 'To ask OUP to continue this task is to invite it to subsidise creative writing' (*The Times*, 4 February 1999).

There are continual accusations in both the British and US press of slipping standards in British publishing. Spelling and grammar are full of inconsistencies; there are tales of academics being asked to deliver pre-edited manuscripts in return for an additional advance. All these things lead to badly produced books, which the reading public *do* notice. How long will it be before US funders insist that one edition must suit both markets and only pay for the process at one end (and given that the US market is five times the size of ours, guess which end it will be?).

Cultural pessimists complain that our national failure to see culture as a component of the welfare state, consistent with other aims such as social integration and participation, is a huge mistake. Soon all that will be left of our once thriving literary culture will be marketing, they moan, and Britain will be nothing more than a tourist attraction.

That's one view. On the other hand there is cause for great optimism in the industry. Never before has there been so much space devoted to selling books, and reading itself is a growing pursuit. Literary fiction is getting a much wider readership (eg Louis de Bernières, Vikram Seth and David Guterson are all on the bestseller lists). It is estimated that there are now more than 30,000 reading groups throughout Britain; in the US Oprah Winfrey's book slot recommends a book a month to an audience of 21 million. Literary prizes have given huge new emphasis to books and selling them through supermarkets presents them as an everyday staple commodity. Bookshops are in high street locations and are far more enjoyable places to visit than many other retail experiences (comfortable chairs and coffee available). So does it matter that choice is the same in every chain shop? Bestsellers can have a transforming effect on publishers' revenue and profitability, and allow them to take more risks.

As for the gentleman publisher, should his decline really be lamented? It may be true that, as one former publisher told me, 'literary merit, friendship and loyalty' have gone from large parts of publishing, but previously bookshops couldn't afford to be on the high street. By treating the book trade as just another form of retailing, and increasing the discounts, today they can be there. As for the traditional editorial nurturing offered by publishers, should the author have to rely on a third party to tease out the best book they have inside them?

Perhaps today writers get their nurturing elsewhere – membership of the Society of Authors is up and meetings are increasingly well attended. The role of friend to big authors seems to have shifted to literary agents, and certainly the wholesalers play a far more important part in shaping public taste than they did five years ago. In any case, the active pursuit of the 'special voice' is certainly not dead, and survives in independent companies such as Granta, Fourth Estate and Bloomsbury who are doing better than ever before.

The publishing industry is also opening up; getting into the industry doesn't seem to be so difficult these days. There are now 13 universities running under- and post-graduate courses in publishing and, provided you can fund yourself for an extra couple of terms, they have a very good record of finding you a job afterwards. To get into publishing today, you are far less likely to have to become a secretary first, or have a famous parent.

But still, as we reach the end of the century, there are a lot of people to be convinced of the merits of the book. Celine Dion, age 29 and one of the world's best selling singers, concluded a recent contribution to the 'Day in the Life' of column in the *Sunday Times* as follows:

> Sometimes I wake up and have potato chips in bed. Not plain, but barbecue or ketchup or whatever. Sometimes I read fashion magazines. I don't really read books: there's not enough space in my life. When I have an empty space in my brain, it's cool, it's OK. I don't want to fill it with anything.

Now there's a challenge for the new millennium!

Alison Baverstock
October 1999

1

How and Where Books are Sold

Until about five years ago, dealing with the retail trade was wonderfully simple for publishers. They had their own dedicated retail outlets (bookshops) that in the main sold only books. Even those that were shops within shops (eg the book department of major department stores) were run by booksellers rather than general retailers. Most booksellers did not want to retail anything else.

Although there were squabbles – most notably about the different terms available according to the number purchased and the delivery times publishers achieved, dealings for the most part were organised and timely; promotional and selling cycles were stuck to by all parties. And cooperation levels in the industry as a whole were high: the two trade organisations (The Publishers Association and The Booksellers Association) debated the issues raised and senior figures in the industry would give up their time to train their future competitors at Book House Training Centre.

Today books still sell through bookshops, but there is now a wide range of other outlets through which books are sold.

> Never before has so much square footage been devoted to promoting and selling books on the high streets.
>
> Jonathan Chowen, preface to BA Annual Report in 1997

For example books are sold in supermarkets, at garden centres and historic houses, through book displays in schools and colleges and in the workplace, through national newspapers offering direct sales for books featured or reviewed: indeed anywhere the paying public might possibly decide to buy a book.

The new selling outlets have meant publishers have been forced to change their working practices. Booksellers might be understanding if authors delivered late and the books were consequently delayed. Supermarkets are not. There was an standard-size dump-bin that publishers used to offer bookshops. Supermarkets want their own, designed to fit the various different specific layouts of their stores. In the case of garden centres or locations unused to stocking books at all, the shelving may have to be provided too.

How are most books sold?

Table 1.1   Market share in the book market

| | Volume | | Value | |
	1997	1998	1997	1998
Bookshops*	35	36	39	41
Book/stationery stores**	20	18	22	20
Supermarkets/chain stores***	12	12	7	8
Other retail#	11	10	9	8
Total retail	78	76	77	77
Book clubs	11	12	11	11
Other direct ##	7	8	9	9
Total non retail	18	20	20	20
Total other not stated	4	4	4	3
Total	100	100	100	100

*including large and small chain, independent, bargain and religious bookshops.
**eg W H Smith/Menzies, Sussex Stationers
***including Woolworths and the Early Learning Centre
#eg toy shops, department stores, service stations, gift shops, CTNs
##eg off the page, through school, via the workplace, via the Internet

Source: Books and the Consumer 1997–98, © Book Marketing Limited 1999

These figures show a significant increase in supermarket selling in recent years – estimated by Euromonitor as one per cent of total book market in 1994, and an interesting increase in book club sales, again estimated by Euromonitor as nine per cent of the market in 1994. (Source: Euromonitor's report *Books: The International Market*, August 1995.)

Table 1.2   The market for books in the UK by value 1990–97

(£ million, current retail selling price)	
1990	1997
1,517	2,745

Source: Euromonitor Consumer Europe 1998–99 from national statistics

The layout of the book world

The most remarkable trend in the book business in recent years has been the consolidation of interests. There are now five major publishers (Transworld, Hodder Headline, Random House, Penguin and HarperCollins); three major wholesalers (THE, Gardners and Bertrams) and three main bookselling chains (HMV including Dillons and Waterstones, W H Smith, and Borders UK, which includes Books Etc). The large multimedia groups to which the publishing houses belong have interests in magazines, films and television, and there are further crossovers, as the recent purchase of Hodder Headline by W H Smith revealed.

Some examples of the concentrations of interest

In 1998 the top five publishers of adult fiction accounted for 65 per cent of all books bought; the top ten publishers of children's paperback fiction for 80 per cent of sales (source: BML).

Although the overall number of bookshops has remained fairly constant for the past few years at around 3,300, and the number of publishers similarly so at around 3,000, there is now a huge disparity in size terms between the smallest and the largest organisations.

The effect of polarisation on smaller operators

Publishers

Small publishing companies are having to be more focused and to think longer term. The larger corporations can afford to make publishing decisions on the basis of vanity or prestige – signing up big names that will attract buyers – while smaller companies are having to take a longer term view by developing product that will last. A prime example of this trend is the publication of *Longitude* by

Fourth Estate; the way in which the book was singularly packaged and marketed has provided a long term sales phenomenon, that flatteringly has attracted imitation from much larger houses.

Sheila Boundsford of the Independent Publishers Guild commented that although their membership stays around the 340 mark, each year new ones join and larger firms get bought up and so cease to qualify as members. She sees everyone being careful, but indications of how business is going, like attendance figures at their annual conference, look good (people don't go to conferences when their businesses are doomed). She commented that members are increasingly looking outside the traditional trade for business. Small publishers can benefit from offering direct sales through Web sites, direct mail and other deals with membership/subscription lists, reader offers, and so on. The growth in direct sales of books, which have increased significantly ahead of the retail sector in recent years, particularly in terms of the volume purchased, can be seen as part of this trend (source: BML).

For the small publisher the future is likely to be niche publishing, for precise market areas that the publisher understands and can develop a relationship with.

Booksellers

According to figures provided by Book Track,[1] today independent bookshops have around nine per cent of the market as opposed to 38 per cent of the major chains and multiples. They also estimate supermarkets and mixed multi-stores as having around 9 per cent of the market.

The hobbyist bookseller has probably gone forever; as has the notion that buying a bookshop is a suitable occupation for a semi-retired gentleman. To succeed in bookselling today, you have to like retailing and be able to spot new market(ing) opportunities. Independent, non-chain booksellers must reinforce links with their local communities in order to survive. This is particularly pertinent with smaller chains like Ottakars targeting towns where there is an independent bookshop but no branch of a larger chain.

There is certainly evidence that booksellers are being much more efficient in their buying: certainly returns over the period have fallen dramatically (as a percentage of net sales, returns on consumer books fell from 20.1 per cent in 1995 to 11.6 per cent in 1997).

Authors

Authors have not benefited from the polarisation of interests. It is largely they who fund the discounting of books that goes on in chain stores. Almost all publishing contracts include a high discount clause, and this is exploited to the author's disadvantage when publishers and booksellers want to discount titles, despite the fact that the publishers at the same time benefit from lower per-unit production and distribution costs. The argument that higher sales compensate for lower royalties does not always work.

Authors complain to the Society of Authors of feeling bewildered, that they lack information on who is now publishing them and that they have lost personal contact with those who commissioned the book: patchy or inadequate editing is a common complaint. Instead of nurturing authors to write, larger houses frequently find it more convenient to turn big names such as media or sporting stars into authors, supplying the services of a ghost writer if necessary.

Interestingly, some would-be authors have looked outside traditional publishing for a more personal service. For example, Amo Libros offers an editing service for manuscripts and then will assist authors through publicity and promotion of the finished product. From a standing start three years ago, the company now produces 30 titles a year. Vanity publishing has always been an option, but Jane Tatam of Amo Libros claims that not all those she helps have failed to find a commercial publisher: many are seeking more control, or just more information, about how their brain child is presented to the wider world. Others see niche marketing opportunities (eg lecturing or training) which a published book would enhance, and that they could profit from, without sharing the proceeds with a commercial publisher.

The Net Book Agreement (NBA)

Until 1995 the Net Book Agreement underpinned the book trade in the UK, offering retail price maintenance on the majority of titles published. This meant that a net book could not be sold to the public at a price lower than that fixed by its publisher, and it was up to the publisher to decide which titles were net and which non-net. So, unlike almost every other type of retailing, it was the producer rather than the retailer who fixed the price of the goods being sold and incentives to purchase, such as free offers, were not allowed on net books.

There was extensive debate about how abolishing the agreement would affect the market. As market conditions have altered in so many ways since its demise (most notably with the development of the Internet and the arrival of Borders), it is impossible to make sensible comment on the real effect of its going.

In general though, the demise of the agreement has greatly strengthened the hand of the larger publishers at the expense of smaller ones, the chains at the expense of independent bookshops, and the wholesalers have grown hugely.

The proportion of the population buying books has not increased since the NBA went; those people who do buy are spending more. The main reason for their greater spending has been an increase in book prices. Most books are still bought by the highest income groups. *The Family Expenditure Survey* (The Stationery Office, November 1998) has shown that neither the availability of discounts nor the wider exposure of books has led to any expansion of the book-buying public, particularly among those not in the top income bracket. The NBA demise has been relegated to a newsflash that temporarily highlighted books and caused a rush into bookshops just after it went. Publishers don't want to talk about it any more; booksellers have other things to worry about.

Who are the main players in the book trade?

The Booksellers Association is the professional organisation for the trade; membership spans all involved in selling books, from chains and independent outlets to some supermarkets. Each year it publishes a list of members (selectable by type of business and available on sticky labels for mailing), holds a conference and hosts several special interest groups (for example there is a Library Suppliers Group and a School Suppliers Group).

As a rough guide to the trade there are several major groups to point out.

Large bookselling chains

The large bookselling chains, such as Dillons, Waterstones, W H Smith (including John Menzies), Ottakars, Books Etc, Borders, Blackwells, Hatchards (part of HMV Media Group) and Easons (in Ireland and Northern Ireland) are enormously important within the book trade. Large discounts can be demanded by them in return for extensive stocking.

The procedures for selling into these chains vary, but certain trends are discernible across the industry.

For example, take W H Smith. Twenty years ago Smith's was probably the main bookshop outlet for browsers as well as more popular purchases, with branches in every high street. Today with the market segmented and more sophisticated they have discovered that what their customers want is popular bestsellers rather than wide range in library-type depth, a service that is offered by Waterstones and Dillons. Books in W H Smith now form part of the wider Entertainment and Interests group, and compete for retail space with videos and music. If new stock lines are added it is usually on the basis of 'one in, one out' – one line removed for every one added.

Smith's now does almost all of its buying centrally; only stock of very local interest is bought at the discretion of the local manager. Publishers take covers and book information to regular presentations to the buying team at the head office in Swindon and stock is delivered there before being despatched to the various locations nationwide. This offers the best possible opportunity for negotiation of discounts.

Covers are crucial to Smith's buying decisions; it's not unknown for them to request a cover alteration before they agree to take a particular title. They are also interested in author reputation, track record of previous title(s) and likely proof of demand. Acceptance of all display material is charged for and there is talk of there being a charge for reps to present forthcoming titles to Smith's. Electronic point of sale (EPOS) at tills dictates most of the reorders: bar codes on purchased titles are read by the computer, stock levels altered and the re-stocking order automatically generated, regardless of local market peculiarities.

Similar developments can be seen in the buying patterns of all the bookselling chains today: increased central control, reduced autonomy for individual local managers.

Key independent booksellers

In addition to the bookselling chains there are a number of key independent booksellers with extensive markets, both in this country and overseas. Most have diversified and now sell a range of stationery (higher profit margins and little space needed), audiotapes and CDs. Diversification is becoming more important as other markets such as library supply become so uncertain.

Many are seeking to database market – build up a list of individuals or organisations (eg small libraries and businesses) for whom dealing with a reliable and friendly third party is an attractive way to buy. Many shops find direct selling makes a substantial contribution to their profits. They, like other independents, have diversified, selling music, artists' materials and stationery.

Particularly important for academic publishers are the bookshops linked to the country's 111 universities and 60 other colleges of higher education. Some of these are owned by bookselling chains, such as Blackwells or John Smith and Sons; others are strong independent businesses such as James Thin. All rely on offering their customers excellent service – the ability to order esoteric titles from any publisher on demand and a 'bookish' atmosphere that harbours loyalty.

Book wholesalers

Wholesalers sell to retailers who sell books. The theory is that they secure large discounts from publishers in return for buying correspondingly large quantities, and sell on to other bookshops at a lesser discount. The range that they carry, although wide (Bertrams carry 160,000 different stock lines from over 1,000 publishers; a medium-sized independent bookshop would probably carry around 20,000), is not completely comprehensive: individual orders for specific titles still have to be sourced from the appropriate publisher or ordered specially by the wholesaler, on the bookshop's behalf.

Ordering stock in this way offers booksellers the chance to amalgamate their requirements from different publishers and save on the administrative hassle of monitoring lots of different orders sent to different addresses. The majority of the wholesalers' accounts are with small to medium-sized independent bookshops (Bertrams estimated 55 per cent of their business is made up in this way) and most bookshops deal with at least two wholesalers. Larger bookshops and the multiples tend to deal, for the most part, directly with publishers rather than wholesalers, as they secure better terms on the wide variety of titles they stock. However, most use wholesalers for customer orders and urgent 'top up' orders.

Wholesalers have invested heavily in systems and distribution in recent years. What they increasingly offer the vulnerable independent bookseller is a 'mother ship' – friendly support backed up by computer links and very fast response times. Speed of servicing is very important. Some publishers offer a 'Christmas hotline' for ordering stock but for the rest of the year three to four days is usual with 7 to 10 more common. By comparison, the largest wholesalers offer a 24-hour service every working day with free delivery provided the minimum order quantity is reached (usually £100 in retail value). This means that the booksellers can use the wholesaler as an extended stock room, saving on storage and cash committed.

The relationship between publishers and wholesalers is full of anomalies. Most publishers are targeting the vast majority of their promotional efforts at booksellers and then competing with their principal accounts (the large wholesalers) for fulfilment of the business. They circulate promotional materials to all the wholesalers, who then pass it on to their customers; but as most bookshops deal with more than one wholesaler, duplication is inevitable. Many publishers complain about the huge power of the wholesalers, but it was their reluctance to fulfil very small orders from independent bookshops that forced so many to rely on wholesalers instead.

Wholesalers now employ their own rep forces to call on bookshops (at a time when most publishers are cutting down on the number of calls made); they stage their own promotions and produce their own catalogues. Their publishing judgement is becoming increasingly important too.

Because wholesalers are experts at judging what will and will not sell they are having an increasingly large impact on what does and does not get published. This has been the case with key accounts for some time (W H Smith's buying decision can make a huge difference to a book's chances of success) but with wholesalers too shaping publishing decisions, publishers are increasingly finding that the imposition of market forces on what they produce and how they go about it is coming from *outside* the organisation.

An undeniable trend over the last few years has been the increasing competitiveness of the wholesale market. Ten years ago wholesalers tended to specialise in the supply of different kinds of titles to specific kinds of institution (hardback or paperback; or supply to schools or colleges). Today economic pressures mean they are competing on every front. One of the consequences of electronic point of sale has undeniably been that orders to wholesalers tend to have become smaller. Whilst it is convenient to bookshops it means the wholesalers face higher transport costs and less predictable cashflow.

The increase in technology has prompted wholesalers to invest huge amounts of money in providing comprehensive, computer stock management solutions for bookshops. These low-priced solutions offer significant cost-savings in the way of increased discount, free order lines and generally much greater control over operating their accounts with suppliers.

Internet solutions are now a standard requirement for bookshops and existing computer systems have been upgraded to incorporate Internet links. Publishers are increasingly using their Web site as an information provider, occasionally allowing order placing and chasing.

As well as the very large firms of Bertrams (now merged with Cypher library supplier), Gardners (still independent) and THE (owned by Menzies), there are smaller, regional wholesalers that serve particular areas of the country, and these have found themselves under increasing financial pressure with the need to invest as well as improve efficiency. There are also smaller wholesalers who supply to particular kinds of outlet, the largest being STL who supply religious titles; other examples include suppliers of gay titles or political pamphlets to specialist-interest bookshops or sheet music to record shops. *(The Booksellers Association publishes a list of book wholesalers.)*

Wholesalers have been one of the main beneficiaries of market uncertainty after the demise of the Net Book Agreement. Both Gardners and Bertrams have reported extraordinary growth in the past few years. For example, Bertrams' sales in 1998 were double what they were in 1995 (the year the agreement collapsed), way ahead of the growth of the market as a whole; from 1997 to 1998 Bertrams' sales grew by 28 per cent.

Library suppliers

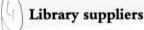

Library suppliers provide the local authority library services in this country with books. Some also supply academic libraries and export titles.

Until the collapse of the NBA this was a highly competitive and shrinking market, but still one that was still relatively stable. In return for a library licence (which the library or appropriate authority applied for), the nominated supplier could provide books at a discount of up to 10 per cent. What amounted to more discount was offered in the form of 'service', which covered a broad range of activities. For example, the suppliers organised approvals collections of books for librarians to examine; handled electronic data to save librarians re-keying the same information; presented invoices in a way the libraries' accounting structures could handle, and 'serviced' titles before they were delivered. The latter could include covering the book, sticking in the date-stamping sheet and making up catalogue cards – the library authority would provide some of the materials, the supplier the labour.

The collapse of NBA meant that there were no longer any set limits on the discount available; market forces apply. The library authority buyers (the usual term is Acquisitions Officer or Bibliographical Services Officer) were not used to receiving large discounts and not unreasonably asked for more, on the basis that if prices were being discounted in the high street there was no reason for libraries to pay the full-list price. At the same time it became increasingly common to put supply out to tender: firstly to comply with EU regulations, secondly as part of the local authority's search for 'best value' – their accountability for public money.

Today this is a very volatile market. Before the collapse of the NBA, library authorities tended to use several suppliers; now increasingly they are consolidating their requirements and reducing the number they deal with, thereby securing the best possible discount as suppliers change their discount structure to reflect turnover. In some cases 'framework tenders' are put together where customers agree to split their requirements between several nominated suppliers on the basis of the latter's expertise and service.

This is a dangerous position for the suppliers who stand to win or lose all on each account. Firms that do lose turnover may try offering their clients more discount to win business back, and their competitors may respond with further cuts. The long-term effects of this trend are to destabilise the market, raise the expectations of customers of the kinds of discount they can expect to receive while rendering firms less able to deliver the service they expect. Firms that are forced to operate at unsustainable profit margins risk going out of business.

A further area of difficulty has been the reorganisation of local government with the creation of new urban centres of responsibility (eg Southampton and Portsmouth are now independent unitary authorities rather than being subject to Hampshire County Council) as well as the dividing up of old county councils into smaller, self-funding units. Each of these new areas of responsibility has its own budget and there are two main consequences for book publishers.

Firstly, book purchase is not 'ring fenced'. Money for books comes out of the 'materials fund', a large and visible target for cost reductions – it is easier to achieve lower operating costs by cutting the book fund than by closing a library or cutting back on staff.

The second is that libraries have less money to spend. Dividing into smaller administrative units increases the running costs whilst reducing the size of the eventual order. For example, if Portsmouth, Southampton and other parts of Hampshire are ordering separately, administrative cover for each order must be provided, whilst at the same time the larger bulk discount their combined total might have generated is lost. Fewer books overall get bought as a direct result. How this impacts on the type of books actually purchased is interesting. The publishers of key specialised titles relevant to the library market (often small companies) arguably benefit, as they are able to target more decision makers in different authorities. It is likely to be the size of the general bulk stock order that gets cut back. All involved in this market have to invest in extra staff to handle increased documentation and administration.

An answer to this has been the development of buying consortia to purchase bulk supplies (books are just one commodity; stationery, housekeeping supplies and so on also feature) at a preferential prices. For example, several counties in the South and Midlands belong to the Central Buying Consortium, which by offering the various suppliers it deals with a certain level of business can ensure its members get maximum value for money for their budget.

A problem for the future is the potential entry of wholesalers into library supply. Publishers give wholesalers bigger discounts than they give to library suppliers (unlike in the US where there is legislation preventing different terms of supply) and wholesalers could use that extra discount to undercut library suppliers. This is not happening at present – the range of servicing required by librarians has up to now proved too costly to draw them into the market – but the recent merger of wholesaler Bertrams and library supplier Cypher drew attention to wholesalers' interest in this market.

The future is uncertain. If library budgets stand still and publishers' prices rise further, there will be additional squeezing in the market. On the other hand the supply chain could change, as intellectual property is delivered through new media such as the Internet. This will have an impact on the margins of the business if not the discounts.

The large library suppliers are all in the Midlands and further north. Many are run from warehouses where librarians can choose the titles they want off the shelves. *(A list of library suppliers can be obtained from the Booksellers Association.)*

5 School suppliers

School suppliers sell directly to schools. This too is a difficult market. The margins on school textbooks have always been very tight, with profits only to be made by selling class sets. In recent years the purchase of textbooks has been very under-funded in schools and the class set largely redefined to mean 'one between two' (see Chapter 13, Section iii).

Since the change of government in 1997, however, new money has become available to support improved literacy in schools, and most of the funding has been used for the purchase of books in primary schools. This has led to the market opening up.

The new governmental funding of books has tempted many smaller independent bookshops into offering school supply (the BA lists 885 such firms). Such operations tend however, to be interested for the most part in mainstream single-copy sales (eg a selection of readers for five- to seven-year-olds from a variety of publishers) on which there are greater profit margins. The proceeds can contribute greatly to the overheads of running a retail outlet.

Educational suppliers offering mainly textbooks have found life difficult in the past few years. Whereas fifteen years ago books made up 15–20 per cent of their turnover, text book sales are now of much lower importance. Today such firms see themselves as being in the business of making life easier for their clients rather than being purely in the business of book supply. Most produce a substantial annual catalogue listing a wide variety of different items in stock. This means schools can order all they need – from blackboards and clocks to stationery and climbing frames (and maybe some books and educational software) – from one central delivery point with one invoice.

Other school suppliers have chosen to specialise in books. For example, Richard Heath of Heath Educational has aimed to fill the advice gap left by the under-funding of teachers' centres in recent years, which can no longer afford to stock inspection titles for teachers to look at. He runs a showroom where copies of every school title are kept for teachers to view (40,000 in total) and offers advice in selecting the course that will best meet schools' needs. This means that teachers can view materials alongside each other and make proper comparisons, and the time taken up sending for sample copies, inspection and evaluation packs is saved. The teachers gain objective and free advice on what to buy.

Along the same lines, Books for Students (BFS) have found that putting together packs of books for specific curriculum or special needs solutions can offer objective guidance, save the teachers time and so attract many purchasers. For example, they put together a reading resource pack of books likely to appeal to boys which drew a great deal of interest. Their stocklists for school bookshops are a time-saving method of ensuring a balanced stock, likely to appeal to specific ages, without school librarians having to wade through individual publishers' catalogues.

Competition for all school suppliers has also increasingly come from publishers soliciting orders directly from schools, some of which have been financially empowered by receiving funding directly from the relevant local education authority. Some local authorities have formed direct book purchasing organisations which can function as book suppliers and advisory services.

Once clear areas of business are now blurring. Today there are several firms who are involved in both library and school supply. In addition, there are a number of more hybrid organisations that organise other marketing initiatives, thereby revealing important trends in the book business. For example school book fairs have burgeoned in recent years.

School book fairs

Selling books to children at the end of the school day can be very profitable, with purchases prompted by 'pester power', weary parents and a desire to support the schools' fund-raising efforts at the same time.

Books and display cabinets are delivered to schools, and then the set-up, policing and money-taking are handled by parents and teachers (so no staffing requirements). The schools are paid a commission on sales in free books rather than cash, which costs the organiser substantially less than a monetary transaction would.

School book fairs are also one of the few opportunities that children get to reveal their own purchasing preferences, and jacket and blurb designs for this market have to be taken into account. For example, book fairs have shown that children love to buy horror and science fiction, categories that adults buying for children are less comfortable with.

Also significant are the many bookshops run in schools. Most schools in Britain have some sort of bookselling activity in the course of a year and there are at least 7,000 school bookshops, mainly in primary schools. These are often serviced by school suppliers who run sticker-based savings schemes for children to save up for the titles they want.

All these initiatives strive to make access to books a permanent feature in schools: a huge service to publishers.

(A list of school suppliers can be obtained from the BA.)

Book clubs

For many mass market publishers, book clubs are the second most important source of sales after W H Smith. Discounts demanded by the clubs can be heavy, often as high as 70 per cent, which reduces the overall profit margin on a title. But if the deal is secured early and the club's requirements can be added to the initial print run, it makes the economics of printing much better. It is the firm's rights manager or director who negotiates and secures book club deals.

The book club market is large in the UK, around 12 per cent by volume and 11 per cent by value of book sales. Roughly one in five adults belongs to a club, and membership is highest in the 15–24 age group and higher socio-economic groups. A few years ago discussion was rife in the book trade as to the effect book clubs had on bookshop trade, the initial assumption being that copies bought from book clubs were sales lost to bookshops. Today the benefits of book clubs to the book trade are more widely seen. They promote books, both generally as something worth owning and specifically the merits of individual titles. They introduce many authors to a wider public and book club promotion material leads to additional bookshop sales.

Bargain bookshops

At first bargain bookshops sold largely remaindered stock and imports.

Remaindering involves selling off unsold stock to specialised remainder bookshops at a heavy discount. No royalty is paid to authors on what is sold; instead they receive a percentage of the total price achieved by the sale. Authors should always be alerted to the fact that their book is to be remaindered – many prefer to buy the stock themselves, perhaps for use at speaking engagements and so on.

'Imports' consist largely of stock brought into the UK from overseas, produced initially for a different market.

Habitual book buyers will buy from a wide variety of outlets, but cut-price bookshops attract customers who do not frequent traditional book trade outlets. Some publishers have taken advantage of this and produce books specially for them. The product has to be *perfect* for the market – these are impulse buyers – but for the right product (usually hardback with an attractive jacket), at the right price (usually around £4.99), the rewards can be enormous. Interestingly publishers involved in this area claim that producing a special version of a 'trade' title for the bargain bookshops has no noticeable effect on bookshop sales, and can produce substantial sales (200,000 plus) in its own right.

Sales through 'non traditional' outlets

Sales that are not made through bookshops, but through the wide – and fast expanding – range of other locations such as garage forecourts, motorway service stations, leisure centres, garden centres, hospitals and historic houses and through direct selling operations are becoming increasingly important to the publishing industry.

Today most of the books (and associated merchandise) that get sold through these outlets go through **merchandising wholesalers** who buy huge quantities of books, and then set up and service displays. The service they provide is not only the mechanics of display (most of the outlets they deal with have no experience of dealing with books and lack facilities for presenting them) but title selection. This is particularly important when many of the venues are visited by specialists and the selection of titles must reflect their level of expertise (for example titles stocked by garden centres or historic houses must be appropriate to the likely level of knowledge of the customers).

Most of the wholesalers involved deal with other compatible items (toys, stationery and so on) not just books. A large amount of what they buy is top title paperback or illustrated non-fiction. They aim to sell 100 per cent of everything they buy (so 90 per cent plus is bought on a firm sale basis); 'printing to sell' means they keep the prices as low as possible (it is rare to sell anything over £10). All are convinced that there is an enormous amount of untapped potential in what is an entirely separate market from the traditional book trade. This is important for publishers as it means their retail sale through bookshops is unaffected. What is more, because (unlike the bookshop market) this is not a particularly time-sensitive market, extended mileage can be got out of material nearing the end of its useful life in bookshops. This is also a market that is expanding very fast: there are about 15 or 20 new garden centres starting to take books for the first time every year. Most purchases made through garden centres are 'self purchases' (bought for the buyers themselves), with paperbacks more likely to sell than hardbacks.

It has taken time to persuade publishers that by dramatically reducing the cover price and selling to wholesalers they stand to make much more money. But producing a book for £3 and selling it to a wholesaler for £4, instead of £10 to the traditional trade, can be very profitable if they then take 50,000 copies on firm sale basis. Publishers often sell to these markets at run on printing cost rather than the full cost of print plus editorial, sales and marketing overheads, but as Ivor Asquith, Managing Director of OUP's academic division (includes dictionaries and trade reference) commented:

> If all your sales are incremental, your profits are excremental.
>
> Quoted in *The Author*, Spring 1988

'Shopping at work' is similarly an extremely fast expanding area. A set of samples is delivered to companies for examination by staff during the week, they are examined by all staff (perhaps in Reception or in the staff rest room), orders collected and a commission paid to the person who organised the promotion (it doesn't matter who does the organising but it has to be someone pro-book). This is proving a very popular method of shopping because it is convenient; most of the books bought are purchased as presents by working women who thereby avoid a trip to the shops on Saturday afternoons. Party plan shopping works on very similar lines.

Most wholesalers want branded products (some publishers' logos carry huge weight), representing quality and value to the market. But the monopolistic nature of supply (there is no other source for certain authors other than the publisher) and the enormous scale of some of the deals on offer has now tempted wholesalers to do the publishing themselves, in particular for illustrated non-fiction. Paragon only produced their first books in March 1994 and are now producing 500 titles a year.

Most of the major publishers now have teams of people exploring the potential for these sales, promotions and other related non-traditional activities. Some firms have set up a direct sales force to explore the market further. It is worth pointing out that the people who fill these jobs usually have a background in fast moving consumer goods or advertising sales rather than publishing. *(A list of firms involved in this area can be obtained from the BA.)*

Selling via the Internet

The cyberspace people are becoming more like booksellers and the bricks and mortar people are becoming more electronic. The gap is going to narrow.

Tim Godfray, Chief Executive of BA in *The Times*, 9 June 1999

See Chapter 7 on selling via the Internet.

What kind of information book buyers like to receive

'Buyer' is the job title for the person selecting stock for shops and wholesale outlets. Remember that book buyers are pro-book. It is their responsibility to select and order titles, and so they are actively looking for information that will justify their decision to choose yours. They receive thousands of pieces of information each week, so make yours enjoyable to read; there should be enough space for the key points to stand out, and enough of a different point of view to make them memorable! You must give them:[2]

- **Brief summary of the book.** Provide a short description of the relevant features of the book. For a novel a short synopsis; for non-fiction a list of contents plus editorial type copy on the differences between this new title and the countless other similar titles already available and selling.
- **Promotional details.** A breakdown of the media spend, if any, is always useful. Precise details are required. It is not sufficient to say 'ads in the *Daily Mail* and *Express*'. Such statements will largely be ignored. Instead it should read 'half page ads in the first half of the *Daily Mail* and *Express* during the week of publication'. Serialisation is also important (which publication and over how many weeks).
- **Selling features.** Factual reasons why this title can be expected to sell in greater quantity than all other similar titles. This can include relevant details on the author, the topicality of the subject, a particularly competitive price, media interest (and why) and so on. Information must be accurate and truthful. It is reasonable to say 'submitted for the BA Christmas catalogue' but not 'included' in the BA Christmas catalogue' before the committee has even sat. (We are on the committee so we know.)

- **Quirks.** Interesting extra information which can provide a feel for the book. This could be unusual facts which are featured, additional information about the author, details about the design or cover. In fact anything which will serve to make the title memorable and differentiate it from all the others that have been submitted that month.
- **User-friendly style.** Information should be light and easy to read; that way it much more likely to be absorbed.

Discounts to the book trade

Discounts are a complicated subject. Publishers don't want to give away more than they have to; wholesalers and bookshops hope for as much as possible: both sides want to ensure their long-term profitability and survival. There are average standard discounts: 36–40 per cent on hardback and 40 per cent on paperback trade titles; 25–30 per cent on academic titles; 17.5 per cent on school titles. It is worth looking in closer detail at the basis on which discounts are decided upon.

1. **Discount as part of a complicated matrix of promotional support.** Key titles are negotiated into bookshops under complicated promotional agreements. These will include the terms under which stock is delivered (firm sale or sale or return[3]); is the title to be merchandised (supported by related branded goods); will there be a window display; point of sale; what position will stock occupy in the shop (where and for how long); will there be a related author event? There is increasing use of promotional incentives in bookshops, for example BOGOF (buy one get one free) deals or 'three for the price of two offers' (which can be very successful for authors with a long backlist).

    Publishers supply back-up promotion material for their titles in the hope that it will be used to attract attention and generate more sales, for example dump bins, posters or materials for a window display. Some either charge for accepting these or ask for extra discount. The bookshop chains (often referred to as 'multiples') now mount their own promotions; they produce catalogues and carry out mailings. The opportunity to appear as entries in such catalogues are sold, at a premium, to publishers who wish to participate, in return for guaranteeing a certain level of stock (this effectively amounts to more discount).

These promotional deals must be negotiated into bookshops title by title. It is worth pointing out, however, that the buying power of the main book chains means that even if titles have been negotiated in under such precise arrangements, if they do not sell then the stores can in practice insist that they are returned before further stock is supplied by the same house.

2. **A great volume of business.** It is obviously possible to offer a greater discount to a wholesaler who takes 10,000 copies of new titles than to the owner of a small bookshop who agrees to take half a dozen. The same argument can be applied to specific support for a single title.

3. **Consistent support for a house's new publishing.** All publishing houses are looking for 'front list support' from those they sell to. This means retailers ordering the books of new authors whose titles have no track record of sales. Any bookshop knows it can sell a certain number of Wilbur Smith, but will it back a new and unknown author from the same stable, who may become a household name in a few years? If bookshops consistently back the publisher, they are often rewarded with extra discount.

4. **Stocking a wide range of the publisher's titles.**

5. **Stocking on terms that are more beneficial to the publisher.** It is better for the publisher's cash flow if a bookseller or wholesaler buys titles on 'firm' sale, as opposed to 'sale or return', and there may be corresponding rewards.

6. **Supplying a particular market or fulfilling a particular function.** If a bookseller is offering to reach a specific market, unattainable elsewhere, extra discount may result. For example, when launched, *The Good Book Guide* was able to demand large discounts on the grounds that it was reaching (largely overseas) markets not traditionally served by the book trade. Direct marketing operations selling business books to MBA students who do not use the retail trade can similarly demand very high discounts.

So what kinds of discount can the large firms secure? In general, paperback discounts will be higher than hardback. For paperbacks discounts of 50 per cent for retail and 62.5 per cent for wholesale are not uncommon. For hardbacks discounts can go up to 50 per cent.

Dealings between publishing house and book trade

The role of the rep

Larger publishers still present information to bookshops via a team of representatives, usually reporting to a sales or marketing manager. In recent years the number of reps actually in the field has been falling, and many of those who do still visit bookshops may spend time merchandising rather than discussing the merits of individual titles.

Today there are many more office-based staff; key accounts managers, marketing and administration staff who liaise with the head offices of retail outlets and negotiate promotional and merchandising schemes. Many of these staff can be office-based.

This is having a knock-on effect on the kind of people who take a repping job and their motivation. With more central control of buying from the chain's head office, and less ability of the individual rep to shape the buying patterns, the 'professional rep' in publishing is becoming less common. Today they tend to be younger and their turn-over fast; many move out of the industry rather than trying to work their way upwards. On the other hand, those who do succeed in negotiating on the company's behalf 'at the hard end of the business', may move easily into management positions in-house.

Organising a representative force

If bookshop sales are vital to the success of your publishing house's list it follows that fully briefing the reps who sell to the trade for you is equally important.

In general, looking after the reps will be the responsibility of the sales manager, who liaises with them on a day-to-day basis. It is usually the marketing department that produces the information that all parties involved in selling the firm's products need: advance notices, catalogues, brochures and individual title flyers.

As they are in daily contact with the market the reps are in a good position to pick up market trends, advise on the likely acceptability of new titles and anticipate publishing opportunities. Consult them and make them feel their opinion is valued. It is a cliché that they are the eyes and ears of your company, but it is true.

What does it cost to run a rep? The basic answer is that it is not cheap. Providing and servicing a car, voice-mail, mobile phone and laptop computer, health and holiday cover and other extras mean that the total package probably costs your company more than double what the rep actually earns. It follows that you should ensure they are able to sell effectively. (An additional perk to the rep is the income generated from disposing of sample copies: they generally get 50 per cent of the retail value within three months of publication; 33 per cent thereafter.)

All reps seem to complain about the amount of paperwork with which they are expected to cope. In general, the sales manager expects itineraries for their five to six calls a day plus details of the orders they secure. Sales managers regularly accompany their reps; good sales managers usually spend about half their time in the field. Some managers alleviate this requirement to be out of the office by appointing regional managers who look after teams of reps.

If you can arrange it, a day spent travelling with a rep can be very worthwhile. Not only will you see the buyer's reaction to your pet projects at first hand, you will also benefit from hearing the rep pass on, in a nutshell, the main selling points. Some firms use freelance reps if they cannot afford full-time staff. They are generally remunerated by commission, probably 10–12.5 per cent of invoice value (ie less discount; they are not paid commission on the full retail price). Freelance reps can also be helpful in reaching specific market segments. For example, mothers with young children who need to be free during the school holidays have been used extensively in selling to primary schools, receiving in return a combination of salary and commission.

In between employing individual freelance reps and taking on full-time staff stands the option of appointing an agency to handle your representation to the trade. This is frequently taken up by smaller publishers, who either join forces under a particular agency or appoint a publishing firm larger than themselves to visit the trade on their behalf.

The key requirement when considering who to team up with is that the various lists to be sold together should be complementary rather than in direct competition. Other factors should also be considered:

- How many reps will be used to promote your books, and how often will they visit your key accounts?
- How much contact will you have with them? Will you have the chance to brief them at sales conferences or other meetings? Will you see copies of their orders and sales reports?
- How many other titles do they carry? In what order do they show them to the buyer? Beware of being 'last out of the bag'.

- Do they visit all relevant bookshops, wholesalers and library suppliers?
- How will they be paid? Will your firm have to pay commission on sales not generated by them but from shops they visit? How quickly does commission have to be paid?
- If the arrangement does not work out, what is the notice period for ending it?

How a rep sells to bookshops

Reps make appointments to see buyers in bookshops; large shops will have a buyer for each department. The rep can expect each appointment to last around 30–45 minutes, and this fits well with the attention span on both sides. The appointment will frequently start with the rep being asked to sign forms that permit the return of previous titles that have not sold. Orders are increasingly taken on the rep's lap top computer. Books are usually sent out as 'firm' orders, on 'see safe' or 'sale or return' conditions.

The rep will arrive armed with a folder containing advance notices and jackets for the titles currently being subscribed: usually two months' worth at a time, three to six months ahead of publication. Good reps will prepare themselves and know the main selling points of all the titles they are trying to subscribe, as well as how they compare with the competition. Time is limited, and the rep will not waste it on pushing books the buyer immediately expresses no interest in. They will also know which titles currently being subscribed are inapplicable, for example engineering titles in the bookshop serving a university where the subject is not taught. I was told by the director of a major bookshop that the time allowed for each title was measurable in the seconds it took to say: 'yes, no, yes'.

As well as encouraging the level at which books are stocked in shops, trade reps play an important role in persuading booksellers to devote extra floor space to specific titles. The in-store promotion material produced by publishers is designed to attract the customers' attention and hence generate more sales. They may include dump bins (to hold large quantities of stock), show cards and single-copy holders (for display on the sales counter), posters and bookmarks, 'shelf wobblers', balloons, badges, stickers, and materials for mounting window displays. Such items can be bulky and their production or distribution is no guarantee that they will be used: this often depends on the negotiating skills of the rep. Increasingly, booksellers charge for display. Publishers may also provide booksellers with leaflets overprinted with their name and address for them to use in their own mailings; again this is often negotiated by the rep in return for agreeing to take extra stock.

Some firms organise through their reps regular (say, six-monthly) presentations to booksellers in an area, perhaps inviting them to a hotel to see a video of the new season's highlights and look at sample materials over a drink. Organising half a dozen such meetings in various regional centres (perhaps Oxford, Cambridge, Birmingham, Edinburgh, Glasgow, Leeds and Exeter) can generate a great deal of goodwill as well as be an effective means of selling.

What information does a rep need in order to sell effectively?
See the section on providing book buyers above, plus hard copies of all materials (book jacket, leaflet, advance information sheet and so on). See also Chapter 4 on different types of promotional format.

Export sales

In 1997 British publishers' exports were worth around £844 million (invoice value, ie after discount), and to this can be added books exported by booksellers and publishers' income from royalties and overseas investments. Large paperback houses may sell as much as 40 per cent of their annual output outside the UK; scientific and professional publishers may sell more than 60 per cent overseas. Sometimes it is only securing a US deal that can be added to the print run that makes publishing academic monographs financially viable.

Selling books overseas offers access to larger markets than are available by concentrating purely on home sales. (The US, with a much larger domestic market, exports only around 5 per cent of titles published. Britain's domestic market is around a quarter that of the US and yet Britain is still the world's major book exporter). The large international publishing and media companies are now truly global, selling and distributing their titles throughout the world via a comprehensive network which reaches from Aberdeen to Auckland. Some overseas markets offer the additional advantage that they are expanding far more rapidly than any similar publishing opportunities in the UK, for example the ELT market (see Chapter 12).

Brewing problems over international copyright

Publishers used to divide up the world into neat chunks for the purpose of copyright sales, so that different editions would be marketed in the US and in Britain. These divisions were largely based on hegemony and old loyalties: the US agreed to keep out of former British colonies (eg Australia and Africa) and Britain agreed to keep out of South America.

This is being heavily undermined by the Internet, which makes it possible for customers to order titles from anywhere, irrespective of territorial agreements on copyright. This situation also puts the bookseller at a disadvantage: if a customer asks to order a US title which is not yet available in this country, and is unable to do so, the customer retains the right to order the book direct. Booksellers are thus left policing an agreement that does not suit their financial interests. This is a real difficulty, made worse at the moment with export margins being cut drastically by a strong pound. Differential pricing for different markets also looks exploitative as buyers start to compare prices and buy from the lowest price.

Looking ahead, the long term and logical outcomes of this are:

● The production of a single English language edition for use world-wide
● Global pricing
● A simultaneous publication date world-wide.

And indeed these criteria are already being adopted in certain niche markets where sensitivity to textual English is less marked, for example with academic titles.

Judging by the success of American television programmes in the UK, one can reasonably predict that the differences between American and British spelling will become less of an issue as time goes by. There is an undoubted fear in Britain that with so much of the industry now American-owned the result may be that the one English-language edition will be American rather than British.

Trade discounts on exported titles tend to be higher and payment periods longer (60–180 days from the date of invoice, depending on the shipping time), but the customer generally pays carriage. Royalties paid to authors on overseas sales are lower than those paid on home sales; the percentage paid is commonly based on actual receipts after discount, not on a title's selling price.

The export market and you

How your company approaches overseas markets will depend on several factors: the size of the company; the current (or potential) value of export sales and where the company has rights to sell. How that commitment is expressed can range from a fully fledged overseas company to reliance on freelance reps who sell the firm's products in return for commission.

It may be up to the marketing department to produce materials for use overseas, or the export sales department may take responsibility for this themselves, producing specific material independent of UK marketing plans.

It is worth noting that knowledge of export markets seems to be an assured route to the top in publishing. Many senior managers have spent periods either travelling as export reps for the company or running overseas offices. There are several reasons why this experience is beneficial in the long run.

Working overseas you have the opportunity to build up patronage, perhaps from a fellow expatriate manager or from visiting UK staff. This can be exploited on return to the UK. Just as important is the chance of early responsibility. As well as being the official face of their company in a large market (frequently a whole country), overseas managers have to attend to all aspects of the publishing business: distribution, invoicing and credit control, marketing, editorial and so on, at the same time as motivating and manoeuvring their way through local political and cultural difficulties.

Most of the selling overseas is done face to face, whether through the local trade or to academics in the pursuit of adoptions, and as the local rep you can be identified closely with the success (and, of course, failure) of your endeavours.

Different levels of commitment overseas

1. **The UK publishing house founds or buys a separate company which publishes UK titles and also, perhaps, commissions some of its own, selling directly to the local market.** The local company handles distribution, representation, promotion and so on, either receiving special editions of UK marketing materials or preparing its own. As an example of this, in recent years many US publishing houses have bought British publishing operations, and at the same time gained a

foothold in the EU. Now British publishers are starting to buy companies in the US.

2. **The firm pursues co-edition deals with other publishers to sell to specific overseas markets.** Depending on the subject matter and level of the title, a separate edition may have to be produced (or licensed) or it may be exported as it is. For example, when pursuing co-edition deals for sales to the US, the spelling and packaging of a children's book would have to be made sympathetic to the local market and a special edition probably produced, whereas a high-level monograph could probably be exported as it was.

3. **The firm appoints a local stockholding agent for a particular market that takes some or all of the UK titles, and handles promotion and distribution to the local market.** Such an agent could be a bookseller or a wholesaler, or perhaps another publisher. Again, the agency either produces its own promotion material or receives special editions of UK materials. Smaller bookshops in the territory order stock from the agent.

4. **The firm deals in a specific area on the open market – direct with the local book trade and individual customers.** As with UK sales, depending on the amount of stock suppliers take, some accounts will get bigger discounts than others. Some of the larger local accounts may sell on stock to smaller ones.

    Links with the market are generally maintained through an export sales manager, UK-based but travelling overseas for a number of months each year. In larger firms an export sales director may be supported by the services of a number of additional reps. The marketing effort may also include direct marketing straight to customers in their homes/place of work.

5. **The firm exports through UK suppliers who are themselves exporting, for example, booksellers or agents, or employs freelance reps.** Booksellers are increasingly soliciting orders from overseas by direct mail.

    There are a number of freelances working overseas, perhaps concentrating on representing the related products of several UK publishers to distinct markets, for example one sells high-level journals through exhibitions in Eastern Europe. Many are language specialists and have moved out of full-time publishing to concentrate on what interests them and to gain more freedom. They generally receive a contribution per title represented towards their expenses and then 10–15 per cent on the net sales value (ie after discount) of the orders they take as commission. Sometimes they receive commission on all the orders taken in the territory, even those not secured by themselves.

These various methods of approaching overseas markets can be combined, as market size and ease of keeping in touch dictate. For example, a large publishing house may have a separate company in certain countries in Africa to which UK managers are sent on secondment and which the UK export sales director visits regularly to bring news of forthcoming editorial projects and to explore the potential for further penetrating the local market. But within Europe the same company may deal direct from the UK with local suppliers, sending out UK-based representatives on regular visits to boost trade.

General trends in export sales

It is worth pointing out that in the penetration of export markets there is a general tendency to move away from agency and licensing arrangements and to seek instead overseas establishments that promote the main edition and therefore the publisher's overall brand at the same time. The consequent ending of many long-established arrangements has caused bad feeling among those who have promoted loyally for years, only to find that their service no longer fits a multinational publishing ethos of the group in the 1990s.

At the same time, overseas sales of titles for which you have only purchased the rights and not originated the materials yourselves, are increasingly threatened by selling mechanisms that are able to ignore copyright such as the Internet. Some publishers have responded with a policy of never offering for sale to the consumer a product that they have not developed themselves, ie a corporate decision has been made not to buy rights.

Involvement with selling overseas may include some or all of the following activities:

- **Producing extra copies of your promotional material for overseas markets,** ie adding their requirements to your print run. They may require changes to be made before the material is printed, for example the omission of prices, the offer of inspection copies and all but the most basic details on the order form.

If no order form is required, replace it with a blank space for over-stamping.

You may be asked to send film of your promotional materials to overseas offices, for them to amend and print, but I have found that the anticipated savings are never as large as initially hoped. For example, in dealings between the US and UK, US paper sizes are different, and tone and spelling of the text usually needs completely reworking. It is probably as cheap to pass on a finished copy of a leaflet and allow a local designer to use it as the basis for something similar, or to send your text by e-mail file or on disk and allow the market to adapt.

- **Routinely sending out copies of your promotional material to those representing your company's interests overseas.** This provides them with the basic title information they need to produce their own.
- **Producing special promotion materials especially for use overseas.** This is mainly done by publishers in this country producing books in the UK solely for the overseas market, such as some ELT/ESL materials.
- **Briefing overseas managers on their visits to the UK on how you promote.**
- **Soliciting direct orders yourself.** This is most likely to be done through the mail and space advertising. If possible, printing should be handled as a 'split run'; the information you send overseas should omit reference to the UK price if it is lower than that for overseas customers, and payment should be requested with order. If this is impossible (eg a space advertisement in a journal for which one edition circulates both at home and abroad) you will have to add a paragraph stating the conditions on which orders are accepted from overseas customers.

Ask to be included on the circulation list for overseas promotion materials; it can be fascinating to see how different designers and copywriters promote the same titles.

External help

British Trade International (part of the Department of Trade and Industry) can provide subsistence grants to help with the costs of attending meetings overseas. Don't forget to keep the British Council up to date with your promotional information. It regularly sends copies of UK publishers' catalogues and promotional material to contacts in the book trade overseas, and frequently act as a valuable first port of call for export reps starting their travels. The Publishers Association regards advice on exporting as one of the key services offered to members and publishes a digest called *Book Development Council International (BDCI) Brief* 10 times a year.

Book fairs

The world's major book fair is held in Frankfurt each autumn. There publishers gather to show their wares; rights managers to sell and deal; and hangers-on to acquire the famous 'Frankfurt throat'. For children's books the annual Bologna Book Fair in March is important and many UK trade publishers take a stand at BookExpo in America (what was the ABA meeting). This alternates between Chicago and Los Angeles.

In the UK the London Book Fair gets larger each year, becoming much more significant not only for the UK but also in terms of the number of overseas visitors that it attracts. There are other specialised fairs such as the annual Socialist Book Fair held in Camden Town Hall and science fiction conventions. Watch the *Bookseller* for details of forthcoming events.

Information on the book trade

Understanding the book industry will never be an exact science but will always demand creativity, discipline and faith.

John Mitchinson, The Orion Publishing Group, presentation to
NBL Conference 1999

For information on what is selling, and where, the following are very useful:

- Book Marketing Limited (BML), reports and a most interesting annual conference
- Book Track (owned by Whitakers)
- Book Data
- Book Watch
- PA and BA for trends and surveys
- the trade press.

For addresses and contact numbers please see Appendix 4.

The trade press

Last of all, a word on the trade press, which it is worth keeping informed of all plans and achievements relevant to those who sell your books. Anything that is likely to have an impact on demand for a particular title should be passed on: sudden topicality; publicity coverage arranged; the dramatic sales of the author's last book and so on.

The *Bookseller* is the main vehicle for information, and is very influential within the trade. *Publishing News* is widely enjoyed. Other relevant titles are listed in the appendix.

In addition, if you are promoting mass market titles likely to be sold through confectioners, tobacconists and newsagents, don't forget to keep *The Grocer* magazine up to date with your information – it has a special section called *Confectioner, Tobacconist, Newsagent (CTN)*.

It is a very good idea too to keep an eye out for coverage of the publishing industry in other, more general, newspaper and magazine features. Such reports tend to be much more objective as they are written without the cosy insider's view. For example, a subscription to a general marketing magazine such as *Marketing Week* keeps you up to date with what those marketing products *other than* books are up to; bear in mind that the marketing stimuli they send out will undoubtedly affect your market.

Notes

1. Source: Book Track Plus TNS, 1999.
2. I am indebted to a bookseller speaking on a copywriting course I ran at the Training Centre at Book House who provided the basis of this list. If you recognise it as yours, please contact the publishers so that we can credit you!
3. See Glossary.

2

Marketing in Publishing: Planning for Effective Promotion

Marketing at its most effective appears simple: the slogan so appropriate that it is instantly memorable; the sales letter that makes a product sound so desirable the reader fills out the order form immediately. Yet this simplicity is not easily achieved. It depends on a complete understanding of both designated market and product; an understanding that emerges only through detailed planning and research.

All too often in publishing, immense pressure on the time available means that planning and research tend to get forgotten in the rush to get something written down. The habit of planning marketing strategies – aims and objectives – is an important one to acquire. Drawing up a marketing plan acts as a mind-focusing exercise, encouraging clarity of thought and helping you to prioritise. And, of course, carefully planned campaigns stand a very much better chance of achieving their goals.

It is increasingly the case that an effective marketing plan is vital in acquiring as well as selling books. Agents or authors offering titles to prospective publishers will place considerable importance on the suitor companies' ability to present (and deliver) coherent marketing plans.

What you are up against

The number of books published each year is useful background knowledge as you start to plan your marketing activities: it should make you aware of the difficulty of your task. Whitaker reported that nearly 104,634 books were published in 1998, a 4.6 per cent increase on 1997. At any one time there are around 800,000 books in print, a figure that goes up by around 65,000 each year (some go out of print each year and are not reprinted). By comparison the grocery trade in the UK is nearly 50 times as large but launches only one-fiftieth as many new products.

An understanding of the breadth of the market should help you to guard against complacency. You may be very familiar with the impending publication of a forthcoming title, having seen it on the production schedule for so long, but can you think of any reason why the bookseller should be equally familiar with it? (If you want instantly convincing and depressing proof, take a trip along to your nearest bookshop and examine the shelf on which the forthcoming title will hopefully sit, and in what company.)

Over half the books sold each year are sold through bookshops, so time spent in them trying to understand more about the market for your titles is seldom wasted. If you can get a local bookshop to take you on, a couple of days helping out will teach you a huge amount. Try arriving when the post is being opened one morning to see how much information a shop receives in a single day; notice how much gets rejected without even being looked at as simply inappropriate. Even if you cannot work in a shop, do acquire the habit of visiting bookshops at regular intervals. See how busy they are (particularly in the run-up to Christmas); watch how customers peruse the stock; listen to the scanty information they have about the titles they want.

The aim of all this is to encourage you to stop viewing your list of titles as an interesting whole, united by its single publisher, and rather, as the bookseller will see it, a collection of individual products, for each of which rejection is the easiest option, and reasons for stocking need to be fully spelled out.

What is more, books compete for both the consumer and business purse with a whole range of other products, not just other books. A business person may select an online computer service rather than an expensive reference work; a windsurfing enthusiast may prefer a video on techniques to a new book; the teacher an audio-visual package to a new language course. And the amount of advertising trying to direct our pattern of spending is enormous.

So where do you start in trying to develop coherent plans for your marketing? Perhaps by considering what marketing means.

customer needs a variety of different sources of information may be used: specialist knowledge from your authors; socio-economic data; mailing list research; relevant directories; the sales pattern of related products, and so on.

The right product

The right product is the one that customers want, or one that they will be prepared to want – and pay for – once they have been informed of its existence. The manufacturer's initial concept should be refined until it meets this standard.

Applied to publishing this can include changing the level at which the book is pitched, the cover or number of illustrations, or price to meet the anticipated needs and preferences of the market. Although active involvement in this process may well occur only higher up the publishing tree, you should bear in mind that the author's first submission of text is not necessarily what finally appears in print. Appropriate and professional presentation to the market is a very important part of the publishing process.

The right things

The right things are those that need to be said to convince the potential buyer to purchase. That does not mean listing every possible sales benefit, but concentrating on those most relevant to the market. For example, tyre manufacturers could stress a variety of different product benefits: competitive price; road-holding ability; value for money and longevity. They usually concentrate on a single one: safety.

Taking the selection of sales benefits a stage further, what offer in combination with your product is more likely to persuade the buyer to purchase? General advertising yields lots of examples: the free extra if an order is over a certain value; the complimentary voucher that accompanies student bank accounts; the cast-iron guarantee of a refund if the customer is not completely satisfied. Since the demise of the Net Book Agreement both publishers and wholesalers have set up similar promotional deals.

The right way

This means the right creative strategy (style of copy, format, design, typography and so on) that allows the message to speak clearly to the market. For example, when selling business information to companies your tone probably needs to be clear, professional and centred on the competitive advantage you are offering; one or two colours may suffice. If writing copy for point of sale material to be used in children's book departments, the image chosen must both attract children and sell through to those who will make the buying decision; the visual appeal must be instant.

The right time

The right time is the best time to be selling. Advertising fireworks in April or Christmas decorations in July may achieve sales but will probably not produce the best possible results. Pharmaceutical companies producing drugs for seasonal illnesses frequently secure the best response if they time their mailings to doctors carefully, for example, by sending information on hay fever remedies when the pollen count is high.

The best time to mail schools with information on an educational publishing programme is when they are thinking about how to spend their forthcoming budget (January to March) or at the beginning of the new school year (September). If you mail during July there will be no one there to read what you send. On the other hand, mailing university academics during the summer holidays will frequently find them still at their desks but, in the absence of their students, with more time to read and consider your sales message.

The right place

The right place is the selection of appropriate sales vehicle, the place where the largest number of your prospective customers will read your message. For example, to reach primary school teachers you may decide on a mailshot, space advertising in a relevant publication or to instruct a team of freelance reps to take your product into schools. All three are different ways of reaching the same market.

How to draw up a marketing plan

Basics

A good way to start drawing up a marketing plan is to make a list of all the standard promotional boosts received by every title published by your house. Not only will compiling such a list give confidence, it will also be useful when you have to speak to authors or agents about promotion plans for a specific title. (Often these standard promotional processes are so familiar that they are easily forgotten.)

If the task of setting up these procedures is yours too, the following list will be helpful.

An advance notice or advance information sheet   *A1*

This is usually in the form of a single sheet of A4 paper and includes all the basic title information: a brief description (blurb) and author profile; bibliographical details, price and expected publication date; key selling points and features. The 'AN' or 'AI' is sent to reps, booksellers and other interested parties, normally six to nine months ahead of publication.

Inclusion in catalogues and seasonal lists   *spring autumn Catalog.*

Most general publishers produce two six-monthly catalogues (spring and autumn); others produce a new books list three times a year or *+ several* even quarterly. Academic and educational firms usually produce *list* a separate catalogue for each subject for which they publish. Catalogues generally appear six months before the books featured are due to be published.

Advertising

Are there any standard features in which all your firm's titles are listed? For example, are there standard space bookings for the spring and autumn export editions of the *Bookseller*, regular title listings in *The Times Higher Education Supplement* or a Sunday supplement?

Despatch of covers to major bookshops and libraries

Your production department can arrange for extra book jackets and covers to be printed. If you have these stamped on the back with price and publication date they can form useful display and promotional items when sent to bookshops. A basic mailing list could be buyers at your key accounts (ask the sales manager for contact names). Alternatively, the Booksellers Association can rent you bookshop names on sticky labels. The best time to circulate is four to five months before publication. Similarly, jackets can be sent to large public libraries.

'Silent salesmen' [4]

There are a number of other possible homes for your material which take little effort to reach but may result in extra sales.

These include sending information to:

- The British Council, which promotes titles abroad
- *Books in Print* (published by Whitakers)
- Various booksellers who produce their own catalogues
- Relevant associations
- Appropriate media and press to stimulate features or the demand for review copies (see Chapter 8).

The marketing manager of one major academic publishing house concluded that 95 per cent of their sales were achieved through such intermediaries.

Specifics

The checklist above should apply to all your titles. For marketing plans for individual titles, a number of considerations needs to be thought through before you start planning.

What is your strategy?

What is your company trying to achieve through marketing? To launch something new; to raise the profile of an existing product or to probe and eventually break into a new area of publishing? You need to know the goals to stand a chance of achieving them.

The very best marketing is grounded in a clear understanding of both product and target market. Only if you have this will your copy be relevant and personal, your advertising seen by those who need to read it in order to buy. Research is the only way to achieve this.

Researching the market ('the right people')

Market research should have been of fundamental importance to the commissioning and development of your company's products. You now have to find the groups of people who need what you have to offer and persuade them to buy.

The marketing for an existing product can be defined as follows in decreasing levels of interest:

(a) People who have bought/used such a product or a related product before; people who need such a product now

(b) People who used to but do so no longer
(c) People who have never done so.

What is the market like?

What kind of people are they? Is purchase likely to be by males or females; are there socio-economic indicators, or area biases (most mailing lists are selectable in these respects)? Database and software companies can now offer very sophisticated socio-economic analysis of your mailing lists; this is mostly done by postcode analysis but can also draw on additional information such as the examination of house name or first name of householder. The following table of social gradings is also widely referred to and so may also be useful:

Grading	Description
A	Upper and middle class; higher management and administrative or professional
B	Middle class; intermediate managerial, administrative or professional
C1	Lower middle class; supervisory, or clerical and junior managerial
C2	Skilled working class; skilled manual workers
D	Working class; semi- and unskilled manual workers
E	Those at the lowest level of subsistence: state pensioners; widows with no other earner; casual or lowest grade workers.

Gathering this kind of information will help you to decide on the right promotional approach.

Other questions to ask yourself about the market

- What needs does the market have? How will the product you offer improve people's lives? How much will they benefit? How much do they want it/need it?
- Who is the product for? Who will buy it? *for children by parents*

    These two questions are not identical. Think of the advertising of children's toys on television at Christmas, designed to encourage children to ask for the products that parents and other adults will buy. Equally for educational publishers, new materials may be preferred and recommended by classroom teachers, but it is departmental heads or head teachers in primary schools who make the buying decisions.

- How big is the potential market? How does this compare with the title's print run? What percentage of the market do you have to sell to in order to make the project profitable?
- How much will the market pay (and how will they pay – if they are buying for work, how much can they spend on their own account without having to get a second signature to approve the purchase?)
- How much does your product cost? Will price rule out any important markets? For example, academic libraries are more likely than individual lecturers to buy high-priced monographs but are there enough libraries in the market to make publication worthwhile? Corporate libraries may be able to afford the latest information but can public libraries? By targeting your message to one market will you alienate another (and possibly larger) one?
- How has it been marketed in the past and with what success? If the product has come to your house from a competitor, try to get copies of the promotion material they used. Was marketing one of the reasons the author decided to change houses? If so, what where their chief complaints?

Once you have established the primary market, who else might need it? Is there anyone who certainly won't buy it? (You can perhaps capitalise on this in your promotional information.)

Researching the product ('the right product')
This means finding out all you can about the product you are to promote. Who is the author: bestselling or unknown; always published by your house or new to the list; available at the time of publication for interviews; with other titles in print? Look at the title. *Confessions of a Showgirl* will give you an idea of the content.

If the book exists in manuscript form try to get your hands on a copy. The number of books you have to look after will dictate the amount of time you are able to spend on each one. For example, a major new English scheme brought out by a primary education publisher should be examined in detail. If you have 15 monographs a week to promote, looking closely at them all will be impossible; you will have to rely on what the editors have said about them.

Even if you don't have access to the manuscript, search the editorial *and* marketing files for information – not everything of relevance finds its way from one department to the other.

Most publishing houses have an evolutionary cycle of forms, altered product details passing on to second- and third-generation versions of the original. As you look through these you will acquire an understanding of the title and how it has developed. At one stage in the cycle (perhaps with the 'presentation' form or 'A' form, the name varies from publishing house to house) it will have been brought before a formal marketing/editorial meeting and approved. On this form a note of the anticipated print run and first-and second-year sales will have been made: here are your targets.

Study the contents list. Ask yourself (or the editor) why the book was commissioned. What market needs does it satisfy? Are there any readers' reports in the file (reports on the manuscript before a decision to publish was taken)? There should also be an *author's publicity form*. The amount of time authors spend on compiling these varies but a fully completed one can be an excellent source of information: who better than the author to tell you who should buy the book?

If you are promoting a book that is already published, look at previous advertisements. Find out from the customer services department what the sales and returns patterns have been. Ask the reps what the market thinks of your product; what do they call it?

Study the competition. Early in-house forms and the author's publicity form should list any major competitors to a forthcoming title, or say if a publishing project has been started to meet a major market opportunity. Bearing in mind that the competition may not just consist of other books, start gathering information on what your product competes with and how it is promoted. Book fairs are a good time to collect other publishers' information and catalogues; scan the relevant press for ads. You can pay a press agency, such as Romeike and Curtice, to clip the advertisements of your competitors for you, but you will get a better general idea of the market if you scan the relevant media yourself – as well as early warning of any new competition.

If there are still unanswered questions ask the book's editor about contacting the author. Be prepared; ensure that you have read all the information the author provided about the book before you ring. There is nothing more annoying for an author than to spend valuable time filling in a questionnaire only to be rung by a marketing person who has clearly not read it. Do your basic market research first: you don't want to give the impression that someone with no understanding of the market is responsible for promoting the title. The author's reaction to such a call would probably be panic, followed by a sudden phone call to their editorial contact.

If you are unsure of a book's content or subject matter it may be best to get the author to check your promotional copy. Similarly, can the author help with testimonials or suggest individuals who might give the book a recommendation that you can quote in your advertising material? The recommendation of one expert will be worth ten times what you can think of to say.

The telephone can tell you a tremendous amount about the best way to market a book. Has any teleselling been done on this book, or a related title, in the past? As well as yielding orders you gain a great deal of product information. If the market is easily identified try ringing a few prospects, or consult a directory for contact numbers. You will be surprised how many people find it flattering to have their opinion sought about the need for a new product; librarians can be particularly helpful.

By now the project should be starting to come alive. Start refining your thoughts by answering the following questions about the book or project.

- What is it?
- What does it do?
- Who is it for?
- What is new about it?
- Is it topical?
- Does it meet a new or rediscovered need?
- What does it compete with?
- What does it replace?
- What are its advantages and benefits?
- How much does it cost? What value does this provide?
- Are there any guarantees of satisfaction?
- Are there any testimonials and quotes you can use?

Does the product satisfy any human needs?

Several copywriting gurus have outlines basic human needs, in the belief that any piece of advertising copy should aim to appeal to at least one. For example:

- to make money
- to save money
- to save time and effort
- to help your family
- to be secure
- to impress others

50

- to belong; emulate others
- to be popular
- to attract attention
- to improve oneself
- to avoid loss or trouble
- to further your career
- to gain pleasure.

A new business information title may offer the reader a valuable competitive edge and the chance to make money, a new novel a pleasurable read.

Take this a stage further and make a list of selling points (features and benefits) and put them in order. Successful advertising comes from making the message credible and comprehensible: there may be lots of benefits but the potential buyers need only two to be convinced. The important thing is knowing which two: if you include them all you may confuse.

Put a copy of this list in the front of the title file: it will be useful later if you have to acquaint yourself with the product in a hurry, perhaps before meeting the author or having to write an advertisement or press release at short notice. This will save you reinventing the wheel.

What you say ('the right things')

The words used in a marketing campaign are often referred to as the *creative strategy*. The next chapter will provide ideas on how to make your copy relevant and effective; suggest new promotional themes and much more.

For now I would just recommend that you nurture a general interest in all advertising copy; don't confine your study to the *Bookseller* alone. Start looking out for copywriting techniques that do and do not work and think why in each case. Keep two files, one of ideas you like (and can copy), the other of mistakes to avoid. It is daunting to realise how much advertising effort (and expenditure) goes entirely unnoticed. Get on as many mailing lists as possible to see how other firms are selling through the post.

Keep file copies of every piece of promotional material you produce along with a note of how they performed. This will help you to plan marketing strategies in the future and save you repeating expensive mistakes. Reading through such a file from time to time also acts as a valuable lesson in objectivity.

Where do you start?

The following checklist may be helpful to get you started:

1. Think about where and when your promotional material is to appear and what it is trying to achieve.
2. Plan your schedule. Where does copy have to be and when?
3. Think about the market. What needs do people have that will be fulfilled by your product? What will motivate them to buy?
4. Draw up a list of product benefits to the market.
5. Put them in order of importance.
6. The most important should form the basis for your theme.
7. Start thinking about the headline, bullet points and paragraph headings for your body copy.
8. From them on it's a lengthy process of writing and rewriting, reading aloud and putting to one side to read later. Remember to intersperse your writing with plenty of breaks: you can't keep up an intensive concentration for long and still be working at your best.
9. When you think you have finished there are several ways of testing your copy. You can buy a computer program to analyse the complexity of your sentences, the number of personal words used and the readability level. A less expensive option is to try your copy out on colleagues at work; get them to read it aloud to you. Better still, show it to someone completely unconnected with your work and ask if they find it:

   (a) interesting
   (b) persuasive
   (c) clear
   (d) believable
   (e) motivating – do they know what to do next and how to fill in the order form?

The format ('the right way')

Deciding on whether to produce a cheap two-sided flyer or a full-colour four-page brochure is often where most marketing plans start. It's a much better idea to allow the decision on format to grow out of an understanding of the market and the product. For example, given absolute creative freedom to change format and words of an existing mailshot you would be lucky to put up your response by more than half a per cent. You'd be far better off reviewing the selection of lists or to thinking through the product benefits in fuller detail and coming up with a new offer.

Nevertheless, armed with a marketing strategy to reach your customers, there is a lot of scope for lateral thinking on promotional format. Bear in mind that it is the slightly unexpected that secures attention. There are various ways to attract, such as different sized envelopes for mailshots; new sizes for space advertisements, and so on.

Always be aware of the impression you are creating: large promotion budgets do not necessarily lead to better sales; indeed, over-lavish material can directly contradict your sales message. For example, full-colour material to promote a product supposedly offering good value for money can lead the consumer to conclude that the price is unnecessarily high, pushed up by the cost of the sales message. On the other hand, when selling a high price product through the post, attractively produced promotion material, giving an impression of the quality of what is available, and the beauty it will add to the customer's home, is essential. Look out for the advertisements for multi-volume encyclopedia sets or other collectables which show the products beautifully lit in prestigious surroundings and often provide the appropriate shelving as part of the deal.

Sometimes it may be advantageous to use cheaper materials or to make your message look hurried. Stockbrokers who produce 'tip sheets' deliberately go for a no-frills approach. If time has to be allowed for design and professional layout, the information is stale by the time it is received. Similarly, look at the fund-raising mailshots sent out by charities; they are usually printed on recycled paper, stressing an urgency and need that would be entirely defeated were full-colour brochures enclosed. But when it comes to their Christmas catalogues they print in full colour to put the merchandise in its most advantageous light.

Getting your timing right ('the right time')
When is the best time to promote to your market? When do you need your marketing materials to be ready by? Start working back through your diary, allocating time to all those involved such as designers and printers. See the example schedule in Chapter 8 on direct mail.

Planning too far ahead can be as bad as leaving too little time; it allows everyone the chance to change their mind and the project to go stale. Responding and rising to the challenge of occasional crises for copy is good practice but in the long term it is best not to survive on ulcer juice alone. Even if you are desperately short of time, try to let the copy sit overnight: what seems very amusing at 5.30 one evening may appear merely embarrassing the next morning.

Media planning ('the right place')

What are the best media through which to convey your promotional message? Should you use press advertising; posters; cinema, television and radio advertising; direct mail; display material; public relations; stunts; free samples? All are elements of the promotional mix, tools at your disposal.

Let's take press advertising as a specific example for further examination. Which magazines and journals do your target market read? Consult the author's publicity form and note where they suggest review copies should be sent. Talk to editorial and other marketing staff. Make a short list and look up the rates in BRAD (see bibliography). If they are within your budget ring up and ask for sample copies as well as details of their *readership profile* (useful ammunition when they start pestering you for a booking and you want a reason to say no).

If you decide to advertise, do you plan to take a single space or a series? If there is one magazine or paper that reaches your target market you will probably get better results from taking a series of advertisements, perhaps featuring a different product benefit each time, rather than spreading the same message over several different magazines. If you go for a series of adverts you should get a discount.

Having decided which media you will use, study them. Can you get yourself added to the free circulation list? Look through the pages. Which adverts do you notice? Is this because of effective copy and design or placing? Where is the best place to be? In general, go for right-hand side, and facing text, never facing another advertisement (most people skip past double page ads). Can you get next to the editorial or another hot spot such as the crossword or announcements of births, marriages and deaths? Space on book review pages may be cheaper than on news pages, but by opting for the former will you escape the notice of a large number of your potential buyers? If you are planning to offer a coupon, can it be cut out easily?

Read the letters, look at the job adverts – a close examination of these will tell you who is reading the magazine. If it is a weekly, is any advertiser writing topical copy? Does the lead time allow for this? Is it paid or controlled circulation? When you start writing you should be aiming your message at one individual reader – can you picture him or her?

How much can you spend on marketing?

Chapter 11 on budgeting will look at costing promotion campaigns in more detail. But before you start sketching out your plans you need a rough idea of how much can be spent. This is usually based on:

(a) a percentage of anticipated revenue from the project
(b) a percentage of the firm's turnover
(c) a sum unrelated to these but designed to get the promotion off to a good start. For example, to launch a large reference work, a new journal or to celebrate the arrival of a new author at your publishing house, you may be offered a sizeable budget in the hope that future sales will repay the initial investment.

Whom to tell in house

The last part of drawing up an effective marketing plan is letting the right people know what you are doing.

First of all, inform the reps. If your marketing plans are likely to result in increased demand from the public, it is vital that they know. As a result they may be able to persuade bookshops to take more stock and hence produce more sales.

Even if your plans are simply up to schedule, do send a copy of each forthcoming promotion piece to the reps; it is embarrassing if the customers they visit know more about marketing plans than they do.

Second, inform all those on whom you rely. If you offer telephone and fax numbers for direct orders (and you will probably reduce the response to your direct marketing by at least 50 per cent if you don't), make sure they are up and running before the adverts appear or the mailing goes out. Do the receptionist and people manning the switchboard know what you are offering? If calls come through to your department does everyone who might answer your phone know what to say? Persuading other people to answer your telephone can be difficult; try offering an incentive: a points systems resulting in chocolates or wine for every order taken in the department. Leave a basic list of prices or details of the current promotion beside your phone.

If the magazine you are advertising in offers a reader-reply scheme do you have something ready to send out to those who respond? A telesales script for following up a mailshot? All these things – and more – need thinking through beforehand.

Notes

1. A more detailed examination of the meaning of marketing, supported by full explanation of techniques for conducting a company audit and drawing up a detailed marketing plan, may be found in the companion volume to this one, *Are Books Different?*, Alison Baverstock, Kogan Page, 1993.
2. Competition entry for a definition of marketing in publishing, *Bookseller*, June 1992.
3. The first four elements come from Professor Michael J. Baker of the Department of Marketing at Strathclyde University, the final two are my own.
4. I owe this effective term to Tim Farmiloe of Macmillan Press.

3

Techniques for Writing Successful Copy

Having told friends and acquaintances that I spend most of my time copywriting, and then being asked detailed questions about copyright law, it's probably worth saying right now that promotional copywriting is producing the words that make up the campaign; it means selling in print.

A copywriter's key objective is not to show they have a novel in them or display a noteworthy style, but to get customers to buy the product; to put across what I believe is our main aim:

A believable promise aimed at the right audience

The first rule for would–be copywriters is that there are no rules. The very practice of laying down rules for writing would result in wooden and stilted copy; 'formula writing'. Nor is past skill at literary criticism any guarantee of success. You may have thought a degree in English literature, or a high 'A' level grade, excellent grounding for a future to be spent writing copy; but many such worthy candidates find freedom from linguistic rules awesome or even off-putting.

Suddenly you have an immense amount of freedom: to start sentences with 'and' or 'but'; to use dashes rather than colons and semi-colons; to miss out the verb in a phrase altogether if the message is clear without it; to ignore the skills acquired during précis lessons and repeat your basic sales message again and again, each time in slightly different words. All become techniques at your disposal in the wider aim of attracting attention to the product you are promoting. And to this greater good must also be sacrificed any self-conscious style you have developed, the erudite tone which tutors praised in your essays. The viewpoint or character of the copywriter should be entirely transparent, allowing the product to shine through. The copywriter's aim was summed up in the following exchange of letters in *The Daily Telegraph* in 1995:

Copywriters' fault

Sir – While we're on the subject of punctuation (letter, Jan 30).

Advertisements. They've done a lot of harm! By putting in full stops where they're not wanted. Making sentences without verbs. Or even subjects. No wonder young people are confused.

They never see connected, correctly punctuated prose. Ever.

Cynthia Harrod-Eagles, Northwood, Middlesex.

Copywriters' craft

Sir – Cynthia Harrod-Eagles misses the point about copywriting (letter, Feb 4). The craft of copywriting is all about preaching to the indifferent. It is designed to communicate not to educate.

There are, I suggest, worse things than a predilection for full points. Worse things than forming sentences without verbs or subjects. Worse things, indeed, than splitting infinitives. And one of those is splitting hairs.

Copywriting demands an agile brain, a wide general knowledge, a high IQ and so intimate an understanding of the Queen's English that one can abuse it with impunity.

Patrick Quinn, Eddleston, Peeblesshire

The first correspondent is a novelist, the second a copywriter.

Having said there are no general rules for successful writing, this chapter will be devoted to making suggestions. I will start with four basic principles and then continue with ad hoc suggestions.

The four basic principles

1. *Think in detail about the market and the product before you start working out what to say.*

Before you write a word immerse yourself in an understanding of the market you are writing to and the product you are writing about. Why do people need it? How does it compete on price with the competition? How will they pay? What other options do they have? Can you picture a member of the market? Your copy is far more likely to be effective if it is personal. Summon up an image of a typical member of the market and then explain to them one-to-one.

Useful tip. You will find it easier to get on to other people's wavelengths on a regular basis if you start varying your own reading habits. So don't just read the same newspaper or watch/listen to the same news programme every day (it will simply confirm your judgement that everyone is as reasonable as you are). Read different ones; tabloid and broadsheet; commercial and public service and see how different media report the same stories.

2. *Avoid grammatical howlers.*

If you are promoting the written word it's vital that your sales message is error-free.

Check your work carefully for mistakes such as the combination of singular verbs and plural subjects, misspellings, and in particular, avoid the split infinitive. *This is not because it is wrong, but because most people believe it to be so.* The split infinitive will attract the attention of many who ignore far more casual uses of the English language; they will stop reading your message and start congratulating themselves on catching you out. Their conclusions will be that if a publisher can't get such a basic grammatical point right their books must be unreadable.

Watch out, too, for the confusion of similar words with different meanings: accept and except; principle and principal; affect and effect.

3. *Avoid isms.*

Make no assumptions about the market you are writing to, you will offend part of it when (not if) you get it wrong.

For example, ensure your copy is not sexist. Do not write to the business community as 'Dear Sir' or assume all nurses are female. You must qualify every 'him' with an 'or her' to show that what you say is equally applicable to both sexes. Alternatively, it is now acceptable to use plural pronouns (eg they, their, them) with singular subjects (eg anyone).

Some markets are particularly sensitive. Schools today are at the forefront of promoting equality of opportunity. All teacher training courses emphasise its importance and most schools have a written policy on the subject. You may write a brochure to schools of complete sexual equality, yet include in your accompanying letter a couple of references to the masculine pronoun alone, and your material will start arousing the wrong kind of reaction. People who might have ordered will use the reply envelope to let you know how strongly they disapprove. (That does not mean sexist language is offensive only in mailshots – just that direct mail is one of the few advertising methods that gives you direct feedback.)

The same rule applies to all the other 'isms' of today: racism, ageism and so on, although in these cases, as it is harder to offend through words alone, you should pay particular attention to the illustrations that accompany your text.

4.   *Avoid the predictable*.
Do not write exactly what the market expects: we do not bother to read an advertisement if from a cursory look we already know (or can guess) the content. This does not mean that you have to compensate by tending towards obscurity or outrageousness, just that to be interesting – and therefore get read – advertising should be slightly unexpected. And just to prove that rules exist only to be broken from time to time, an occasional cliché can be the copy-writer's best friend, if skilfully used.

How to learn more about writing well

Formal training can be difficult to come by. Your principal option is to learn on the job, from other people you work with/for and from the wider world of advertising. Teach yourself by gaining access to all the advertising material you can. Watch what your competitors are producing and compare it with the past and current efforts of your own publishing house. Build an awareness of what makes for good and bad advertisements. Learn to recognise good copy and formats that get frequently repeated, in particular those that are used in direct response advertising: they must work. Read a good book on the subject (see the Bibliography) or ask to go on a copywriting course (see the training section in Appendix 4).

Acronyms and other ideas

Generations of copywriters have found the following acronyms useful. These are followed by some examples of other techniques and ideas worth considering. This chapter will finish with a look at two parts of the promotion piece for which the copy is particularly vital: the headline and the order form.

Acronyms are words formed from the initial letters of other words, for example NATO, SWALK (sealed with a loving kiss) and the more recent TLI (three letter initials). The publishing industry seems to embrace the use of initials with particular enthusiasm; each house has developed its own terms.

AID(C)A

AIDA has been around for over 50 years: it is one of the best known acronyms. Originally, it served as a structure for writing direct mail letters but it works equally well as a guide to writing press advertisements, leaflets, telemarketing scripts and other promotional formats. It was recently updated with the addition of a 'C', and so now stands for: Attract, Interest, Desire, Conviction, Action.

Attract

What is it about an advertisement or piece of promotional material that first attracts the reader's eye? It may be a stunning photograph, an attractive layout, a message on the envelope of a mailshot, a personalised name and address at the start of a sales letter, a headline or slogan on a space advertisement or billboard.

Whatever it is, if you start thinking about the process of attracting attention and start noticing what grabs yours, you are well on the way to writing successful copy yourself.

Interest

Once you have secured the reader's attention, your next task is to keep it: advertising guru David Ogilvy reckoned five times as many people read the headline as the text beneath. You must develop the copy in such a way that the reader stays with you, absorbing the sales message as he or she goes.

Explain the benefits of the product; use subheadings to assist readers who want to 'skim' before they read in detail; talk logically through the sales points in a tone that is friendly without being either condescending or patronising.

Desire

As you stimulate interest, create desire to own or benefit from the product you are describing. Be enthusiastic: it's worth having! Will the reader be one of the first to benefit from this new kind of information source? Are stocks limited? Is there a pre-publication offer so that the reader will save money if the order is placed before a particular date? Has it already taken America by storm? Provide all the reasons you can to create the desire to purchase.

Conviction

Provide proof: testimonials; review quotes; how long it took to develop and trial the material now about to be published; the current sales trends; your cast-iron guarantee which shows your company's great confidence in the product.

Action

Lastly, direct the reader to take the action necessary to secure the product you have described. What is the publication date and where is it available? If you take direct orders make it easy to do so: offer freepost; the chance to order by telephone, fax or computer link and pay by credit card. Restate the comforting guarantee: if the buyer is not completely satisfied there is a full refund.

FAB

Features, advantages and benefits: a useful checklist to ensure that your copy is relevant and interesting to the market. Many copywriters get no further than listing features. These need to be converted into what really interests the reader – benefits.

Two examples here, one from general advertising, the other from publishing.

1.   New Snibbo toothpaste contains newly researched ingredient XPZ2. (feature)
     Which reaches the plaque that covers your teeth, even in hard to reach places. (advantage)
     Which means you and your family need newer fillings. (benefit)

2.   This new maths course has been extensively piloted in schools to ensure it meets the needs of a wide range of abilities. (feature)
     Which means the whole class can be using the same material at the same time. (advantage)

Which means you get more time to concentrate on individual needs. (benefit)

The same principle was also neatly summed up as: sell the sizzle, not the sausage.

USP

The search for a *unique selling proposition* for every product was at its height in America in the 1950s. A USP is what makes a product different from everything else on the market; if one was not immediately apparent it had to be invented.

Here are some examples of a USP providing an identity for products that are in reality very similar to others on the market:

Treets: The chocolates that melt in your mouth, not in your hand.
Esso: Put a tiger in your tank.
British Airways: The world's favourite airline.

Today the practice is no longer obligatory. Some products are deliberately very similar to their competitors (known as the 'me too' market) and are best promoted on the basis of similarity, value for money or simply how strongly you feel about a product. John Hegarty of advertising agency Bartle, Bogle and Hegarty commented:

Advertising has moved from the UDP to the ESP, or emotional selling proposition. Product quality differences are far less, because technology has moved forwards so much. So today it's a matter of how you feel about a brand.

Sunday Times, 18 April 1999

Nevertheless, if your early product investigations make you aware that the title you are promoting is unique (new to the market; a completely new look at the subject; new format etc) make the most of it.

WIIFM?

Everyone reading promotional material or responding to advertising has this question in mind, and if the question is satisfactorily answered they will keep reading, right to the end. The message is: *What's in it for me?*

And lastly:

KISS

Explain yourself clearly. Don't be over-complicated or verbose. In other words: *Keep it simple, stupid*.

As an example of all these suggestions in action, see how they relate to the advertisement opposite. Note how every feature is turned into a benefit, the copywriter (Bob Osborne) identifies himself closely with the market and the day-to-day problems faced by teachers.

Techniques for effective writing

Write clearly and logically

Having established all the sales benefits of the product you are promoting, rank them and use them in order: one idea per sentence, one theme per paragraph. Your final copy doesn't need to make use of everything you have thought of!

Use short sentences. David Ogilvy reckoned that the first sentence of advertisement body copy (the text that follows the headline) should contain no more than 11 words. Thereafter ensure sentence length is varied to avoid monotony. Use words from everyday speech (demotic language), and don't use long phrases where single words would do, for example:

use		*instead of*	
	most		a great deal of
	respected		widely acclaimed
	consider		take into consideration.

Georges Simenon (creator of Maigret) deliberately stuck to a vocabulary of just 2000 words so that his books could be understood by everyone.

Use short words (often Saxon in origin) rather than long ones (often from Latin), for example:

And can you really blame them? By the time many below average ability pupils reach the fourth year they are sick to death of Maths. They need something new. The secondary survey said "...in 60 per cent of schools visited HMI considered that new courses (in mathematics) should be developed for the less able pupils."

You know what they need - something fresh, amusing and lively.

A chance to get a taste of success and achievement. Something which will still work even though half the class were away last week.

Are worksheets your answer? Or do you feel that they may have had enough of worksheets too?

MATHS FOR YOU is a new two book course for **CSE**. It is extraordinarily lively. Each page is clear yet interesting. It's flexible to use (because it's mostly self-contained spreads). And it really does work.

Please have a look at this course. At the very least you'll gain some good ideas. And at the best, you might cut out the graffiti altogether.

Please send me an inspection copy of the books ticked below:

Maths for You Book 1 by Duncan and Christine Graham
——— price £3.25 non net

Maths for You Book 2 by Duncan and Christine Graham
——— price £3.25 non net

Name _____

School _____

Address _____

To: **Bob Osborne, Hutchinson Education, FREEPOST 5, London W1E 4QZ**

Figure 3.1 *This appeared in 1981 – today many more direct ways to get in touch would be offered – but note how it has lasted the test of time; it still feels fresh and immediate*

news, facts	*not*	information
find		discover
show		demonstrate
now		immediately.

On the other hand, the occasional use of long words can attract attention, particularly if they are surrounded by monosyllabic terms that throw them into further relief. Prince Charles' 'carbuncle' was well chosen. Positioned among short familiar words it had an added bite:

'... what is proposed is a monstrous carbuncle on the face of a much loved and elegant friend.'[1]

Similarly, the linking of very different words can be most effective (oxymorons). Ryvita created the 'inch war'; conditioners have offered us a solution for 'thirsty hair'.

Use vivid terms, not hackneyed:

vivid	*hackneyed*
hate	dislike
adore	love
cash	money.

Use active verbs, not passive, for example:

you can see	*not*	it can be seen.

Better still, use an imperative:

see how ...

The present tense implies action, for example:

research shows	*not*	research has shown
the author talks to	*not*	the author was interviewed.

Steer clearing of advertisingese and over-used words. I am grateful to Justine Crowe, of Words Worth Booksellers for the following list of words that make her yawn. They appear in order of frequency:

unique ('almost unique' is even worse and makes no sense)
major
moving
timely
exciting
a must
heart-rending
outstanding
hilarious
exceptional
invaluable
revolutionary
essential
brilliant
remarkable
eye-catching
compelling
absolutely fabulous
original
unputdownable
wicked (in particular of children's books)
author at the height of his/her powers
… and nothing is quite what it seems
… nothing will ever be the same again
… she is left holding the baby, literally
… this book is bound to be a success
… more frightening than anyone could
    have imagined in their worst nightmares.

So as not to be negative, here are words from recent campaigns that did catch her eye and got her reading the rest of the copy:

high-rolling	enrapturing
twizzling	engrossing
exuberant	vital
banal	frisky
bizarre	striking
abrasive	inestimable
eye-washing	incomparable.
delirious	

Justine commented: 'I believe the secret of good copy is enjoyment. If I, as a buyer, find that I am relishing what I read in my "bumf", I will enjoy actually selling the product and buy more from you.'

You should also avoid publishingese – words that mean different things to those involved with books from the rest of the population. For example, the heavily over-used 'accessible', which to the rest of the world means you don't have to stand on a step ladder to reach it. Similarly, avoid using in-house jargon – most of the population haven't a clue what a 'C format paperback' is.

Get to the point. Avoid long flowing sentences of introduction. Home straight in on the main benefits to the reader. When dealing with complex subjects with which they are not wholly familiar, many copywriters use the first paragraph to work their way into the subject; to demonstrate their understanding. Readers are not interested – get on with what is in it for them. It is remarkable how often simply deleting the first paragraph will improve the readability of copy.

Don't be clever or pompous, even when you are writing to an audience that is either or both. Imagine you were explaining the benefits to a prospect face to face; you would be concentrating on the product not your presentational style. Many people assume that when writing to academics or high-powered business people they should produce a suitably lofty tone. Avoid this. It slows the reader down and impedes access to benefits. What is more, if you are not expert in the subject, you may get the jargon wrong or sound patronising. Academics get enough tortuous prose from their students.

Don't drone on about your company. The average reader could not care less; it is the specific product that has attracted their attention. If there is information that is relevant to the product give it, but spare the reader the rest of the potted company history. The following is plenty:

> This new 20-volume work comes from the publishers of the respected *Everyperson Encyclopaedia*, and was researched and written with the same accuracy and attention to detail.

Avoid flowing passages of purple prose, even if you are particularly pleased with them. Indeed, your own admiration for sections of your work should be your guide to what needs deleting. If it stands out to you as a particularly good use of words it will probably strike the reader in the same way, and slow down reading flow. Or as G K Chesterton put it: 'Murder your babies'.

Tell a story, talk to the reader, adopt a tone of sweet reason

This is best achieved by completing the research on the product, noting down the main sales points and then writing from memory. By doing this you explain the benefits to yourself as you write, and your copy is more likely to be convincing.

Overcome any objections the reader may think of while reading, perhaps by using question and answer panels, for example:

Why is this new biography needed?
Who will use this manual?

Don't be controversial or provide anything for the reader to argue with: the result will be that they stop reading altogether, either to analyse their reaction in more detail or through sheer annoyance. Your sales message is wasted.

Let the copy flow. Use linking phrases so that the text reads fluently. Copywriter Roger Millington calls these phrases 'buckets and chains'.

And of course …	For example …
At the same time …	This includes …
Not to mention …	In addition …
Did you realise …	On the other hand …
After all …	Finally I must mention …
Just as important …	Two final points …

Make your copy personal. This means using 'you' rather than 'one' or 'they', and relating the examples you use to the interests of the reader. For example, instead of:

One-third of the population will develop cancer at some time in their lives; for 20 per cent of the population it will eventually be terminal.

try:

One in three people get cancer; one in five die from it.

or:

You have a one in three chance of getting cancer; a one in five chance of dying from it.

Quote actual people rather than statistics, for example, instead of:

20,000 copies sold.

try:

20,000 art lovers have already bought this book.

Keep editing

Write long and then cut back to the essentials. Are there still words that are not really necessary to the sense and which you could manage without? Delete extra adverbs and adjectives: they slow the reader down. Avoid estate agentese, a bland and predictable prose, where one adjective is never used where two can be squeezed in (a practice that seems to be spreading with alarming rapidity):

this perfect and lovely ground floor flat
convenient and well-positioned house
useful and timely book.

You don't need both; think of a more original alternative.

Structure the layout of benefits and selling points

Don't oversell: don't provide more selling points than the reader needs to reach a buying decision. One or two may be plenty.

Don't end the page or column of copy with a full stop; make the text 'run over' so that the reader is encouraged to continue.

Writers of mailshots often save the biggest benefit for the end of the sales letter, perhaps putting it in the PS (regarded as one of the most highly read parts of the letter). There will be hints that this big benefit is coming for this who read from the start to encourage them to keep going.

Divide up your copy

If you walk along a street of terraced houses with no front gardens you will find your eye is automatically attracted to the first gap: perhaps a side street or a house set back from the road. Look at a page of text and the effect is the same: see how your eye is sucked into the spaces.

There is another reason. Most of us are short of time, and faced with a page of text (even if we have written it) we 'skim read', homing in on the features we find most interesting. Use this information to manipulate your readers, encourage them to be attracted to the sections and features most crucial to your message.

For the same reason think carefully about asking for text to be set 'justified' (right and left margins vertically aligned). Use a ragged right-hand margin to attract the reader's eye into white space.

Aim for visual variety. Ensure your paragraphs and sentences are of varied lengths. Short sentences attract attention: try this technique at the beginning or end of paragraphs. It works.

Use bullet points (heavy dots at the beginning of each line) for a list of short selling points. Beware of over-bulleting just because you can think of a large number of benefits to highlight: the text can end up looking riddled and the effect of sharpening the reader's attention is lost. Five or six is plenty.

Subheadings attract attention to your main selling points; each one can be fully explained in the paragraph that follows.

> Try indenting paragraphs for extra emphasis, using both the right hand of the page and the left for maximum effect.

Number your paragraphs.

Use <u>underlines</u> and CAPITAL LETTERS (sparingly though).

Print in **bold** or in a different typeface. Laser printers and desk top publishing machines can produce a variety of wonderful effects, but do be careful that your finished text doesn't resemble a sampler designed to show the machine's capabilities rather than an advertisement.

Put copy in boxes.

If your material is to be printed, put a tint behind the box, or reverse the text out (use reversed-out text sparingly as it is harder to read).

Many readers who cannot be bothered to read a whole page of text will have their attention caught by illustrations. So ensure every picture has a caption, and that the captions pass on the main sales benefits. Tables and bar charts divide up the copy and, armed with captions, reinforce your message.

Give facts not opinions

Qualify every statement you make. If you don't, doubt may creep into the reader's mind as to the validity of your arguments. So instead of:

widely used in major companies

say where:

in extensive use at ICI and BP.

This prize-winning book ...
Winner of the 1999 Belling prize for scientific research.

This new work is based on extensive research.

These two volumes are the result of over 20 years' research in the Wedgwood family archives, the British Museum and other sources. Publication marks the first time that the subject has been explored in such detail.

Review quotations are more valuable to the reader than your opinion, but when deciding which ones to use, choose those from journals best known to the market, even if slightly less complimentary than those that appeared in lesser known journals.

Don't make the reader sound stupid

You probably don't realise that this new research has been published.

Sounds patronising and may alienate, particularly if the reader does realise! How about:

Market research showed us that many people did not realise that this new research was available. I am therefore writing ...

(ie, shifting the blame from the reader to the publisher.)

Using the negative

The use of the negative can confuse your message. You risk your reader:

(a) missing the negative or

(b) associating the negative with your product.

So, instead of:

> If you do not find this book essential to your everyday work we will refund your money.

try:

> You will find yourself consulting this book every working day or we will refund your money.

Humour

Avoid humour unless you are a very good writer. As Claude Hopkins said:

> 'No one buys from a clown.'

Repeat yourself

Someone once spelled out the basic theory of writing a direct mail sales letter, and the practice can be extended to many other promotional formats where there is space to develop an argument, such as brochures and press releases:

> Tell them what you are going to tell them
> Then tell them
> Then tell them what you have just told them.

Having said repeat yourself, do so in different words each time, don't be boring. Probably the dullest start to any advertisement is to repeat either the title of the book or the headline. Equally yawn-worthy are:

> This new book is …
> This new title is …

Get used to using a thesaurus

The most difficult word to find a synonym for is 'book'. Try the following:

new edition, title, report, work, text, study, or qualify the book as a casebook, sourcebook, reference book.

Other ideas for attracting attention

- **Feature the author.**   Is he or she controversial, newsworthy, interesting in their own right? Allow the new book to be promoted on the back of the name; to the media the personality is often more interesting than the fact they have written a book.
- **Invent/use a character.**   Several primary school publishers have lifted characters from their software programmes and illustrated schemes to enliven their promotion material.
- **Offer a firm guarantee.**   It shows complete confidence in your product and can compensate for asking for money up front. Challenge the reader. Are you offering the best value for money, a fantastic read or your money back? You'll be surprised how very few people claim refunds; far more will be impressed by your immense certainty that your product is excellent.

General advertisers can link their promotions to themes the public will find interesting. In *The Craft of Copywriting* Alastair Crompton lists the following:

animals   babies   cars   disasters   entertainment   fashion
holidays   money   royalty   sex   sport   war   weddings.

Think how closely this list follows the chief headline interests of the tabloid press.

See also Chapter 6 on direct marketing; Chapter 9 on other promotional ideas: competitions; incentives; free samples; news sheets and much more.

On accepting criticism

Lastly in this section, the urge to alter someone else's copy must be one of the hardest temptations to resist. Faced with almost any piece of text, one can always think of a better way of wording it. As part of the management process, copy shown for approval tends to mean copy changed (otherwise there is no evidence of managerial input).

When others try to change what you have written, do try to distinguish between valid criticism and the desire to meddle. Being objective about your own work will help you when you come to commissioning copy from freelances.

Topping and tailing your promotion material

When looking at an advertisement or promotional feature most readers instinctively do two things:

1. They look at the headline.
2. They look at the bottom of the page to see who is advertising.

This means that the information presented in these two places is absolutely vital. A good headline can grasp the reader's attention and set the tone for an interesting advertisement; an effective 'signing off block' can restate the main sales benefits and urge the reader to buy the product.

Yet still many publishers' advertisements start with information that is interesting to themselves rather than their customers. 'New from Snodgrass and Wilkins' is accurate, and may even be interesting if the firm has a world-renowned geography list and the feature appears in the *Geography Teachers' Review*. Too often, though, this approach is the inevitable start to a huge range of advertisements, simply because the copywriter doesn't have time or – dare I suggest – can't be bothered to think of anything else.

Similarly, if you were a rep and had just spent 20 minutes selling a product to a potential customer, the very last thing you would forget would be to ask for the order. Yet many publishers forget the Action stage of AIDCA. What is the point of stimulating interest, desire and finally conviction that your product is the one for them, if you then fail to make it clear how to obtain it?

Here follow some ideas for getting advertising material off to a good start, and for rounding it off to ensure that it produces the right results: orders.

Headlines

● At the risk of stating the obvious, the headline should go at the top of the page or space. Flick through any recent newspapers or magazine and you will see how your eye is attracted to the bold headline, wherever it appears. If it is sited in the middle of the page and is sufficiently interesting for you to carry on with the rest of the text, you will find yourself reading what is immediately beneath the heading, even if that point is halfway through the explanatory copy.

- Advertisements attract attention if the copy or look of the material is personal and relevant. So if you are writing for a specific market, name it:

  Calling all mothers!
  Important information for all maths teachers.

- Target benefits to the audience as specifically as possible. Which of the following headlines would be of most interest to Sally Brown, new promotions assistant at Heinemann?

  How all promotions departments can work more effectively.
  How all new promotions assistants can do their jobs better.
  Promoting books? How you can do your job better.

- Don't be ambiguous or clever. Blind headlines (which can only be understood once the rest of the copy has been read) are best avoided. If meaning is only semi-apparent most readers won't bother to investigate further.

- One of the most reliable techniques for starting a headline is to ask a question:

  Why? What? Where? How? Who? When?
  How will this book save you time and money?
  Why is everyone talking about this new novel?

- Start your headline by saying something controversial (preferably something which stimulates debate rather than causes an outright denial and the reader to stop!).

- Feature a strange word.

- Use catchwords that are instantly interesting.

  Now   Free   Introducing   Announcing   Secret   Magic
  Mother   Unique   Money off   Save £££   Sale
  Offer closes   Guarantee   Bargain.

- Include a promise.

  A completely new kind of DIY manual: satisfaction or your money back.

● Feature news or a new way of using the product you are promoting.

Why each year over 100,000 new businesses fail.

● Use a quotation. David Ogilvy reckoned if you put the headline in quotation marks you increase recall by 25%. So if you have testimonials at your disposal use them at the top of the ad; or put a comment of your own in inverted commas.

'How your company can benefit from the latest techniques in marketing'.

For backlist titles, are there any favourable reviews that will serve as headlines?

● If you are mailing your information, put an eye-catching headline on the envelope. State your best offer or start a story but don't finish it so the reader is encouraged to open the envelope and read on.

How spending £100 on a new reference work will help your company save thousands more ...

If your budget won't stretch to overprinted envelopes a cheaper solution is to have a *slub* produced. A slub sits next to the postage-paid symbol on a franking machine and is reproduced every time an envelope is stamped. The cost is small and the technique works well for simple slogans:

Out now
Who's Who 151st edition
30,000 biographies
From A&C Black

Ask the person who looks after your company's outgoing post about having one produced.

Coupons and order forms

● Once you know how much advertising space has been booked, or how big your leaflet is to be, the order form should probably be the first thing to be designed. If potential customers are motivated to buy, it is essential that they find it easy to order. If your order form or coupon is difficult to complete you will reduce response.

- Learn from the experts how to compile a form that is easy to use. Insurance proposal forms and the annual tax return are excellent examples of clarity. Both provide reversed out white space for anything the customer has to complete; you can see at a glance if all the required information has been given.

- An order form should be a mini version of the advertisement, restating all the main selling points. Start with the chief one:

  Yes, I would like to save £50 on a set of the new *Children's Encyclopaedia*.

- Do be aware of the number of people reading the magazine or journal in which your advertisement will appear; it may have a far wider circulation than just the original subscriber or purchaser. So if you are providing a tear-off card or coupon for response, ensure that your address and number for telephone orders appear elsewhere on the advertisement. It does happen that you cut out an order form to send, and then find the address is back on the advertisement, in the magazine, wherever that is.

- It is essential to provide numbers for telephone, fax and e-mail orders, preferably freefone if you are targeting consumers at home. It is reckoned that as many coupons get cut out but don't get sent as do come back. Make sure the system for answering it is up and running by the time the promotion goes out. (Ring all the numbers on your order form before you pass for press, just to make sure they are what you say they are.)

- All direct marketing companies are now collecting e-mail addresses and you can also rent lists of e-mail addresses in the same way as you rent a mailing list. Regular Internet users like doing business that way.

- The position of the order form. It should be on an edge, preferably the bottom right-hand edge of a right-hand page so that it can be cut out with the minimum of disruption to the text. A better option is to ensure your coupon backs on to another ad (rather than text) as readers may be unwilling to chop up journals that are kept for reference. Do ensure your coupon does not back on to another coupon.

Lastly, a checklist of useful tips on preparing orders forms that produce results:

1. Call the form something different: entitlement opportunity; invitation to a demonstration; estimate; hotline; information request; free sample request form.
2. Include an envelope so the recipient does not have to hunt for one. Use freepost or business reply for offers to consumers. For business-to-business mail it does not make much difference.
3. Put a time limit on the offer.
4. Offer a free gift for a prompt response. (Your warehouse is probably full of suitable items.)
5. Keep the shape simple – no complicated cut-outs, however pretty they look. You may have seen coupons the shape of the British Isles or telephones but I bet not many get returned.
6. Give telephone, fax and e-mail hotlines. Put little diagrammatic symbols next to them to attract attention, so customers can find the numbers in a hurry and don't ring the wrong one by accident.
7. Leave plenty of space for the customer to write his or her name, address and postcode. (It's expensive for your customer services department to have to question the information given. Ask customers for a contact telephone number in case of query.)
8. Repeat the benefits on the order form.
9. Repeat the terms of the offer.
10. Test cash up front versus approval.
11. Announce which credit cards you accept by showing little pictures of the cards – it attracts attention. Provide enough space to write the *whole* number, legibly; avoid little boxes. Be sure to ask whether the card name and address are the same as the orderer's. Provide a space for writing the additional information if necessary.
12. Name your product on the order form and show a picture of it if you have room.
13. Test third person copy against first person.
14. Test putting all the facts (ISBN, number of pages, etc) against minimal facts.
15. Use rushing words to encourage the reader to act immediately – 'rush', 'express', 'now'.
16. Personalise by pre-addressing. Find out the cost of laser printing the details on the order form. If this is too expensive,

try sticking the address label on the order form and use a window envelope so it shows through for posting.

17. Test integral coupons against separate coupons.
18. Test charging postage and packing against giving it free, or make it conditional on the size of order. Similarly, test offering free insurance for larger purchases.
19. Add extra tick boxes: for a catalogue; to hear about future titles in the same field so that customers keep in touch with you even if they do not want to order now.
20. Try different colour order forms, or use spot colour on an integral one.
21. If your order form is not being perforated, print a dotted line with scissors around the order form to show where it should be detached.
22. Include a second order form.
23. Stick real postage stamps on the reply device and ensure they are visible through the window of the envelope before it is opened: this increases the reader's perceived value of your mailing package.
24. Ask for all the information on your order form that you think you may need in future when you come to contact your customers again. (But beware: if you ask for too much information you may put your customers off responding.)
25. Make it clear to whom cheques should be made out.
26. Offer the option to buy on standing order (less hassle; no obligation to purchase; a possible discount).
27. Code each order form for different mailing lists.
28. Ask for the name of a friend to whom information on your products should be sent.

Notes

1. 30 May 1984, Royal Gala Evening to celebrate the 150th anniversary of the Royal Institue of British Architects at Hampton Court.

4

Different Types of Promotional Format

The early stages

Before considering the variety of different formats your promotional material may take it is worth thinking about what gets said about a product on its journey through a publishing house.

The very first information the marketing department receives will probably be the initial in-house alerting form to say the product is definitely going to be published. This may be accompanied by a copy of the author's publicity form. The short description or 'blurb' offered will probably have been written by the author or editor, perhaps a combination of the two.

A word of warning. The more you become familiar with copy you don't understand, the more you will come to *assume* you know what it means. Your initial reaction of bafflement will, however, be exactly that of all the other non-specialists – sales reps, non-specialist book-sellers, librarians and others who may consider ordering the title on someone else's behalf. Never assume, either, that English is the recipient's first language.

So get involved early. If you don't understand the blurb, feel it is too wordy or lengthy, attempt to unravel the meaning *now* rather than accepting that, at this stage, the information is still 'for in-house use only' (it almost never is). Ask yourself whether you really understand the key features of the book. Are they lost in description? Even for a highly technical title the key selling points or reasons the book has been commissioned should be instantly obvious.

Remember that the results of your efforts will last: information prepared at this stage will be loaded on to the company computer database for retrieval and use in a variety of other guises ranging from catalogue copy to an advance notice. Once a blurb is in existence it is extremely hard to change.

Advance notices or advance information sheets

How to write an advance notice that people will read

An advance notice is usually the first opportunity to alert both the firm and the wider market to the forthcoming publication of a new title. It is sent to bookshops, wholesalers, the company's reps and overseas agents, and any other parties interested in the firm's publishing programme.

Ideally despatched six to nine months ahead of publication (less in the case of 'perishable' titles), it needs to be with wholesalers and bookshops to allow time for the subscription of orders; further ahead if the information contained is to be catalogued and included in their own promotional material, or the subject of a special publisher–retail promotion.

Because an advance notice is usually drafted by the editors it is often viewed as an editorial document. Forget that, its task is to sell.

The proposed text is usually sent to the marketing department before it is printed. If this is the first chance you have had to take a detailed look at the proposed title copy, it is vital that you do so. Make sense of what you read, edit and amend, and submit your efforts for approval. Try to improve readability by shortening sentences or adding bullet points to highlight key features. If your efforts at simplifying are rejected on the grounds that the author is a specialist on the subject and he/she wrote the blurb you are attempting to unravel, gently remind critics that bookshops and reps receiving the information will not be specialists; like you they should understand what they receive.

Relevant brevity is best. An advance notice serves to tell busy bookshop buyers why they should stock the title; to provide the rep or agent with sales ammunition. Don't feel every inch of space has to be covered: densely packed copy is very off-putting.

What information should be included in an advance notice?

- Author, title and sub-title (actual, not a working approximation)
- Format (actual dimensions, not in-house jargon)
- ISBN (complete, ie 10 digits plus a valid check digit – the final number in the series) and extent
- Imprint
- Series
- Publication date and price. Be realistic not optimistic: publishers get a name for the accuracy of their predications
- Discount, if special (this is essential if it's different from the norm)

- Short blurb
- Brief author information, including brief sales history of previous titles and editions if relevant. Where the author is based (the rep for that area will want to persuade the local bookshop to take stock)
- Who is it for?
- Key selling points. What is new about it? What needs does it meet? Why did your house decide to publish? Why should the bookseller stock the title? Why is the book better than the competition? (These are probably best set out as a series of bullet points.)
- Scope – ie broad description of what the book covers
- Contents. If they are long and complicated, stress 'main features/papers' first
- Key promotional highlights arranged so far. If you have already arranged for the title to be serialised in *The Sunday Times* at the time of publication, say so. If it is a book with a strong regional flavour, say you will be targeting the local radio station. If the book is one of your lead titles for the season and so has an enormous promotion budget, pass on the information
- Details of illustrations, colour or black and white
- Binding
- Dumpbin information (quantity, mix, price and ISBN)
- Point of sale information (what will be available and when)
- Address, telephone and fax numbers of the publisher.

Some publishers put the title in bold or underline it and then repeat as often as possible on the grounds that they are reinforcing the words in the readers' mind (the same technique as in radio advertising). The reader, on the other hand, gets used to recognising a familiar block of copy and skips past. It may never get read. Far better to use the space to explain why the book is being published.

Catalogues

The production of catalogues is one of the main regular activities of those marketing books.

Successful management of their preparation and production is vitally important – not only do they stimulate orders by presenting the firm's wares in an attractive light, they are part of the regular selling cycle which the trade is used to responding to and hence expects. Catalogues are also a lasting form of promotion: once the initial ordering has been done, few are thrown away. For example, in bookshops they continue to function as reference material for enquiries and specific requests; in schools as the reference point for topping up stock levels.

Amassing title information (including all the last minute entries that will suddenly appear), checking publication and bibliographical details, rounding up illustrations, dealing with design and production – all involve a tremendous amount of detailed work.

How often catalogues are produced depends on the type of list being promoted. Many general houses produce six-monthly catalogues (usually autumn/winter and spring/summer) to fit in with their marketing and selling cycles, the catalogue forming the basic document for presentation at the sales conference that precedes each new selling season. Mass market paperback houses may produce catalogues or stocklists every month, usually three months ahead of the month of publication. Educational, academic and reference publishers often produce a separate annual catalogue for each subject area in which they publish. In addition, most houses produce a yearly complete catalogue which lists title, author and bibliographical information for their entire list.

The copy contained in a catalogue should vary according to the anticipated readership and use, the marketing department adapting the basic title information as appropriate. To get ideas on how to present information clearly and attractively study both the catalogues of your competitors and those of firms which have nothing to do with publishing (eg consumer goods sold by direct mail). The following tips will also be useful.

1.   Space for major titles

Ensure that the allocation of space in your catalogues reflects the relative importance of your various publishing projects – it's very reassuring to customers to know they are buying a successful product.

A major scheme or series should stand out as such to the reader: reviews, illustrations and sample pages can all be added to impress. The same goes for backlist titles that are still widely used by the market: if the publisher gives them a poor allocation of space the market will conclude they are scheduled for extinction. Catalogues selling consumer goods often repeat key items within the same edition. So however quickly the potential customer flicks through, the chances are they still note the products the firm really wishes to push.

HOW TO WRITE SALES LETTERS THAT SELL
2nd Edition
Drayton Bird

KEY SELLING POINTS
- **New edition of the established best-seller**
- **'If you manage to take on board just half of the suggestions, you will never write a dud sales letter again'** *Business Matters*
- **'Drayton Bird's clear, concise advice on what really matters in a sales letter is a welcome relief'** *Marketing* **Magazine**
- **Packed with examples of sales letters proven to have excellent results**

READERSHIP & MARKET
- **Sales and marketing professionals**

DESCRIPTION
The right piece of direct mail can produce excellent response rates and have an extraordinary effect on a business. But why do some sales letters achieve spectacular results whilst others are instantly consigned to the bin?

Drayton Bird, the internationally renowned expert on direct mail, reveals the secrets of creating successful sales letters in this best-selling book. Packed with examples of real sales letters, it includes plenty of advice on what to avoid as well as what to include. Key topics are covered in the author's readable style, including the secrets of persuasion; planning a letter which will get replies; creating offers that get responses, and; timing mailings for maximum effect.

MARKETING & PUBLICITY
- **Extensive direct marketing to members of the Chartered Institute of Marketing, the Marketing Society, the Institute of Directors and other professional groups**
- **High profile editorial and advertising coverage in the national, regional and business press**

AUTHOR INFORMATION
Drayton Bird has over 40 years' experience as a copywriter, creative director and latterly as Vice Chairman and Creative Director of the world's largest direct marketing network, Ogilvy and Mather. Today he runs the Drayton Bird Partnership, which handles marketing activities for clients both large and small. An internationally celebrated speaker and featured columnist in *Marketing* Magazine, he is also the author of the best-selling *Commonsense Direct Marketing* and *Marketing Insights and Outrages*, both published by Kogan Page.

Published: September 2002		Territory: World	
Subject Category: Sales/Marketing		320 Pages	Size: 234x153mm
Paperback £18.99		Band: 01	Order Form Ref: 07
ISBN: 0749438762		Previous ISBN:	0749414316

KOGAN PAGE

120 Pentonville Road LONDON N1 9JN
Tel: +44 (0) 20 7 278 0433 Fax: +44 (0) 20 7 837 6348
www.kogan-page.co.uk info@kogan-page.co.uk

Figure 4.1 *A sample advanced notice for a recent title from Kogan Page*

As a guide to how much space to allow for different titles try comparing sales figures (real or anticipated) with the available space. At the same time, do try to avoid a rigid space allocation, which is very boring to the reader. For example, the common practice of giving all the big titles a double page at the front of the catalogue, a page each in the middle to the mid list and then putting the 'also rans' as a series of small entries at the back, carries a clear message as to what is and what is not important.

What most interests the recipient will probably be what is new or revised, so make clear use of flags and headlines to attract attention.

2.   Order forms

Include an order form (or an inspection copy request form) with each catalogue and monitor the response. Not all orders will come back directly to you, but if you take a note of the recorded sales before a catalogue goes out and a second reading a certain time after most orders have been received, you will have a reasonably accurate picture of how effective the material was. Some publishers take their monitoring a lot further, comparing space allocated with orders, producing an analysis of revenue per page. Such information over a number of years will enable you to assess the merits of different layouts and the effect they have on sales.

Similarly, you can test the benefits of order forms that are bound in as opposed to loose inserts or stiff order forms that fold out from the cover; those which require the customer to list titles selected against those which provide the information, requiring only a tick to purchase. Different methods of payment too can be tested against each other. One final tip. Have you noticed how consumer mailings often enclose two order forms with any catalogue? In so testable a medium it must be working. What other tricks can you learn from them?

3.   Layout

Presentation of information within a catalogue should be clear.

On each page it should be instantly obvious which section is being referred to; perhaps by the use of 'running heads' showing section titles along the top (eg imprint and fiction/non fiction). Educational publishers often use running heads to indicate the age for which material is designed or the curricular subject area.

Ensure there is both a table of contents (highlighting key new products with page references) and an index; both are vital for accessing information in a hurry.

4. Cover

Put product(s) on the front of your catalogue; far more interesting to the recipient than 'new autumn books from Doods and Co'. Can you imagine consumer mailers putting only the words 'new items from us' on the front of their catalogue? They want you to start reading product information as soon as possible. If not a product try a really attractive and appropriate illustration. Educational publishers have been known to produce posters for schools of popular catalogue covers.

For catalogues that will be used in one-to-one selling, for example by the rep visiting schools or bookshops, a light coloured background on the front cover allows notes to be written, and noticed later on by the recipient.

For lists aimed at a particular vocational market (eg school books, ELT materials) a letter, perhaps from the editor, on the inside front cover of the catalogue can attract wide readership. It should always have a signature and look like a letter. Such a start to the catalogue can serve to introduce the list, attract attention to particular highlights and express an interest in the readers' ideas for publications (always a good way of ensuring the catalogue gets retained!).

5. Illustrations

Include as much illustration as possible. Covers are the first choice, particularly for a series. However prominently in the copy you write 'series', the sight of a group of covers is more eye-catching and hence effective.

Avoid featuring covers that are too subtle and 'designer' in appearance. What you see at full size will disappear when reproduced at postage stamp size. Similarly, check that the titles on reduced covers are still legible.

You can also use illustrations (always with a selling caption), sample pages, photographs (perhaps of the materials in action) and line drawings.

6. Academic catalogues

Full author affiliations and contents are vital. Which qualifications/academic level do the various titles prepare students for?

Most publishers in this area encourage academics to send for inspection copies if titles are likely to be featured on recommended reading lists. Make sure that you word these offers carefully. For a title that has a large prospective purchase among students, what you want is the academic to wave the book in front of the entire class and recommend purchase. If they are worried about maintaining 'mint condition' so the book can be returned, they may not do this for you. In practice many 'inspection copies' either get retained by the academic or returned and pulped. Ensure you get what you want out of the system – promotion direct to the right market.

Try to keep entries to a single page, avoiding the practice of taking a few lines over to the next one. The fate of catalogues mailed to academics is often for specific entries to be cut out or photocopied and circulated with a view to purchase. Carrying over copy makes the task more difficult and is annoying.

7. Last-minute entries

However well posted your catalogue deadlines are, last-minute copy on books that simply must be included will always appear. Bear in mind that if you wait for every last correction you will never get to the market, *and getting to the market when the market is expecting your information (and when your competitors' details will be there) is what really matters*.

If your deadline is past and the costs of remaking pages to include a particular important extra title are unjustified, try including the copy on a 'stop press postcard'. This can also function as an order form/inspection copy request card.

Leaflets and flyers

Flyers are cheaply produced leaflets. In general, I would count anything with a fold or more than two colours as a leaflet, single sheets as flyers.

If you are producing a range of flyers for insertion in mailings and handing out at exhibitions, do make them look different. I once produced a range of slim science leaflets advertising titles. Each one was printed in black ink on yellow paper, one-third A4 size. The results were very eye-catching, but when attending a conference I noticed that delegates examining our stand clearly assumed that they all advertised the same title. Thereafter I used a different colour stock for each leaflet.

The information you provide will depend on the purpose for which the leaflet/flyer is to be used, but in general try to make the format suit as many possible anticipated needs as you can. You can then add a letter to turn it into a mailshot; enclose in journals as a loose insert; send out with a press release to provide further title information; insert in parcels. Give details of how to order; the space can be left blank on a bookseller version for over-stamping with the shop's name and address.

Direct mail shots

See Chapter 6, Direct Marketing.

Press releases

See Chapter 8, 'Free' Advertising.

Presenters

Many trade publishing houses produce these for reps to use when presenting new titles to bookshop buyers. Presenters often form substantial (at least six sides of A4), glossy summaries of media and promotional plans and spend for individual titles and their supporting backlist. Usually produced in full colour, they are often laminated or at least varnished.

When bookshop buyers are busy and reps have little time in which to attract their overstretched attention, such promotion pieces can play a key part in getting the importance of the title and its associated image across quickly. Hopefully, a corresponding commitment to take stock follows.

Posters, showcards and point of sale

These are produced by publishers and distributed to bookshops to attract customers' attention to major books, series or imprints at the place where they are available for purchase. The market's understanding should be instant, so such material should not be too copy-heavy or clever (eight words on a poster site is usually plenty). Sometimes they are not even put up in stores who accept them, but serve to demonstrate to the bookshop that a publisher is highlighting a major product and so form an effective method of ensuring advance orders.

Dumpbins, which carry multiple copies of a key title, are often produced to encourage booksellers to take a large quantity of stock. These usually have a header which slots into the top of the box to attract attention. Use this space creatively – avoid repeating the book title here, as it will be repeated on every cover beneath.

The days of one-size-fits-all for dumpbins have gone forever. Several bookshop chains now refuse to take them altogether, on the grounds that they interrupt the shop's designed environment and they have their own material. You may be required to produce dumpbins to the exact requirements of other outlets such as super-markets – usually worth it if a large stock order results.

Other point of sale items may include give-away items such as balloons, bookmarks, badges and mobiles.

Space advertisements

See Chapter 12, Approaching Specific Interest Markets.

Advertorials

Advertorials are advertisements that masquerade as editorial copy. In an editorially biased magazine or paper, David Ogilvy reckoned six times as many people read the average editorial feature as the average advertisement.

Use the same typeface, caption illustrations in the same way, and use the same 'editorial' style. You may find that – Advertisement – or Advertisement Feature – is printed by the magazine at the top of your space, but your message will gain in authority and readership and more people will remember it. For precisely these reasons some magazines do not allow advertorials. One word of caution. Be careful that you don't end up paying for what the magazine would have printed free, as a feature.

Along similar lines is 'sponsored editorial', whereby the customer takes advertising space in return for a commitment from the maga-zine to provide editorial coverage.

Information for telesales campaigns

See Chapter 6, Direct Marketing.

Radio ads

Radio ads have been used very successfully for books in recent times. The launch of many commercial radio stations (eg Classic FM, Capital Gold) have offered cheap opportunities; tying the commercials up with promotional offers such as competitions can secure a wealth of coverage at very competitive prices.

Most memorable ads tell a story, as was used in this very successful promotion from Orion on Classic FM.[1]

Thirty-second radio advertisement for The Glass Lake by *Maeve Binchy*

Telephone distort applied to Sally throughout.

Sound effects:	telephone ringing tone.
Female:	Come on!
Sound effects:	click as telephone is picked up
Sally (telephone distort):	Hello?
Female:	Sally? Is your Mum there? I've got some great gossip for her.
Sally:	She won't come to the phone.
Female:	Won't come to the phone? Why not?
Sally:	*Reading*.
Female:	(surprised) Reading! What's so good?
Sally:	*The Glass Lake*. It's the new Maeve Binchy.
Female:	(echoing on the other end) New Maeve Binchy? *The Glass Lake*. *That's* why nobody's rung me all week.
Sally:	Nor me!
Female:	*That* should keep your parents' phone bills down!
Sally:	Shall I get her to call you back?
Female:	Of course not! I'll be reading *The Glass Lake*.
Sound effects:	phone put down.
Voiceover:	*The Glass Lake*. Maeve Binchy. In paperback now from Orion. Even better than a gossip with a friend.

Classics revisited

A target detail from The Bowmen of England which records the last time the longbow was used to lethal effect... in France in 1940.

Pen & Sword, the military publisher founded by Leo Cooper, has long enjoyed the highest reputation for its battlefield guides, military histories, biographies, personal accounts and monographs of men and women at war. The rapidly growing market for military history — Professor Gary Sheffield described it as 'the new rock 'n' roll' and one national retail book chain sells more military history than any other branch of the subject — has prompted Pen & Sword to reach out to a wider readership.

This week sees the launch of *Pen & Sword Military Classics*. This is a series of trade or B-format paperbacks, which will cover all aspects of military history from ancient times to the late 20th century. All are re-issues, most are illustrated, some have new forewords or afterwords, but what they all have in common is a flowing, jargon-free narrative that will encourage the newcomer to the discipline to read further. And all for between £5.99 and £7.99 a book.

There is a wide range of subjects, and the first four titles reflect this. Donald Featherstone's *The Bowmen of England* describes the pre-eminence of the longbow in the Anglo-French conflicts of the Middle Ages, with a postscript telling of the last time the longbow was used in battle to lethal effect — in France in 1940. No other weapon dominated the battlefield as much as the longbow and it was a winning factor in every major battle from Morlaix in 1342 to Patay in 1429.

Ronald Lewin's *Life and Death of the Afrika Korps* recounts the phenomenon of Rommel's armies in North Africa, and since the Korps had the social characteristics of a well-ordered family, Lewin wrote the book as a biography. John Masefield's classic memoir *The Old Front Line* was written shortly after the battle of the Somme by the Poet Laureate who had spent months at the front and was familiar with the conditions endured by the men. With a new introduction by Martin Middlebrook, this is a poetically evocative contemporary guide to the Somme battlefield that can still be used by the visitor to the battlefield and enjoyed at home by armchair strategists.

Robin Neillands' *Wellington and Napoleon* contrasts the Corsican conqueror of Europe with the 'Sepoy General' who was unemployed in 1806 but who defeated Bonaparte's troops in battle after battle in the Peninsular, and who went on to become the victor at the Battle of Waterloo. Wellington, his men said, "didn't know how to lose a battle" and Napoleon never learned to counter his adversary's infantry, which cost him dear at Waterloo.

Future titles, in a list of 26 to be published in 2003, include Professor Tim Travers' *The Killing Ground*, an incisive analysis of the strategy which led to stalemate and trench warfare, a revised edition of Nigel Jones' personal guide to the Western Front, *The War Walk*, Philip Ziegler's *Omdurman*, and Dudley Pope's matchless tale of mutiny and revenge in the 18th century Royal Navy — *The Black Ship*.

Charles Hewitt, Managing Director of Pen & Sword Books, comments: "Marcus Clapham and Clive Reynard have assembled a superb range of titles, and subscription orders from UK and overseas booksellers and agents have already led to a big increase in our initial print orders. The support the trade is giving to this series fully justifies our biggest-ever marketing spend on promoting this exciting new series."

While reviewing Antony Beevor's *Berlin: The Downfall*, John Sexton asked why military history was enjoying such an upsurge in popularity. In answering the question he wrote: 'It remains the case that any pleasure to be derived by the general reader from military history is unlike the pleasure to be found in other forms of scholarship. It's not merely an addition to knowledge or insight into the past. Military history is ultimately about what men will put above life itself; what they will kill for and what they will die for. That is its special power'.

"This series has it in spades," enthuses Hewitt.

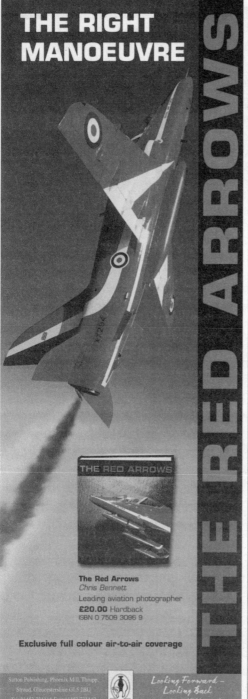

THE RIGHT MANOEUVRE

THE RED ARROWS

The Red Arrows
Chris Bennett
Leading aviation photographer

£20.00 Hardback
ISBN 0 7509 3096 9

Exclusive full colour air-to-air coverage

Sutton Publishing, Phoenix Mill, Thrupp,
Stroud, Gloucestershire GL5 2BU
Tel: 01453 731114 Fax: 01453 731117

*Looking Forward –
Looking Back*

www.suttonpublishing.co.uk

Transport and Militaria Books special

Pre-flight briefing for a Red Arrows team in Sion, Switzerland

A snapper's life at G Force 6

by Claire Bott

Few people who are not members of the precision-trained team of aerobatics Red Arrows pilots are allowed to share the flight deck, but photographer Chris Bennett has done so "about 120 times". And he has written about his experiences — along with his photos of the spectacular displays — in a new book for Sutton Publishing, *The Red Arrows*, which gets behind the scenes in a way that, Bennett believes, few books on the aerobatic team manage to do.

"So many books don't really go into the team itself," he says, "What I've tried to do is explain what it's really like to fly with them." But then, Bennett is no ordinary writer-photographer. For a start, his original reason for getting in to aerial photography was not a fondness of photography per se, but rather his long-standing love of fighter planes.

"I had an interest in military jet fighters, and I came up with an idea for a book mainly as a way to get to work with fighter jets." The book, *Superbase Bitburg Eagle Country*, published by Osprey in 1989, was Bennett's first photographic commission. "I literally had to go and buy cameras in order to do it."

After specialising in fighter planes for a little while longer, Bennett decided to widen his field, and has now worked on subjects as diverse as Harrods and the QE2 liner. "What I enjoy about photography is the diversity. Most photographers tend to specialise in one area or another." Bennett, however, has continued to spread his net as wide as possible. But fighter jets were, and have remained, his first love. And as he points out, the Red Arrows are the pinnacle of that particular tree, at least in this country. "One of the reasons I originally wanted to work with them is that jets are my favourite subject, and from a British point of view, the Red Arrows are the top."

So, after he put forward his idea to produce a book on the team and was rejected by the RAF, Bennett tried again. And again. And again, until finally, at his fourth try, persistence was rewarded, and permission was given. That was in 1996, and the book, *Red Arrows: A Year in the Life*, was published by Deutsch in 1997. Since then, Bennett has flown with the team many times. "I have maintained a relationship with the Red Arrows where I am kind of an official photographer. They know I'm trustworthy in the air, and there is a lot of mutual respect."

And when in the air with the Red Arrows, Bennett's reliability is very important indeed. He usually goes through several rolls of film per flight, and should he drop one while changing it over, the danger of having a small, unsecured object rolling around under the pilot's feet would force him to land the plane. And once on the ground, if the film had happened to roll away out of sight, the jet would have to be stripped down and the film found before the jet could take to the air again.

When you consider that Bennett is often making film changes while the aircraft is looping and rolling hundreds of feet above the ground, you begin to realise how important it is that he should be dependable, steady and sure-handed. What's more, he has to take all his photographs without jolting, or even touching, the control column, which, in the confined space of the cockpit, can be tricky.

Besides all this, there is the effect of the acceleration, which can go up to six Gs (six times the earth's gravitational pull). Bennett knows to his cost just what that means — on one occasion he was bending over his camera, reloading film, when the pilot went up to six Gs without warning him. "Suddenly my helmeted head weighed six times more than normal. Try as I might, I could not lift it. I even pushed on my chin with my right hand, but to no avail." The next day, Bennett was in agony from his wrenched neck and shoulder muscles, barely able to move. These days, he makes sure that when the G forces are going to go up to that extent he is sitting upright, with his head braced and his camera on his knee. He only takes photographs during the 'moderate' G forces of about 3G, and even this gives him burning pains in his shoulders from having to hold the camera steady against such a force.

"It's one of the hardest things I've done in photography," Bennett says. "Everything has its challenges, but for real, sheer responsibility and hard work, flying in jets is the hardest." In spite of this, it is still the part of his job that Bennett loves most. He once planned a career in commercial aviation, but gave up the ambition on realising he had no real desire to become "an air taxi driver". He says he doesn't know quite why the possibility of trying to become a fighter pilot himself never occurred to him, but feels his current profession gives him the best of both worlds. "I get to fly in lots of different jets, with different people, in different places. I just touch the subject, then I go and do something totally different, so it doesn't get a chance to become just going to work again."

And it never has become just a job to Bennett. It's still a thrill for him to fly in a fighter jet, and he still feels like pinching himself when the Red Arrows take to the air with him on board. He regards himself as privileged to be allowed to experience that, and asks rhetorically, "How many people would love to be here, to fly with the guys?"

The Red Arrows is published by Sutton on 24 April, £20.00, ISBN 0750930969

Figure 4.2 *Two examples of sponsored editorial (also often referred to as editorial features) kindly provided by Publishing News*

Note how during the commercial the title is continually repeated to get it across to the audience. Repetition is important as people often listen to the radio while doing other things; their attention is not totally focused.

This ad was broadcast over a two-week period. During the third week a competition was run (a question asked each day on the Henry Kelly show) and in the fourth week the announcement of the winners was trailed and then made. The company thus got four weeks' exposure for the price of two. Although it was not possible to quantify how much of it was due directly to the campaign, because of other factors involved, subsequent sales were 40 per cent up on those of the author's previous book.

Television ads

The chance to prepare these will occur rarely in the lives of most publishing marketers. When publishing houses can afford to mount television campaigns they usually assign them to specialised agencies. But there is no harm in knowing the tricks of the trade: it will make you a more discerning buyer of out-house services, and you may get a crack some time. Small budgets can pay for regional television and radio advertising and new channels may offer further opportunities.

If you are choosing between press and television as the best medium for a campaign, in general the less there is to explain about a product the better suited it is to television. Cheaper, mass market, products too work better on television; if customers are being asked to spend a lot of money they need a fuller explanation of benefits than is possible during an average length advertisement. An alternative is to give a telephone number for further information at the end of the commercial.

Classified ads

Classified advertising is one of the cheapest methods of promotion. Copy is usually typeset by the publication in which it is to appear.

With little space, no illustration and lots of similar advertisements to compete with, try to use the variables that are at your disposal to attract attention. Experiment with different type densities, capital and lower case letters. Quote established authorities such as professional qualifications. Give an incentive to do something now, such as ring for a free catalogue.

For ideas on how to handle the medium well consult the classified section of one of the magazines well known for its amusing and effective entries such as *Time Out* or *The Spectator*.

Semi-display ads

A step up from classified advertising, semi-display allows borders and illustrations. Don't take the permission to use reversed out text too seriously, it is hard to read. Do allow plenty of white space around the advertisement – it serves to draw the eye in. Have a look through your local Yellow Pages to see how effective – or otherwise – the use of a small advertising space can be.

Writing book jacket/cover copy

The information on a cover is usually drafted by the editor in consultation with the author. What appears is very important: it often forms the basis of a decision to buy. If you watch how customers in a bookshop assess a new title, you will see that the almost general sequence is look at the front cover, turn to the back for basic information on the title, and if this looks sufficiently interesting, to flick through the contents or read the first couple of pages.

The copy should cover all essential sales points:

- why it is interesting (often achieved through a sentence on the front cover – or 'shout line' that is either atmospheric or pithy)
- what is new/unique about the book
- what it is about (briefly)
- who it is for
- the scope
- the author's aim in writing it
- the author's credentials for doing so (previous well-known titles)
- any quotable extracts from reviews/experts
- bibliographic details.

The words you use should also give a flavour of the kind of book inside. So don't make a highly complicated sociological textbook sound like an easy read for all comers, or a 'beach read' sound like a contender for the Booker prize. If someone has been misled by one of your cover blurbs before and felt let down by the contents, they may be wary of buying from your imprint again.

As regards layout of jacket blurb, do make the text easy to read: don't centre the text or fit it around 'cut out' pictures so that the reader has to work hard to understand. Keep both sentences and paragraphs short and punchy.

How much of your jacket blurb will actually be read is debatable. Most readers will home in on the beginning and perhaps the end of the text, as Wendy Cope brilliantly captured in a blurb that appeared on the back cover of a promotional piece to advertise *Making Cocoa for Kingsley Amis:*

> Brilliant, original, irreverent, lyrical, feminist, nostalgic, pastoral, anarchic, classical, plangent, candid, witty – these are all adjectives and some of them can truthfully be used to describe Wendy Cope's poems. Very few people bother to read the second sentence of a blurb. Or the third. Most of them skip to the end where it says something like this: a truly spectacular debut, an unmiss-able literary event.

Notes

1. I am grateful to Orion for permission to reproduce this advertisement. Script written for Orion by Hugh Bulford and Cathy Douglas.

5

The Design and Printing of Promotional Materials

Design

Once copy has been written it needs to be presented in a suitable way for printing. This usually involves the services of a designer.

You may have an in-house design department who will work for you. The advantages are speed and accessibility – you can go from draft copy to on-screen approval of the final image in one afternoon. Alternatively, it may be left to you to commission the work out of house, either by using a firm of designers or one of the local free-lances that serve your company.

Whereas at one time every publishing house had its own in-house design department, today many are finding it more cost-effective to recruit such services out of house when they are needed rather than paying for them all the time. Publishing tends to be a very seasonal industry which results in some equally frenetic promotional cycles. A firm may require the services of several designers one month, but only a month later have very little for them to do. On-going promotional items (catalogues, advance notices) are often produced on desktop publishing machines by in-house staff. But the assumption that effectively laid-out material can be produced by secretarial staff, without any proper training on the equipment they are using, is usually a mistake.

Whoever you decide to use, do remember that the brief is yours. You may not have a design qualification, but nor will the market, and your common-sense ability to distinguish between what is easy to read and what is not is just as relevant.

What is good design?

In the context of the preparation of marketing material, a well designed piece of information is one that encourages the designated market to read it, to absorb the sales message and act on the recommendation to buy. Good design should stimulate without swamping; be implicit rather than explicit. Kate Hybert of Hybert Design commented: 'A well designed piece looks as if it was really simple to lay out; like it always *had* to go that way.' If readers starts admiring decorative borders that frame text will they remember to return to reading the list of product benefits?

Prepare yourself to recognise good design. Start scanning both the publications you are likely to advertise in and the general media for advertisements, and assess their impact. Read Ernst Gombrich's *The Story of Art* (Phaidon) and David Ogilvy's *Ogilvy on Advertising* (Prion). Visit art galleries; ask to look through designers' portfolios or your company's promotional archives, read relevant magazines such as *Creative Review* and *Design Week* and let your awareness of design grow. At the same time, it is important to try to keep up-to-date. Design is as volatile as clothing and car style – fashions change and design styles can look just as outdated as last season's fad.

How advertisements are read

The designer needs copy. As the person who either wrote it or commissioned it you will probably do a final check before you pass it on. You will start to read at the top of the page and work your way methodically through, looking out for spelling mistakes or verbs that have been used too often. (You may well miss some; it is very difficult to proofread your own work, particularly so on-screen.)

If, on the other hand, you can imagine yourself coming upon the text cold, or perhaps seeing it for the first time in its final form as an advertisement, you will realise that your reading habits are in reality much more haphazard. Uninvolved readers wait for their attention to be attracted, allow their eyes to flit around the page looking for something of interest and certainly do not feel duty-bound to read everything that is provided. They may look at the headline or picture, perhaps at the caption. Their eye may be drawn in by quotation marks – someone else's opinion is much more interesting to them than the view of the advertiser. The vast majority will get no further.

If their interest is stimulated they may look to the bottom right-hand corner or the back of a brochure to see who is advertising. Only then will motivated readers start on the main text (or body copy).

The reaction of potential readers to your marketing information will be the same. You cannot take their interest for granted and so must use all the means at your disposal to encourage: through the words you use, the illustrations you provide and the design layout that unites them.

For most publications there is also a style and order in which the articles and features are read. Awareness of this can help you present your sales information in the way most likely to ensure it gets noticed. Start observing your own reading habits. The most obvious one is a desire for ever-quicker access to information. The ability to 'zap' on screen if we are not interested has made us all more impatient to understand at once whether or not the information is relevant to us. This means that all advertising material has to work harder and quicker to draw a response.

In search of a quick review of what a magazine includes, many people flick through from the back forwards. Similarly, it is common to start reading a newspaper with a speedy trawl through the pages, allowing one's attention to be grabbed by particular headlines. Some people pause to read the articles beneath, others return to them later having scanned specific sections of the paper where they habitually find items of interest: the gossip column, the home news or the letters page. Many papers provide a series of 'news in brief' paragraphs on the inside front pages, allowing the reader to quickly grasp the essentials of the stories on offer that day; page references indicate the more detailed articles within.

Mailshots are read in a particular way too. Chapter 6 on direct mail will give further information on this but in general the letter gets read first, the headline, the signature and PS being the most highly noted parts. Look at the next one you receive and you will see how the senders have anticipated your reading habits.

How to find a designer

If you have an in-house department the choice of whom to use is largely made for you, although if there is a particular designer whose work you like try to steer it their way (difficult if the studio manager has other ideas). Finding freelance designers or local firms can involve more legwork, but in most towns where there is a demand for design you will find local services available. Ask your colleagues and printers that you use. Look in the Yellow Pages or in directories of freelances. It is important to bear in mind the level of services you require. An individual freelance designer with his or her own desktop publishing machine may be ideal for small jobs such as basic advertisements and flyers. For the creation of high-profile point-of-sale material or highly illustrated catalogues by a specific deadline you may need to commission a larger design group, to ensure that there will be additional staff to work on your job should a crisis strike.

You should certainly ask to see the portfolio of previous work of any designer you consider using. Look to see if the designer has done similar work to that which you need. Why not ask in-house designers to show your their portfolios too, as a guide to the kind of projects they have worked on in the past?

Once you have found a couple of designers whose work you like and who respond well to a brief, hang on to them. While I would not recommend relying solely on one designer – you need to ensure you have other options – I would advise against spreading your work too widely. Give those who work for you a decent amount of business so that they have a real incentive to please you.

To get an idea of the prices designers charge, pass on printed copies of a couple of previous jobs and ask for an estimate of what they would charge for preparing something similar. Compare this with the actual invoices you received. If they are far too expensive I would tell them so and use someone else rather than become a routine haggler. You may get a special price once but if you are consistently beating suppliers down below what they feel is a fair price you will earn resentment and they will be less inclined to help you when you need a favour, for example a job that needs doing in a real hurry.

You may call in a new designer to discuss a potential project but if you end up asking for their rough design ideas make it clear whether if what is submitted is acceptable they will get the job. Alternatively, agree a rejection fee of say 10 per cent of the fee.

Time is likely to be an important factor. Ask for an estimate of how long the job is likely to take and when you can expect a first visual. Most freelances live with the difficulty of juggling a variety of different jobs (it is impossible to predict what will arrive when and dangerous to say no). Establishing a time schedule for your particular job at the outset means it won't be left until last.

The designer's point of view[1]

Always remember when commissioning graphic design that a good designer will not only try to meet your project objectives but also take pride in what they do, so the more you can involve them and communicate your objectives the better.

The best design results are always obtained by clients who have a clear idea of what they want and can express it effectively, providing as much as possible of the information needed about the project at the *beginning* of the job. It is a pleasure to work with clients of this kind, we can take a pride in our creative efforts truly meeting a need, and their bills are always lower because they change their mind less often.

So what kind of clients end up paying more than they should? Obviously this is a difficult thing to talk about – a client is a client after all – but in general problems often arise if there is no written brief. There are:

- Clients who don't know what they want until they see it.
- Clients who know exactly what they want but can't communicate it to us.
- Clients who require visual after visual until we extract a brief from them, with both sides getting increasingly frustrated in the process.
- Committees are often difficult – we may deal with one person within an organisation but that person may need approval from several others who may not be in agreement with the requirement for the job (or even whether it needs doing at all), let alone how it is to be handled. The result is often the compilation of several design ideas with a dilution of the original concept, just to get the job out, with very little sense of satisfaction.
- Clients who pass back lots of amendments individually rather than collating them and passing back one set. It is very time-consuming to do amendments and it follows that the more sets arrive back, the higher the costs will be. Don't forget too that lots of sets of amendments can cause confusion and a greater risk that the job will have errors.

Here is one final point of my own for your guidance when dealing with external suppliers. Do remember the power of saying thank you. So if you are pleased with a job, do tell your suppliers. I suspect that many clients fail to do so because they assume that if the customer shows that they are very satisfied, the bills will go up in future. In fact absolutely the opposite is the case. There is nothing more rewarding than providing a service that is appreciated, and if your working relationship is flourishing, your creative bills may well go down.

The various stages involved in getting something designed and printed

Designer and printer speak

Definitions for commonly used terms and abbreviations are included in the Glossary.

1. You provide a brief

Writing a brief is a difficult thing to do. What you need to provide is a structure within which the designer's creative juices can start to flow, not a straitjacket to inhibit the good ideas which you alone would not think of. If you are too prescriptive the designer may respond with just what you ask for; thereby denying yourself access to their professional expertise.

The brief should cover a number of important facts, and should be written down.

- What you are hoping to achieve. How you want your market to feel when they receive it and what you want them to do as a result.
- The market you are targeting: who, where and why?
- The copy: how much; which are the really important sections?
- The relevant illustrations. You may need to commission special photographs (pack shots, point of sale shots, perhaps studio-sets and so on). These can be arranged by the designer or you may have your own in-house photographer to organise. Do bear in mind, however, that the arrangement, proportion, and colour of the illustrations will be an important part of the design of the promotion piece; so if you plan to use existing illustrations your designer needs to know before starting work. Captions provide an excellent spot for passing on key parts of your sales message. Reproducing covers also gives those reading your advertisements the chance to recognise your products in the shops.
- The budget you have available for design.

- How many colours you wish to print in.
- When you want the finished job by.
- The sort of the promotion piece you have in mind (try not to be closed to suggestions – the designer may come up with a better idea than you): leaflet, space advertisement, poster, etc. Include details of the format (size and extent) and provide a sample of what you want if you have one.
- What are you going to do with it? If it is to be mailed, the overall size and weight must be considered in relation to postage bands. If the paper is to be very lightweight the design will have to be planned accordingly to reduce the 'show through' of printing ink.
- If you are planning a space advertisement in a magazine, as well as a sample of the magazine you need to state: how the design should be provided, for example on disk with a laser proof, as an ISDN for bureau output (Integrated Services Digital Network – the use of a telephone line for the exchange of data between computers); screen ruling (the number of dots per inch); size; the trimmed page size; and bleed. If it is to be produced as film, your designer will need the appropriate film specifications (eg whether positive/negative; emulsion up/emulsion down). These details will be given to you by the publication concerned. If you are booking the same advertisement into several publications do not assume they all require it in the same format or size.

A choice of design approaches

I tend not to ask a designer to come up with a couple of alternative ideas on how to present information. I prefer all the effort to be channelled into thinking of one presentational idea that really meets my brief rather than two in which most of the design time has centred on making them different from each other. On the other hand, when producing designs to be approved by a meeting or outside body more than one may be advisable. Bear in mind that two or three choices presented to a meeting will nearly always result in a decision (whether a straight choice or combination of bits from different versions). This is a useful technique when dealing with difficult committees.

The copy you give the designer should be your final draft, double spaced and printed, with headings clearly marked. Assuming the copy has been prepared on a word processor you can pass it over on disk or send it as an e-mail file directly to the designer, faxing a hard copy at the same time. Doing this means that you save paying for the keying in of copy by the typesetter and the errors that may result from this. It is a particularly useful practice if you are responsible for a highly complex subject area where spellings (and in particular names) are elaborate and the possibility for new errors when keying is high. It does however mean that the copy you pass on must be absolutely perfect: all the typographical changes will be charged to you.

2. The designer provides a first visual

The effective handling of type is a vital part of the designer's job. Using your brief on what kind of job it is, the designer will decide on the typeface (there are 5,000 to choose from), the size of type, the width of the margins and so on; lay out your text to these specifications; and then provide you with a visual to show what the finished job will look like. Today most designers have typesetting as part of their on-screen design facilities. A visual will show you the format and design layout, the colours, the position of headings and so on.

Once you have approved the overall concept the designer will proceed. If you subsequently decide to change the layout, the amount of copy or any other element of the design, the additional resulting costs will be your responsibility, although it is worth pointing out that on-screen editing means this is a lot less expensive today than it used to be.

You will receive a proof of your job for you to check. Check it carefully. Changes are expensive as they are time-consuming. To lay out a piece of text may take 10 minutes; to go back into it and locate precise errors in specific lines may take just as long. Today most designers send out a black and white proof first for the copy to be checked and then colour visuals at the second stage. They may then send a cromalin proof before passing for press (this is a photographic process using filmwork just before proceeding to plate-making, to check the look of a job).

You may have to circulate proofs in house, and this may be a source of further expense. It is a common failing to be unable to take copy seriously until it has been laid out, and most people to whom you show the proof will feel they have not taken part unless they correct something. How can you avoid the large correction bills that result from late changes?

- Establish who needs to see what and at what stage before you start work, so you don't end up circulating all the various stages of a job to everyone possibly interested.
- Circulate the visual and ask those contacted to initial and return it to you by a certain date as satisfactory. Allow a reasonable amount of time for studying what you send but say that if you don't hear from them you will assume all is acceptable. Don't chase.
- If several sets of corrections are expected back from your colleagues before a job can proceed, amalgamate them before you pass them back to the designer.
- For jobs that have been heavily changed circulate a note of the extra costs that resulted: this should get the message across!

Advice on how to proofread text

My main advice is don't assume this is easy; it's a job that needs your full concentration and there are courses available to teach you how (see Appendix).

I find it impossible to read for sense and to read for typographical errors at the same time. Try the following sequence:

- Look at the headings and subheadings (it is very easy for mistakes here not to be noticed, especially if all the words are in capital letters).
- Read the whole text against what you provided (always keep a copy of what you gave the designer).
- Examine the individual words that make up the text, looking out for spelling mistakes and additional words (eg Paris in the the spring), awkward word breaks and words that are words but the wrong ones (eg not/now, it/if).
- Errors that are easy to miss include a narrow letter missing (eg signifcance) and an extra letter (eg billling or acccountancy).
- Beware of skimming over long or familiar words; an error may be lurking there.
- Read for sense.
- Check the author's name. Twice.
- For mailshots, ring all the telephone numbers quoted and try sending a fax to the fax number given. Double check the postcode for return mail to be sure that has not been changed.

When checking the final proof look out for the following:

- If you have not seen the job since passing on your corrections, check that all have been made.
- Check the position of headings.
- Where copy is split between columns (bottom of one/top of the next) check that the breaks are sensible. Try to avoid splitting dates, proper names and so on.
- Are there any awkward spacings? Too much of a gap at the end of one page, too little space on another? Should elements be rearranged slightly to make the whole easier to read?
- Circulate copies to those who need to see them, making it clear they are for information rather than alteration!

Once the proofs have been approved the designer will proceed to create artwork, which the printer will need in order to create the ink on material. The quality of the final printed image will greatly depend on the quality of the artwork and transparencies that you and the designer provide.

Managing without a designer

It is not always necessary to use the services of a designer. For product information that stresses new information, hot off the press or value for money, an overtly-designed format could be entirely inappropriate. (The most obvious example is market research – the more you 'package' your promotional material and the report itself, the less it will sell.)

If you decide to go ahead on your own, here are a few tips.

Drawing attention to what is important

- Assume that all your prospects have poor eyesight and make your information easy to read: cut down on special effects that jar and detract from the main message. Make it easy for readers to home in on the essential sales benefits of the product you are advertising.
- Ensure the headings and subheadings are clear, put a box around particularly important text or have it printed in a different type-face or colour. Do make sure however that the colour is really legible. Bright colours are difficult to read; most people find 'muddy' colours much easier on the eye.
- Put the main heading at the top of the brochure or advertising space, not halfway through the body copy. This sounds obvious but it is surprising how often a headline appears in the middle of

an advertisement and encourages the attracted reader to carry on reading just there, half way through the sales information!

Variety
- Ensure the presentation is visually varied without being jarring. A good designer will use 'typographic colour' (special effects such as the emphasising of sub headings, underlining, bold text, etc). A great mass of flat-looking text is suitable for the page of a novel but not for advertising copy.

Use of space
- However much you feel you must say to promote your product, avoid over-filling the space. A format that looks confused or 'heavy work' will put the reader off. Use bullet points, vary your paragraph lengths and don't ask for text to be justified.
- If your advertisement is appearing in a larger space (for example on a newspaper page) pictures work better on the outside edges of the space, rather than disappearing into the centre gutter. For both advertisements and feature articles, headlines on the right-hand side of the page tend to be more eye-catching than those on the left.
- The reader does not have to absorb every word of what you say. Allow them to assimilate blocks of copy by scanning the headings. Make the words you use recognisable at a glance by setting in a 'serif' typeface (easier to read); limited use of italics can also be effective. Eye camera studies have shown that column widths in excess of 80 characters are more difficult to read.
- When booking advertising space, routinely ask for a right-hand page rather than a left, and always for a space facing text rather than another advertisement. Most readers flick past double page spreads of advertising. Tell the designer what you have booked and provide them with a sample of the publication.
- Find out what is going next to you, and in particular what is going beneath you. There is a natural tendency for the eye to move down the page; if there is a small feature (whether advertising or editorial) beneath the space you book, it may well draw attention away from your copy. If you are placing a direct response advertisement put the coupon where it is easiest to cut out and ensure that it does not back on to another such coupon.

How many colours?

- The costs of full-colour printing have fallen greatly in recent years, but if it is still beyond your budget, you don't need to pay for full-colour materials to make your promotions stand out. Consider the use of 'spot colour' in newspapers that are predominantly black and white. A good designer can make a two-colour job look extremely attractive but it requires skill.

Design techniques to avoid (because they make your text very difficult to read)

- Don't use upper case (capital) letters too much; they are hard to read and prevent words from being recognised at a glance. For this reason don't put headlines in capitals. (As proof of this, compare the easy-to-read blue and white Department of Transport road signs with those in France, where most signs are printed in capital letters; very hard to read from a distance or in a hurry.)
- Don't make the lettering too large. 50cm is the normal reading distance for a magazine or newspaper; if your lettering is poster size it will be illegible.
- Don't show humans larger than life size; it repels.
- Don't put extensive amounts of copy at an angle – it's very difficult to read (on the other hand a 'flash' across the corner of an advert can be a very effective way of attracting attention).
- Don't reverse too much text out; it is very hard on the eyes (although for limited amounts of text this can be a very effective way of attracting attention).
- Don't place text over an illustration unless the picture is 'faded back' behind the words (even then it doesn't always work).

House style

Many publishing companies have house styles for their advertisements. These usually consist of a combination of border and house logo that can be adapted to create a uniform look to any advertisement subsequently prepared.

For small-scale or routine jobs (eg advance notices) a house style can indeed save you money: typesetters can match new jobs to existing examples and you avoid paying for the services of a designer. But if you have thought of commissioning a house style for all your advertisements, forget it. There are several reasons for this:

- Advertisements are aimed at customers. A house style is designed to please the advertiser not the customer. Most of your customers could not care less whether adverts for your social sciences titles match those for business studies.
- The logo or name is the identifying mark and unifying item for the publishing house. If this is well designed and displayed there is no need for an elaborate house style.
- A house style reduces the space available. Borders take up expensive advertising space and reduce the area available for copy.
- Whilst the use of a border remains a useful technique for high-lighting part of your text, borders around large spaces make the reader switch off to what is inside them. By neatening the space they fail to attract attention to the contents, in effect providing a summary dismissal for your copy.
- Advertising works by stimulating the reader to absorb information. A house style works directly against this principle by implying that all the products featured are the same. Try it out for yourself: flick through a magazine and see how you don't bother to read advertisements of which you already know (or think you know) the content.

3. Graphic reproduction, or 'repro'

This is the conversion of camera-ready artwork into a printing surface, through computer retouching, proofing and colour separating on to film. These days this is usually arranged by the printer, and carried out by art-workers using computers, with any final retouching done on screen.

Repro is a specialist process and will require the use of expensive equipment (a laser scanner, electronic retouching) and possibly labour-intensive handwork before the mechanical process of printing can begin. Costs can therefore be high. For example, for a four colour leaflet requiring several cut-outs from transparencies, complicated tint laying and with a print run of 2,000, the cost of the repro will be as much as for the actual printing.

4. Printing and finishing

Commissioning print may be the responsibility of a departmental print buyer or designer, or it may fall to you. Production of a reasonable job is likely to depend on three factors: your ability to match the job to the appropriate process, a supplier who can produce the goods on time and a competitive price. Coming up with the right combination is more likely if you understand what is involved.

There are a variety of different methods. No single printing method is superior to all the others; all have different benefits for different applications. The two most commonly used for jobs originating in the marketing department are lithography (litho) and screen printing, but you may also find letterpress, photogravure or flexography being used, according to the requirements of the job.

Finishing includes all the processes that turn the printed sheets into the finished product required, for example varnishing, embossing, laminating, collating, folding, binding, die-cutting, assembly, packing and so on. The various services needed may be provided by the printers or, if they do not have what you need in house, organised on your behalf by them. Alternatively you may choose to do the organising yourself.

5. Distribution

Finally, you must ensure that the printed materials arrive where needed, by the required date, by the most appropriate delivery method and in a satisfactory condition. Printers can handle the last two processes for you, but your own warehouse/office may have established contacts with carriers, especially to your regular customers, and therefore be able to offer a better service. Ask for random check copies to be delivered to you before the bulk of your print run reaches its destination. Apart from allowing you to make your own check on quality, you will need them for your records and for any internal circulation necessary (getting stock back from the warehouse after delivery can take a disproportionate amount of effort!).

Requesting an estimate from a printer

Buy a guide to printing prices to use as a basic reference for what you should be paying for printing (Ingram Publishing produce a *Print Price Guide*; address in the Appendix). Two or three quotations should precede any sizeable job. The printer will need the following information from you in order to be able to estimate:

- A description of the component parts of the job
- Their size and shape
- How many printing colours

- How many different versions
- The amount of repro work included, ie the size and number of illustrations and the amount of retouching to be done
- The type of material
- How many copies
- When the finished job is required by
- Where to deliver to and what special packaging is needed
- Any additional requirements, eg coding order forms, numbering, collating, laminating, saddle stitching and so on.

However specific your instructions, the resulting estimate will probably be marked subject to sight of artwork.

If you have a sample of the kind or quality of material you are seeking to produce, do pass it on. It will give the printer a clear idea of your expectations of quality, presentation and so on. Alternatively, ask to see printed samples of a similar kind of work that the firm has handled before. If the quantity required is likely to change (eg export have not yet let you know how many copies they need) ask for a run on (r/o) price, say 10,000 and 1,000 run on. Or ask for a series of quotes: 1,000, 2,000, 3,000 and 10,000. This saves you from continuously ringing the printer for further information.

Which estimate to accept

Price should not be the only consideration on which you award a particular project; you should consider too reliability, service and the likely quality of the finished product. Some publishing houses negotiate contract prices for jobs that occur frequently (these need to be reviewed regularly to ensure competitive rates are being maintained). Other houses cease to bother requesting quotations from habitual contacts. This is usually a mistake.

While I would not recommend relying exclusively on one printer, do not spread your work around so thinly that remembering what is where becomes a headache for you and a very small account for each supplier.

What to do when things go wrong

Output of a design to a cromalin proof, or colour separations before a file gets sent to print, can forestall many problems, but what do you do if you are just not happy with the final job?

Your immediate concern should be the source of the mistake and, if it is the printer's, what they will do to put it right. If you think the material is usable, but below your (demonstrable) commercial standard, a discount should result; if it is not usable they should reprint at no cost to you. The two bargaining positions will be the printer's view of the job as 'commercially acceptable' (they will not want to reprint) and your concern for the reputation of your company (you will not want to send out substandard material even if it is costing you next to nothing). Be very wary of becoming known as a discount merchant and one who accepts poor quality or mistakes.

To avoid the situation arising in the future you need to decide whether the mistake was due to:

- The printer's incompetence – if so, don't use them again.
- Bad luck – if they are putting it right you can try them again, but watch out for possible cost recovery from them on the next job (charging you more than the going rate to make up for money lost last time).
- The development of too casual a relationship between yourself and the printer, for example failure to put instructions in writing or to make specific requirements clear. You can remedy this.

You have one sympathetic ally in the company who will be able to advise: the production director. The Association of Print and Packaging Buyers runs an advisory service which you can consult. You can also consult Pira, an independent printing advisory service (addresses in Appendix).

What happens after a job has been finished

The printer will usually keep the film used to make printing plates for at least a year and should consult you before disposing of it. If you foresee a reprint in the future say so. Do keep track of whether the disks sent by you to printers and designers do come back – buying new each time can be a substantial cost.

Notes

1. Provided by Tracey Cooke of KAG Design Limited, Basingstoke.

6

Direct Marketing

Direct marketing means selling or promoting straight to the customer, without the intervention of an intermediary such as a retailer. This usually takes place via the post (direct mail), but tele-selling, direct response advertisements in the press, on TV and radio, via e-mail or fax and door-to-door selling are all forms of direct marketing.

Direct marketing can be further divided into two types: *direct response* and *direct promotion*. Direct response advertising invites, as the name implies, a direct response back from the customer, for example mailshots advertising particular titles which ask for orders to be returned to the publisher. Direct promotion advertising is more concerned with spreading information about products. The promotional package is still sent to the customer, but while the response may indeed be received straight back it may also be returned through retail outlets such as bookshops or result in orders placed with the firm's representatives. The mailing of seasonal catalogues to bookshops is an example of direct promotion.

Here the collected wisdom of the general public intrudes. Direct mail (or 'junk mail') goes straight in the bin: everyone knows that. Not true. A recent survey published by the Direct Mail Information Service on public attitudes to the consumer direct mail asked those questioned about the fate of the last item they had received. Over 77 per cent of those interviewed had opened it, 59 per cent of the openers had read the contents.[1] For business direct mail the amount opened was even higher (84 per cent was opened by managers with 31 per cent of items acted on positively – passed to a colleague, filed or responded to[2]). What is more, the levels of response have shown an impressive consistency over the past few years despite a massive increase in the volume of direct mail being sent. Consumer familiarity with direct mail has also increased: 73 per cent knew who had sent the sample without opening it, and 54 per cent of those who recognized the sender also knew that the envelope contained advertising. A further 11 per cent knew it was direct marketing but did

113

not know who had sent it.[3] Remember that direct marketing is a very testable means of promotion. You can see within weeks (sometimes days) of sending out your material whether or not it is working, test different offers and different formats to see which produce most orders. Promotions that you see being repeated are obviously drawing a healthy response.

The second commonly held belief is that direct marketing is a poor promotional medium because of the very low levels of response. It is common to hear of an 'industry average' response rate of 1–2 per cent, but no one is entirely sure where this figure came from! A recent survey in *Marketing Week*[4] gave an average of 4.4 per cent for consumer and 1.8 per cent for business mailings. If you are mailing to a 'warm list' of previous customers you may well do far better. For the consumer mailings, 46 per cent of campaigns showed response rates above the average. It is also common for there to be sharp differentials between the response from different lists sent the same mailing piece: your best performing list will typically outperform your worst by a factor of 3:1.

Every direct mail user can probably come up with a horror story: mailings that did not arrive or reached their destination after the 'sell by' date on the offer had closed; leaflets printed upside down, without prices or with no room for the customer's address. Direct mail demands immense precision but a skilfully handled campaign can reward you with not only orders but also vital information about who your customers are.

What are the advantages of direct marketing?

For the right product at the right price direct marketing can be a very cost-effective form of promotion. Sometimes only a single sale will be needed to pay for the entire campaign and make a healthy profit. For example, old London Bridge was sold by direct mail – the entire campaign needed only one sale.

Personal representation to your market

Well done, direct marketing to your customers is the nearest you get to the rep's visit: a personal communication about your product direct to the person most likely to buy it. At the time most convenient to the prospect, you have their sole attention for as long as you are able to hold it.

If you compare the costs of sending a rep to each of the prospects you consider part of your potential market, direct marketing is a very cost-effective medium: postage at the current rate plus list rental and production costs. There are no geographical limits to how far your message can travel; in inaccessible areas the value for money can be even greater as it is difficult for customers to get to retail outlet.

High selectivity

Direct marketing is not a mass medium: it offers you the chance to make a specific sales pitch to a specific market. The increasing sophistication of both in-house and rented lists means that you can pinpoint exactly whom you want to contact with which message. For example, political parties are making extensive use of the medium's potential for by-elections, as local candidates target taxi drivers or small businesses with the relevant information from their manifestos. Direct marketing makes such selectivity possible.

Perfect timing

Through direct marketing it is possible to time the arrival of your sales message very precisely, and to your greatest advantage, eg back to school promotions that arrive spot on 1 September.

Following up your initial marketing campaign is easy

As response comes back from direct marketing you gain new information about those who have ordered, and have the chance to re-mail or telesell to those who have not. You improve your market and product knowledge and make it likely that future campaigns can be even more precisely targeted; you start database marketing.

Good news for cash flow

Most direct marketing campaigns ask the customer to send money with their order, backing this up with a strong guarantee of satisfaction or a complete refund.

What is more, direct marketing offers you the chance to test the popularity of particular products with specific market sectors before you commit yourself to expensive production costs and lengthy print runs.

Excellent support for other marketing methods

Direct marketing should not be seen in isolation: it can provide lots of market research to inform all your marketing activities; gain leads for your representatives; result in extra retail sales; improve your company image and much more.

The growing amount spent on direct marketing

Expenditure on direct marketing in the UK amounts to over £7bn. It breaks down as follows:

Medium	£ million DM expenditure	
	1995	**1997**
direct mail	1135	1628
telemarketing	1175	1835.1
database marketing	548	695.31
contract magazines	22	38.64
door-to-door	233	353.0
inserts	216	262
press display (national)	786	674
magazines display	616	384.3
regional display	325	375.5
television	398	643.3
radio	47	141.5
cinema	2	1.65
outdoor/transport	45	118.2
new media	50	90.65
total	**5598**	**7241.15**

Source: DMA Census, 1996, 1998

Concentrating on direct mail, both the amount circulating and the advertising spend devoted to it are growing fast. From an annual volume of 540 million pieces in 1975, the total for 1990 was 2,272m, and by 1995 this had risen to 2,905m. Volume is rising faster than expenditure in real terms, and as both television advertising time and newspaper space become increasingly expensive, direct marketing looks even better value for money. In the United

States direct mail is starting to rival television for prime position in the media mix.

Whereas at one time direct marketing was considered a specialised field for specific products, its use is growing among more general advertisers. Several large manufacturers are using the medium to promote benefits of brand loyalty to their customers. Of the top 3000 advertisers in Britain, over two-thirds have a specific direct marketing responsibility in-house and spending decisions in this area are taken at a very high level. If further proof were needed of the growth of the direct marketing industry look at the large number of dedicated direct marketing agencies now offering their services.

How do we know what is being sent?

The Direct Mail Information Service (DMIS)[5] monitors the results of the Royal Mail's statistical surveys on direct mail and produces jointly with them the official industry figures on volume, usage and attitudes to direct mail.

The Royal Mail Consumer monitors, by statistical sampling of 1300 families in the UK, how much mail is received by consumers. The figures include all material to come through the door, not just that which is delivered through the Royal Mail, so free newspapers and circulars are included.

Who is responsible for what we receive? Of consumer mail received in this way the DMIS estimates that the average four-weekly household receipt was:[6]

1994		**1998**
17%	Direct Mail	19.5%
12%	Free newspapers	6.9%
22%	Leaflets and coupons	19.1%
49%	Personal mail	54.5%

Analysed by socio-economic group, AB households are receiving more of everything than DE.

Of that 17 per cent direct mail, the various senders may be further broken down as follows:

Senders of consumer direct mail 1990–1998

	1990	**1995**	**1998**
Mail order	24.3	18.2	14.7
Insurance	9.1	10.3	10.4
Credit card	4.7	4.7	★★
Bank/Girobank	7.2	8.3	11.9
Building society	3.3	2.3	1.6
Retail/Store cards	6.7	8.2	11.4
Magazines	6.8	2.7	3.9
Estate agents	1.7	0.5	★★
Manufacturers	4.8	7.2	3.4
Book club	3.9	4.7	3.5
Charity	5.8	6.8	7.8
Gas/Electricity/Water Board	3.3	2.5	4.2
Film company	0.8	0.6	★★
Travel	4.8	★	★★
Entertainment	1.2	★	★★
Government	–	–	1.1
Education	–	–	0.4
Other	11.6	23.0	21.0
Barclaycard	–	–	1.6
Readers Digest	–	–	1.6
BT	–	–	1.5
Total	100.0	100.0	100.0

★Included in other in 1995
★★ Included in other in 1998

Source: Senders of Consumer Direct Mail 1998, DMIS.

DMIS also carries out research into consumer attitudes and behaviour towards direct mail. The biannual *Direct Mail Trends Survey* looks at various aspects of direct mail from how the last piece received was treated (thrown away, opened, etc) to consumer reactions to direct mail (intrusive, useful, entertaining, etc). Comparisons are made with other direct methods of advertising such as telephone selling and door-to-door distribution of leaflets in an attempt to estimate public responsiveness to direct marketing. Other ad hoc surveys are also carried out on specific issues such as the reactions of heavily mailed consumers.

Direct marketing and the publishing industry

No single bookseller could be expected to stock every book published. What is more, many books (in particular those aimed at the professional markets) are very expensive or highly specialised and general booksellers are consequently unwilling to tie up large amounts of capital in stocking them. The publishers therefore promote direct to the end user.

Most publishers do not see direct marketing in isolation, but as one of a number of marketing strategies used to promote their lists. Direct marketing campaigns result in extra orders through the retail trade; titles for which it would not be cost-effective to produce an individual mailshot are included in thematic leaflets or catalogues mailed to booksellers and libraries, and to professional end-users themselves.

At the same time, highly specialised booksellers have developed who target direct selling campaigns of their own. Alan Armstrong Associates and Dawsons Book Division market business books to industrial and government libraries, Wyvern Crest to professional individuals in the workplace. In many cases these booksellers win co-operation from publishers in either extra discount or through subsidy of mailing and promotion costs. It may well be worth exploring possibilities for co-operative promotions: perhaps providing them with copies of your direct mailshots overprinted with their return address, or paying for a leaflet to be included in their mailings. Many subscription agents will likewise include a leaflet on new or existing journals in their regular mailings to customers.

For which kinds of product does direct marketing work best?

- *High price.* As a rough guide, most direct marketing in the book trade is for titles that cost £25 or more. (Of course you may be promoting to gather new names for your database and therefore be well satisfied with a break-even response. In this case you can get away with books in the £15–£20 range.)
- *Products for specific markets and for which suitable mailing lists of potential customers exist.* Check on list availability early and make no assumptions. A list may exist but its owners may be unwilling to release it. The costs of building your own need to be very carefully considered – will it ever get used again or is it an effective investment in your future publishing programme?
- *Books for which the customer is unlikely to visit a bookshop* or a bookshop to stock eg professional and high price reference.
- *Not general interest titles.*

Where to get suitable mailing lists

When considering a direct marketing campaign the selection of the list(s) you will target is critical. Precision is essential. You may have a title that all chartered surveyors in this country would consider an essential desk-top reference. If you make the mistake of circulating quantity surveyors, a large percentage of your market will be missed.

Developing a list mentality

Open your eyes to the possibilities of lists all around you. In direct marketing terms the lists of most value to you consist of:

1. Those who have bought through the mail before.
2. Those who have bought or need a product similar to what you are selling.

The first place you should look for both these categories is among your own previous buyers.

After that lists may be:

1. bought   – outright
2. rented   – from the owner or through a broker
3. built   – by you or a mailing house
4. swapped   – with another publisher or someone selling a related product
5. investigated.

Option 5 offers lots of scope for initiative.

- *Associations* whose membership is relevant to what you are selling are an obvious starting point. Begin by asking if you can put a loose insert into one of their mailings to members. If the answer is no and the association particularly relevant, your firm may like to consider becoming the society's official publisher and so gaining access to names. If there is already an association journal, try advertising with an attractive offer and so gain the names of those who respond. Do they run an annual conference or exhibition at which you can display your books?
- Can the author provide lists of *contacts* or make recommendations?

● What lists can you build from information published in *directories*? Are there any that you publish yourself?

What is available to rent?

Flick through a recent issue of *Direct Response* or *Precision Marketing* and look at the number of companies advertising themselves as list rental and broking companies. You can now start discovering the wide range of lists available, from new mothers to academics teaching at universities, from high earners to purchasers of British Telecom shares. There are business and professional lists, others of consumers' home addresses. A list of list brokers is available from the Direct Marketing Association (DMA).

The variety is not endless. Once you have asked a few brokers for details of the lists they can obtain you will realise that there is an element of duplication in what they offer. Some firms have compiled and developed their own lists which they rent out to direct marketers (eg Reed, NDL). There are several publications (some available on computer disk) which list mailing lists available, for example *LADS* (Lists and Data Sources). Unfortunately, these are marketed by list brokers, so only feature the lists each has available. None of them is comprehensive for the industry as a whole, as is the case with the publication that covers the whole American market *Direct Mail List Rates and Data*, published bi-monthly by the Standard Rate and Data Service Inc.

Dealing with list brokers

Prices for list rental are charged per thousand, depending on the amount it cost to compile the list, now costs to maintain it and how valuable to other mailers it is likely to be. There may be extra charges for any selections you wish to make, eg geographical exclusions or mailing women only. There is usually a minimum charge (often the same as an order of 5,000–10,000 names). List brokers get a percentage of the rental as commission. You will have to submit a copy of your promotion piece in advance, as list owners will not allow their names and addresses to be used to promote merchandise which competes directly with their own. Unless you agree to repeated use of a list (usually through a leasing arrangement), list rental will be on the basis of a one-time use by a single mailer. If you mail the list again or include someone else's material with yours you will be invoiced for a second list rental.

How do list owners know if you use the list more than once? Every list owner seeds their list with 'check-addresses'. They masquerade as part of the list but are in fact the disguised addresses of company employees; an on-going check on who is using the list. Prosecutions do occur.

Questions to ask a list broker about a list you are thinking of renting:

- When was it last mailed?
- For what kind of product?
- With what success?
- What other products have done well with this list?
- Who compiled it and how?
- Does it consist of people who have bought through the post or subscribers? If the latter how did they buy their subscriptions?
- How often is it updated (or cleaned)?
- In what format is it held?
- Can it be de-duplicated ('de-duped') against your own list, so you don't mail anyone twice?
- If it is available on labels only, what format are they (sticky or Cheshire)?
- What percentage are overseas addresses?
- Are Mailing Preference Service registered names removed?
- What does the list owner credit for envelopes returned as undeliverable? (This usually applies only if over 5 per cent of the list is returned.)
- What is the time limit for such returns (normally three months from order date)?
- If you have your list de-duped against the one you are renting do you pay just for the new names ('net names') or for all those on the rented list, even those you already have? In the US net name rental is standard practice; it's catching on over here.
- What percentage of the list are 'hot line names' (people who have just bought)?

If you take a look at the data sheets that list brokers prepare on the lists they look after you will get an idea of the sort of questions you should be asking.

When dealing with list brokers you will find that there is an industry jargon to acquire. For example, 'nixies' are undeliverable items that are returned to the sender and need to be sent back to the list owner for updating/crediting. Another frequently heard expressed is 'I gonned it', meaning 'I marked it "gone away" and returned it to the sender'. If you start reading the trade press you will soon pick it up.

The arguments for renting lists rather than building your own

- Mailing lists go out of date very quickly. People in full-time employment change jobs at the rate of 20% a year (in some fields/age brackets much more often); around 1 in 10 homes changes hands every year. People often underestimate the resources required to maintain a database: dealing with postage returns; rekeying order information and address changes. This is often a full-time job, two by the time you have allowed for holiday and sickness cover. The list holder needs to invest in sophisticated computer systems to store the information recorded: expensive.

- If the market you want to mail is already covered by well-researched and efficiently managed mailing lists, it is cheaper to rent the names and addresses than start from scratch. Your time is better spent negotiating special rates for frequent use of existing lists; your money on compiling specific market sector lists that do not already exist (you may then also be able to sell them to other users to subsidise your costs). Lists which are cheap to build are also cheap to rent, eg schools and libraries.

- It is often easier to exercise control over a supplier than an in-house department. Firms that make their living selling lists have a strong incentive to provide a good service.

- The best mailing lists are those which are frequently used, and rented-in lists will be used more often than your own. List rental companies can afford the complicated de-duplication procedures which save annoying potential customers with multiple copies of your mailings; they can provide addresses in mailsort order which saves you money on postage.

A compromise position is to use an external supplier to hold lists for you, perhaps amalgamating your bookbuyer names with those of similar companies to produce a single and highly effective mailing list.

Building your own list (or database)

If you decide to build your own list, the best place to start is by recording your own customers and past purchasers. There are many areas to be considered: the system on which to hold the names; who is going to update the list; how often you will mail it; how it ties in with editorial plans for the development of your firm's publishing programme (there is no point in storing names for a particular subject area if no more related titles are coming).

The information you record will depend on the capacities of the system you choose and how much you need to access in the future. There are many database management software packages to help you set up and maintain your customer and mailing records.

The following list will provide ideas of the kind of information to record. Some facts are obtainable simply by making your order form a little more detailed, others require keying at the time of order processing or more detailed research.

- Mr/Mrs/Ms/Miss or professional title
- Phone number
- Business phone number
- Fax number
- E-mail address
- Postcode
- What they bought
- How they ordered
- How they paid
- If they did not pay or returned the item ordered
- Total number of orders to date
- Date of most recent order
- Average value of order
- Order history: date, titles, venue
- Source of the enquiry
- Job function
- Position
- Size of company (employees)
- Type of company – SIC (standard industrial classification)
- Turnover
- Age (in bands) for consumer titles
- Other demographic information
- Opt in/opt out. You must get the responder's consent if you have any plans to use the list in a non-obvious way (eg rent to a

third party). 'Fair obtaining' is a requirement of the Data Protection Act.

Other services available to those managing/renting lists

Help from the Royal Mail

The Royal Mail is eager to help advertisers make the best use of direct mail, and a variety of special services has been developed.

There are two ways to allow your customers to communicate with you without having to pay for a stamp: freepost and business reply. The concept of freepost is easier for recipients to understand and so tends to get used in consumer mailings; business reply is used more for business-to-business mailings. They work as follows:

- *Freepost.* The freepost licence scheme operates in the UK only. The licence costs £57 per annum; you pay a deposit in advance towards postage based on the size of your mailing and then 0.5p above the normal postal rate for every response received back.

  Alternatively, and if you are mailing on a large scale, you can use a bar-code response device as part of the address block on the mail that comes back to you. This can be read by optical character recognition (OCR) machines and because the sorting is therefore quicker the Royal Mail waive the additional half-penny charge for every item that comes back.

  The positioning and reproduction of a bar code does require great precision and so there will be extra origination and printing costs as a result (the Royal Mail will need to see ten proofs of the response device before they allow you to proceed). You have to decide whether the size of the mailing and the possible size of the response makes this extra effort worthwhile. Bear in mind too that the appearance of a bar code on the response device may make your promotional material look less individual.
- *Business reply.* A business reply licence on your material must take the form of a business reply envelope or card. The licence number is printed on the envelope and the first or second class indicator goes where the stamp should go, so it is clear to responders that they need not affix one. UK only, costs are the same as freepost. The Royal Mail can supply the specifications for printing pre-paid envelopes and cards.
- *International business reply.* Works in a similar way to UK business reply but for mail going to over 90 countries worldwide.

The licence costs £100 per annum; you pay 40p for each reply received (under 50g). Contact your local Royal Mail Sales Centre for the list of countries covered.

- *Postage paid impressions.* A ppi is printed on the despatch envelopes (at the same time as your message or slogan) and means that items do not have to be individually franked (so can be mailed more speedily). Stock of ppi envelopes can be kept for future mailings. You pay the Royal Mail for what you despatch at the going rate of postage. The right to produce a ppi is subject to account approval with the Royal Mail and there is a minimum printing of 4,000 items. Most mailing houses can arrange this for you. Even if you do not have mailings of over 4,000, if you spend £12,000 a year with the Royal Mail you can have a stock of 'standard tariff envelopes' printed with a ppi number which do not need to be individually stamped. Again, your local Royal Mail Sales Centre can help.
- *Mailsort.* Discounts are available to any mailer supplying the Royal Mail with more than 4,000 items presented in pre-sorted order. Mailsort discounts also supply to mailings of over 1,000 items where they are packets (this is defined as over and including C5 envelope size and weighing more than 60g or more than 6mm thick). Mailing houses may organise sorting for you and then pass back part of the discount.

Companies who are posting large amounts overseas may also qualify for a reduction in the postal cost. The Royal Mail publishes *A Mailsort User's Guide*.

Further information on all these services appears in two free publications: *The Direct Mail Guide* and *The DIY Guide to International Direct Mail*. The Royal Mail also runs regular seminars on direct mail (for dates and details contact your local Royal Mail Sales Centre).

Discounts overseas

When mailing overseas, you can obtain discounts not only from the Royal Mail but also from overseas consolidators. They work by taking a bulk weight discount from Royal Mail International, some of which is passed on to the customer, and prices can vary quite dramatically due to the differing discounts applied. Mailers can either set up an arrangement directly with a consolidator, or use their mailing houses, most of whom have a working relationship with a couple or act as one themselves.

Before asking for overseas mail prices, be fairly certain as to the actual weight and distribution of the mailing – a few grams and a change in destinations can have a significant impact on costs.

Removal of duplicates from your own list

The same person orders twice from you. The first time he notes his address as:

Mr J Thompson
Ivy Tree Cottage
The Lane
Berkhamsted
Hertfordshire
HP4 1JD

The second time he notes it as:

John Thompson
27 The Lane
Berkhamsted
Herts

Both are correct, but are captured for your list as separate addresses. How do you avoid mailing him twice every time you circulate your list in future?

If you suspect that your in-house list contains a lot of duplicates it may pay to have them eliminated by a computer bureau. You provide a copy of the list (by e-mail or on CD ROM for larger lists), they enter a program that spots all the entries with the same post-code or a high percentage similarity.

It is important to point out that this is not an entirely scientific process. Most systems will yield a list of possible duplicates for manual checking and the fastest way to end up with a final list is simply to remove all these possible duplicates (possibly removing valid ones at the same time). Whether or not it is important to deal with lists in any particular way, ensure that the data-processing team are well briefed to avoid queries and delays at a late stage.

Alternatively, many of the good quality de-dupe systems now run on the PC/Windows platform. These enable in-house users to de-dupe effectively, although it is probably a good plan to involve the in-house IT person/department. The software is not cheap (£500–£5,000), so for companies carrying out a small volume of mailings it may be just as easy to do it manually with imaginative use of a desktop database.

Ensure that all your response devices and order forms ask those ordering for their postcode so that you can try to eliminate duplicates in future. A de-duplicated list saves you money on postage and avoids annoying potential customers by sending them multiple copies of a mailshot – this looks highly inefficient.

Merge and purge

For large-scale mailings you could use one of the many computer bureaux to 'merge' the mailing lists you want to try, 'purging' them of names that appear more than once (ie are on more than one list). If the overlap is high you may be able to negotiate a reduction in list rental, paying only for 'net names'.

The procedure works like this: you provide the bureau with a copy of your own in-house list of buyers, you ask the list rental broker to supply each of the lists you wish to rent in the same format. The computer bureau runs each against the other and aims to produce a single complete list with no duplicates.

If you plan to run lists against each other on a large scale, it is worth trying to negotiate a 'net names' agreement. This means that your list costs will be closer to the number eventually mailed than the total of names run against each other (such deals are usually restricted to a percentage of the total). Such arrangements must be determined before you start processing, but a good list broker should be able to help.

Avoid the trap of de-duping the cheapest list first, in the hope of removing more names from the most expensive list. This may lead to the worst quality list forming the bulk of the mailing. Ensure that you obtain a signed data-processing report from the mailing house or bureau handling the output of names. This must be passed back to the list broker for your net names credit. If you are mailing from the same lists on a regular basis, you may be able to obtain a predetermined percentage of additional names. This can save problems later if your total mailing quantity comes below that expected due to a large number of duplicates.

If you are de-duplicating lists and being rigorous about response tracking (see further on in this chapter), ensure that responses are accounted for against *all* the lists the names came from. If this is not attended to, and there is a large overlap between the lists, you risk the chance of not being able to identify your best list.

Don't be disappointed if a high overlap factor between the lists you choose gives you a much smaller mailing total than you had originally planned: the more overlap the better, as it shows your selection is on target.

List analysis

Regular direct marketers want to know more about their customers. There are two main reasons for this. First, they need to better meet their customers' needs (sell more to them now and develop new things to sell to them in the future). Second, they need to find more of them.

The combination of market research techniques and the increasing sophistication of computer hard and software has made possible the development of highly sophisticated information services for mailing list analysis. There are two main options:

1. *Analysis of geo-demographic criteria.* As a basis for the classification, geo-demographic analysis uses electoral role and census information, overlaying with financial, household and age data to produce effective postcode analysis, ideal for segmenting the mass market. For example, CACI offer a system of analysis called Acorn, CCN offer Mosaic.
2. *Analysis by lifestyle criteria* offers a more detailed and personal approach, ideal for pinpointing specific niche markets. A huge number of individuals are questionnaired at their home address. Any individual's response may contain up to 700 different variables, on age, income, spending habits and so on. Key firms here are ICD, NDL and CMT.

Publishers can use the services of such companies in two main ways. It is possible to have your existing lists (for example of customers, past customers and key prospects) analysed, to make your search for more of the same easier. A minimum quantity for a statistically viable sample would start at around 10,000 names.

Alternatively, armed with a detailed profile of what kind of people buy your products you can pull a very specifically tailored list of prospect from the huge databases such companies hold. On consumer surveys, it is possible to sponsor questions or buy responses to a particular question.

This type of analysis is only good for consumer or residential data. For commercial organisations, firms offering this type of resource will carry out a similar exercise using business variables such as SIC (standard industrial classification), number of employees and so on. Alternatively, you can locate good quality lists and match against them.

If you cannot afford market analysis of this sophistication, start lateral thinking: what kind of person needs my product, what else does he or she buy? It was such a thought process that led a major news magazine to try mailing previous buyers of high quality shirts and accessories with very successful results.

For information on firms offering services of the kind described above contact the Direct Marketing Association.

The Mailing Preference Service

Set up in 1983, the Mailing Preference Service is the direct mail industry's answer to complaints from people that:

1. they object to getting 'junk mail'
2. they get mail that is not specific to their interests.

A database holds the names and records the interests of around 160,000 individuals: those who wish to receive nothing at all and those who wish to receive more mail on specific subjects.

This file is available to members of the service who can run it against lists they plan to mail to both exclude and include individuals; the cost they pay for this varies according to the member's annual mailing volume.

Registering with the service to receive more mail offers an excellent way of examining a wide variety of direct response formats and keeping in touch with new promotional ideas. To register, write for a form to the Mailing Preference scheme (see address in Appendix 4).

The Data Protection Act (1984 and 1998)

The Act was originally designed to protect individuals from having incorrect information stored about them on computer file. In addition to all the other sorts of computerised information held in this country, computerised mailing lists have to be registered with the Data Protection Register and the uses to which the information may be put specified. Compilers of lists may only use the information for the purpose made clear to consumers at the time of compilation, hence the appearance of opt-out boxes on order forms (eg 'please tick if you do not wish to be kept up to date with our publishing programme').

The 1998 Act greatly expanded the provisions of the original act. The most significant change was a widening of the original definition of 'processing' of data to include any mention of an individual (before the 1998 Act passing mentions of individuals in lists that were primarily organisational did not count). The new act extends the definition of processing to include all handling of personal information; it also extends the provisions to manually held lists and to individuals at business addresses rather than solely at home addresses. Vastly more sensitive handling of all personal information is called for, notably relating to sexual orientation or religion.

The new act also specifies that data must not be traded with areas where data protection of a lesser standard than the European Union. The most notable fallout from this is likely to be with the US market where data protection is currently of a lower standard.

For more information, consult the Data Protection Web site at www.open.gov.uk/dpr/dprhome.htm

Planning a direct marketing campaign

Planning is crucial in direct marketing. Effective direct marketing campaign planning means being able to both design the overall scheme and pay attention to the crucial details. You should be asking yourself the following questions:

The objectives

- What is my objective? Do I want a direct response or to spread information about my products? If the latter, will orders come back from other sources?
- What is the print run for the title to be marketed?
- How many do we already have orders for?
- From where?
- How many am I trying to sell direct?
- By when?
- What other items can I sell on the back of this campaign?

The market

- Who benefits from the product?
- Who buys it?
- Are the two the same?
- Are they likely to buy in multiples?
- Are lists of the market available?
- From where?
- By when?
- Are there other secondary markets worth approaching?
- Do these lists exist?
- When is the best time to mail?
- Does the customer need to see the product before making a decision to buy (ie must it be available on approval or with a firm guarantee)?

The product

- What is the product?
- What are its benefits?
- What is new/excellent/noteworthy about it?
- What is the history of my company selling similar products direct in the past: are there list successes worth repeating; failures worth avoiding?
- Where is the product available from and by when?

The marketing proposal

- What offers are at my disposal?
- How much will postage and packing be?
- How will I accept payment?
- What guarantee can I offer?
- What is the format of the promotion piece?
- How many do I want to circulate?
- When do I want it to arrive?

Planning a schedule

Once you have established answers to all of the above you need to plan a schedule. For example, for a mailing, work backwards from the date you want your message to arrive on your prospect's desk/doormat. Consider making a 'sell-by' date for offer on material; this will encourage a quick response but means your schedule must be very precise.

Here is a rough schedule of how much time each stage needs:

Response device in the post.	1 week
Time prospect needs to consider the offer and respond.	5 weeks
Best time to arrive.	1 September
Rebate sort and second class post.	1 week
Stuffing the mailshot.	1 week
Printing.	2 weeks
Circulation of final proofs, passing for press. Ordering lists.	1 week
Design and layout, corrections.	2 weeks
Copy approved and passed to designer, visual prepared and circulated.	2 weeks
Finalising copy.	1 week
Copy presented, discussed and circulated.	1 week
Time for writing copy.	2 weeks
Drawing up schedule, briefing suppliers, requesting estimates, sourcing lists, setting up monitoring procedures for mailing response.	2 weeks

Working back and allowing a little extra time, you should start thinking about the mailing at least three months before you want it to arrive. NB: Whereas your list research needs to be one of the first things you do, to establish the size and shape of the market, the actual ordering of the lists should be one of the very last things you do – to ensure absolute currency.

A few other hints before you start

Try to plan ahead. The problem in most marketing departments is the sheer volume of work. Books tend to slip beyond their estimated publishing dates, there are natural convergences of season, eg publishing for the new financial or academic year. You may think you will have time to finalise marketing plans and order list estimates while proofs are circulating but the more planning you can do ahead of schedule the better.

Try to establish before anything is written or designed who needs to see what: the copy; the visual; the list selection and so on. Keep the list as small as possible, but bear in mind that senior managers often take a particular interest in direct marketing plans (their success/failure is provable – and quotable – unlike the majority of more amorphous marketing techniques).

Keep track of your costs by starting a methodical system, either using a spreadsheet on the computer or manually. At the top of the sheet note the title's budget. Divide this between the various component parts on which you need to spend money: design; copy; printing; mailing costs and so on. Next to these figures note the amounts you have been quoted and the suppliers to whom you award the contract. You then have everything to hand for quick expenditure decisions and a ready means of checking invoices as they come in.

Once you have established both a schedule and the rough allocation of budget there are a number of colleagues both in-house and out-house that you need to talk to.

The copywriter

Direct mail is above all a writer's medium. You are far better spending your budget on effective copy than expensive illustrations or photography for your mailshot.

In order to sell the product benefits to the anticipated audience your copywriter will need answers to all the basic research questions listed on pages 131–32. Can he/she have access to all the various in-house forms and so gain an idea of the evolution of the project (on a confidential basis, of course)? Don't forget to pass on all the background information that you take for granted, eg what the product competes with. An effective copywriter will write for a specific format (they may well suggest an alternative to your original idea) and provide you with a rough layout indicating what goes where for the designer.

The designer

Provide a complete brief on what you are trying to achieve and the ideas you have had so far *before* the designer starts work. (For further advice on dealing with designers see Chapter 5).

The printer

Do get at least two estimates for any sizeable job, and get them in writing. Compare them with those listed in a print price guide (see

Appendix 5). Do include all the extras that you require, such as the coding of your response device or the delivery of printed material to your mailing house in Aberdeen.

The mailing house

Whether you are using the firm's warehouse or an external supplier do give them plenty of notice of your forthcoming schedule. Far better to sort it out early than to end up grovelling on bended knee to get your mailing out.

Put all your instructions in writing, making it absolutely clear what goes where in the mailshot. Make up a sample and send it to them, both as a guide to what to expect and for an estimate on the cost of posting. (Incidentally, showing the mailing house your proposed material before it gets printed may also save you money. For example, folding a rectangular leaflet on the short side rather than the long may result in it being hand- rather than machine-stuffed (more expensive), but will probably make little difference to the overall impact. The mailing house will be able to point out these kinds of things.) Anticipate any potential problems, for example what should they do if they run out of stock of any of the components? A letter or order form can be photocopied, but what about the brochure?

Will the size of mailing you are planning entitle you to any discount on postage if it is presented in mailsort (postcode) order? Can they organise the discounts for you? Do you need a freepost licence? Sort out all these details now rather than hold up the printing of your material while you wait for a licence number.

Better still, go and look around the mailing house. Watching a labelling or inserting machine in action is quite mesmerising, and the chance should not be missed.

What to put in a direct response mailshot

The best way to learn about how to put together a direct mailshot is to become a direct mail addict. Get yourself on to as many mailing lists as possible, and study what you are sent.

To do this register with the Mailing Preference Scheme; buy by post rather than from shops; examine the loose inserts that fall out of magazines when you open them; look through newspapers and notice which headlines on direct response advertisements attract your attention and why.

You will soon start to notice that most direct mail packages and formats consist of four standard items:

1. The outer envelope, to enclose the package and carry the head-line to attract attention.
2. The letter, to introduce the contents of the package, the product being sold and the offer.
3. The brochure, to explain in further detail.
4. The reply device or order form.

In some mailshots these components may be amalgamated – for example into a long sales letter that has an ordering coupon along the bottom. Similarly, in the case of space advertisements enticing a direct response (usually called 'off-the-page advertising') all the component parts must necessarily be part of a single space, divided up into various segments. A telemarketing call will be structured in a similar way. But even the simplest direct marketing format will combine the features of the four items listed above:

- A headline with an offer or key benefit
- An introduction
- An explanation
- A means of ordering.

How to make each component part as effective as possible

Your task in putting together a direct mail campaign is to provide enough buying information so that your package is (a) compelling to read and (b) motivates an order. All the advice in Chapter 3 on techniques for preparing successful copy applies here too, but the following hints which are specific to direct mail will also be helpful.

The outer envelope

The outer envelope needs to be sufficiently interesting to ensure the package gets opened. Bear this in mind when deciding whether or not to add a message on the front. The envelope also needs to bear the return address for undeliverable items. It follows that if you are paying to have the envelope overprinted with return details, you may as well include a sales message too.

It is sometimes claimed that for direct mail going to people at work the outer envelope is less important because the post is usually opened by someone other than the recipient. It's a big gamble to take: even if a secretary does open the mail, many people flick through their in-tray to see what is there first; something that looks different may be pulled out and opened. What is more, if the envelope is sufficiently interesting to the secretary, it may get passed on with the contents.

Bear in mind what else the reader will be receiving at the same time (how much, how interesting?) and the time of day when it will be opened, eg most working people open mail sent to their home address in the evening.

- Provide a 'teaser'; start a sentence that sounds interesting, but don't finish ...
- Say something controversial
- Print on both sides of the envelope
- Make the envelope an unusual shape
- Add a quick checklist on the back for the recipient to either request more information or have themselves deleted from your list.

The return address can be either your own or that of your mailing house, who can then batch up returns and send them to you at regular intervals. If your organisation is new to direct marketing, the latter suggestion avoids negative internal publicity.

The accompanying letter

The sales letter is the one essential component for a direct mail package. Time and again research has proved that packages with a letter pull more response than those without. Sometimes you can dispense with the brochure altogether, just send an effective letter and a suitable means of ordering.

Why is this? A letter is a highly personal form of communication. Watch how you react to the next mailshot you receive. If the sender is not immediately apparent, you look for explanation. The almost general reaction is to extract the letter, turn it over and look for the signature and company name at the foot of the second page.

How to write an effective direct mail letter
- Your copy will work best if it is personal: can you picture an individual recipient of your material? What does he/she look

like; what does he/she wear/read/watch on television/do at the weekends?

- Make your tone conversational and personal, not stilted. Be reasonable and logical. Don't overclaim: it sounds ridiculous and discredits your sales message. If you can, make your copy topical and newsy; fascinating to read. Check for readability by reading the text aloud.

- Keep your sentences short so the copy reads well. For the same reason, avoid very long paragraphs (around six lines is fine). Don't use too many adjectives or complicated verbs, they slow down the reader's pace.

- Start with a headline stating the main benefit you are offering: what the product will do for the recipient; how much time/effort/money the reader will save by buying.

- Try starting the main text of the letter (what comes after 'Dear Reader') with a short sentence to attract attention. Alternatively, try asking a question.

- Introduce the offer, and explain the benefits. Your copy should be laden with benefits rather than features; what the product can do for the potential owner rather than a detailed description of the contents. Repeat the message (in different words) to be sure your key points come across – not everyone will read from start to finish.

- Use bullet points for the main selling points; these can always be expanded in the main brochure. Numbering the selling points can be effective, but don't give too many (four is plenty).

- Underline key benefits for extra emphasis, blue underlining apparently improves the response still more (although do not over-use this technique). You can use the second colour for your signature at the bottom of the letter too.

- Provide enough information for the reader to make an immediate decision to buy. Describe in clear detail what the reader is expected to do next, ie how to order.

- Mention all the other items in the mailing. Provide a short cut to the order form for those who have already made up their minds to buy and do not need to read the brochure.

- The final paragraph too needs to be strong, to urge a positive reaction to the product and your offer, and to provide the motivation to fill in the order form straight away.

- Another very important part of the letter is the PS (apparently the second most widely read part of the letter after the headline). Think of a really important reason for buying and put it there.

- Don't make assumptions or use jargon, even when mailing your own buyers list. You will almost certainly get it wrong and may sound patronising.
- For business-to-business mail you may be using a job title rather than addressing a named individual. Bear in mind that at least a small percentage will have moved on and the mailshot should make sense to the next incumbents (who may never have heard from you before).
- Length. Long copy usually outsells short copy provided it is:
  (a) being read by the right person, ie the right list has been chosen
  (b) relevant
  (c) interesting.
  However, do bear in mind that if your letter is designed to create leads for the sales force, it's not a good idea to make it so long and detailed that the recipient has no need to see a rep. If you go for a two-page A4 letter (the standard) do break for the page end in mid-sentence on something interesting.
- Never say that someone will follow up the letter with a phone call to find out if the recipient is interested: it's a real turn-off.
- Layout is important: *make it look like a letter.* Whatever wonders your in-house desktop publishing machine can offer, resist the temptation to try out gimmicks on your sales letters. Don't get it typeset in anything other than a plausible computer face. If you want to look really hard-up, choose a typewriter font such as `Courier`. Ensure your finished copy looks varied. Make the paragraphs different lengths, give sub-headings, allow plenty of space to attract the reader's eye.

Who should the letter be addressed to?

Direct mailers spend a great deal of time agonising over this. Computers have made a range of personalised mailshots possible, but if price rules this out can you make a specific greeting to the job title you are mailing? For example: 'Dear Senior Partner' is better than 'Dear Sir/Madam'.

You may find that it is simply too expensive and too labour-intensive to produce a different header for each batch of letters you send out; if this is the case then 'Dear Reader' is probably your best option. Think about what greetings you find patronising – 'Dear Decision Maker' may fall into this category. Try testing to see if improving the precision of the greeting makes your response any better.

Who should sign the letter?

A similar decision awaits you at the foot of the letter. The person to sign the letter should be the person the recipient would expect to sign. I would therefore favour reserving the letter from the chairman of a multinational or managing director of a publishing house for a possible optional extra item in the mailing. In academic and educational publishing some marketing departments get the relevant editor to sign mailshots on the grounds that their letter will be treated with more respect by the recipient. Don't be afraid to fiddle with your job title if appropriate. For example, I got a very poor response to 'Product Manager' when handing out my business card at a conference for (arts) academics; as book lovers they felt it was inappropriate and an inelegant use of English. In future direct mail shots to arts academics I change my title. Science academics might have been less concerned; teachers of business studies might have thought it highly appropriate!

One final point. A letter is a very personal communication, and obviously you should avoid offending any of your reader's sensitivities. But don't worry unduly if you get a few angry letters protesting about the content of your mailshot. One copywriter told me that if you don't get a couple of cross letters per campaign no one is reading your material. What you should do is notice how you react to receiving a personal letter in response to your sales information (you usually feel rather uncomfortable) and realise the power of direct mail.

The brochure

The brochure serves the same ends as the sales letter: it explains the product benefits to the recipient. The sales points will be those covered in the letter, but explained in different words and ways so that the information seems fresh and interesting.

- You have more room in the brochure to explain your product and answer questions that, were the recipient examining the item for sale (for example in a bookshop), they could answer for themselves.
- Give precise and believable information about the product, not vague puffery.
- Again, stress the benefits to the recipient, not the key features you are most interested in.

Checklist for writing brochure copy

When writing copy for direct mail brochures I have a standard list of questions which I seek to answer.

- What are the key benefits of the product to the market?
- Who is the product for? (You can give a list of professions or job titles.)
- How can it be used? (Give examples of problems solved through using the product how it might be used in the recipient's everyday work.)
- Who is the author? (What are his or her qualifications; experience; appointments and previous publications relevant to the book, national and international?) If possible, include an author photograph. This should be captioned with the name. Remember that a well known name is not the same as a well known face; but if the author is extremely recognizable, use the caption to link their name to the product. Captions get read before body copy.
- What interesting facts are included? (General, interesting information in a brochure tends to get read.)
- What is the scope (ie breadth of coverage)?
- What are the main contents (or main revised sections for a new edition)?
- What does it replace?
- Who has reviewed the title and in what?
- Has anyone the market has heard of and respects said anything interesting about the book? (Testimonials.) If not, is there anyone who might be persuaded to do so?
- What does it look like? A photograph of the book cover is useful. If it is not yet available get your designer to make up a 'dummy'. Browsers in bookshops would want to know what the books they intended to purchase looked like; allow direct mail purchasers the same opportunity. If the title is expensive and has an impressive format or long extent, ensure the book is shot from the side, spine upright to show the value that the high price represents.

  The appearance of a photograph is particularly important if you are selling high price publications such as multi-volume reference sets. Your copy should imply that ownership endows prestige to any home: show the books beautifully lit in the best possible surroundings. If the book is one of a (collectable) series of titles, show other companion volumes.

- What is in it? Again, the browser in a bookshop would want to flick through a title they were considering buying. In a mailshot you can select which pages you reproduce to show the book to its best advantage. Use arrows with captions to make sales points. The same goes for illustrations from the book: all must have captions. (Captions are more often read than body copy.)
- When is the book due to be published? What are the publication details? (You should give extent; number of illustrations; number of entries; date available and so on.)
- Who else should see this mailshot when the recipient has finished? When mailing institutions, try printing 'route instructions' on the top of the brochure to suggest which other people should read your mailshot: the librarian, the head of department and so on.

For advice on brochure design see Chapter 5.

The reply vehicle

The reply device is your point of sale; it must:

(a) stand out in the package;
(b) be easy to use and;
(c) invite response.

Remember that the overall level of response to your material will always be in inverse proportion to the level of commitment required. It is therefore essential to make ordering as potentially trouble-free for the customer as possible. If you can supply goods on approval do so; if not ensure there is a complete guarantee of satisfaction (restated on the order form), such as a money-back guarantee, to allay fears and establish trust.

Format – what kind of reply vehicle should you go for?

What you enclose in your mailing will depend on the kind of response you are soliciting (how much information you need before taking the sales process any further) and how much budget you have available.

Cost will probably be an important consideration. In general, separate order forms attract a higher response than integral ones that have to be detached from the brochure or letter. Of the latter, perforated forms tend to do better than ones which require the recipient to find a pair of scissors, but again the extra finishing costs more. If budgetary constraints mean that you cannot perforate, show a pair of scissors and print a dotted line along where the cut should be made. Be wary of approving order forms which require the recipient to destroy the reference material. If it is an expensively produced brochure they may well pay you the costly compliment of putting the form to one side to be photocopied later, thus leaving them with their information intact. More lost sales.

In a brochure with an integral order form, probably the first thing to be laid out should be the coupon. Never cramp the coupon in order to make room for all your brochure copy; cut the copy instead! For similar reasons, never produce a cleverly shaped coupon which is time-consuming to clip, or one which is in an awkward place to cut out (bottom right-hand corner is best); many readers won't bother. If clipping the order form requires the reader to lose part of the brochure, don't put anything vital on the back of the coupon. Most people like to keep a record of what they have ordered until it arrives.

Some firms produce a complete sheet of paper as an order form with arrows marking where it can be folded to turn it into a mailable item (a 'self-mailer'). Others leave it to the responder to provide the envelope, perhaps making it easy for them by supplying them with a freepost or business reply address.

If you decide to provide a reply envelope ensure that the order form fits into it. For one of my early business mailshots the order form when cut out was slightly larger than the reply envelope mailed with it. I assumed people would fold the form to fit. A good percentage of the responders trimmed it so it fitted the envelope exactly, thereby obliterating the codes on the bottom of the form which showed from which list the order had come!

For separate order forms the cheapest format is probably the reply postcard with blank spaces for the customer to complete on one side and a freepost address back to the publisher on the other. But if you are asking for complex information you will have to send an envelope as well: very few customers will fill in a VISA number on the back of a postcard for all to see!

Information gathering

An order form is your chance to compile accurate information about your customers in the hope that you can sell to them again.

What kind of space should you provide for your customers to fill in?

Do bear in mind that the more information you require, the more space you need to provide. At the same time, remember that asking for too much information may mean the recipient is either offended (consumers can spot an attempt to load them on to a database) and puts it to one side to deal with later or it never gets filled in.

Offering a box for each separate letter of their name and address can be annoying to fill in; the boxes are usually far too small. If instead you provide lines for the name and address and mark underneath the vital information you need (first and second names, county, postcode etc) you can ensure you get a valid address. Ask for block capitals, which most people will write 'joined up'.

Other tips for making order forms work harder

- The small print. The quicker you are able to describe how it works the better. 'Offer subject to our standard terms and conditions, available on request' covers most eventualities.
- Special offers push up the response. They can be used in different ways, for example to get money in more quickly or boost the average level of order. Learn from the other mailshots you receive: an additional free gift if you spend more than a certain amount is very appealing. The free gift need not cost you much. It could be some item you already have in stock that is not selling well so has a higher value to the market than to you who must store and count it (and maybe subsequently pulp it).
- Free draws for swift response likewise attract replies. If you try this on a regular mailing to the same list be sure to announce who actually won: it boosts credibility and creates a club atmosphere. Try a pre-publication offer or, for projects that are even further from completion, a 'pioneer supporter' price: this can work particularly well for expensive multi-volume sets that take years to come to fruition and helps to subside your development costs. The incentive should be relevant to the audience and not necessarily to the product you are selling.
- Involve the reader on the order form. American publishers pioneered the technique of asking the recipient to stick stamps showing the covers required on the order form; this can be a particularly effective technique for promoting backlist titles if they are well known. Similarly, UK catalogue firms ask you to stick down 'Yes' or 'No' stamps.

- Repeat the offer and the name and address of the publisher on the order form. If it gets detached from the main part of the information package the reader will still have the details they need to order.

- Offer the option of a standing order for year-books. To libraries this may be a welcome chance to obtain important information reliably and without hassle. Stress that an invoice will be sent each year before the book is despatched so it is perfectly possible to decline a particular issue. Put the discounted and non-discounted prices side by side, with a line through the latter to show that a bargain is available (attracts attention).

- Postage and packing. Don't just assume that you have to print the same conditions as have always appeared. Can you experiment to make the structure of your additional charges cleaner and clearer? The quicker you describe how it works the better.

  Postage for specific weight bands is fixed according to Royal Mail scales, packaging is at your firm's discretion. 'Postage and packing' together can be levelled as you decide best, either as a total sum or as a percentage of the amount spent (bear in mind that most people cannot work out a percentage other than 10% in their head and a hunt for a calculator slows the process down – more lost orders). Consider, too, that the public's perception of postage is often that it costs more than it actually does – and books are heavy items. Some firms make quite a lot of money from carriage. Alternatively, try an offer with free postage and packing, maybe for orders over a certain value. This may well push up the overall response rate to justify the extra costs incurred. If you are doing this, write 'FREE' in the subtotal box on your order form to make the point more clearly.

  The quicker you are able to describe how 'p & p' is charged the better. Some firms use free postage and packing as an incentive to order, or offer it free for orders over a certain amount in value. If you are doing this write the word 'FREE' in the subtotal box on your order form to make the point clearly. If earlier on in your copy you have stated the price as '+ p & p', restate the total price payable on the order form.

  If you ask the customer to work out the p & p payable and add it to the total value of the goods ordered, and then receive cheques for less than the sum due, it is probably deliberate. Bank the money; it is not worth rejecting the order to obtain the extra 10%.

145

If goods you are sending out in the post are not easily replaceable and may get lost in transit (for example highly expensive reference sets, or the last few copies of an edition you are not planning to reprint), the Royal Mail offers insurance at the time of posting at very competitive rates.

Coding your order form

Ordering devices need to be coded so than when orders start to come back you can see which mailing lists have produced them. The cheapest way to do this is to run a felt-tip pen down the side of a wedge of leaflets and record which colour went to which list. A step up from this is the more reliable 'scratch coding'. A different code is assigned to each list, eg five lists could be coded respectively: A B C D E, all five codes appearing on the initial printing plate. Once the quantity for the fifth list (E) has been produced the last digit of the code gets wiped off and the quantity for D is printed. Scratch coding will increase the costs over a straightforward run for your printed materials but is much cheaper than the printer producing split runs for individual codes. Ask how many 'up' the printer is producing at one time: this gives you the number of mailing pieces on the plate at the same time and the number of changes that consequently must be made each time the machine is halted.

Your order forms can be coded with much more sophistication; in specific places, with more detailed codes and reference words, even with sequential numbers, as needs dictate. But bear in mind that with each additional specification the costs are likely to go up.

As the orders come in then either:

(a) ask if the list source can be entered when the sales information is entered on computer by customer services for invoice and despatch note creation. You should have regular reports fed back to you. Or:
(b) keep a manual total of how many each list has produced.

Do look through completed order forms to see how your customers react: is the space provided adequate; is it clear what information you require? What mistakes regularly occur in completing them – ie what do your customers not understand?

Keeping a standard order form

If you are to produce direct mail regularly it is useful to keep a standard order form on (computer) file. Find out from your customer services department the conditions on which you will supply titles: the approval periods; how you accept payment, from which credit cards and so on. Do you require a signature from the customer? Do you need to print a disclaimer, eg 'prices subject to change without notice' or 'subject to fluctuating exchange rates'.

Other items you could consider including in your mailings

- Information about your Web site.
- An extra order form. Once your customer has ordered they will still have the opportunity to buy again. Code it so you can see the response it generates.
- A checklist of all the related titles you publish.
- A 'recommendation to purchase' form for recipients working in institutions (academic and business) to pass to the librarian. Most new academic and company library purchases are the result of recommendations by the other staff.
- Another letter. Perhaps a 'lift letter' from a satisfied customer or famous admirer of the product or a 'publisher's letter', say from your firm's managing director or the book's editor. Such a letter need not come from someone famous, just someone plausible. For example, when mailing schools the ideal candidate would be a head teacher or subject adviser. Charities use the technique in fund-raising mailshots; for example, enclosing letters from field workers describing the value of their work.
- A sheet of quotations from published reviews of the title you are promoting.
- A news sheet on an existing product. Even best-selling titles can become boring to the market. How about a news sheet describing developments being made by the editorial team; how the material is being used by some buyers? It's all good stuff for promoting the customer's perception of your product and hence their loyalty.
- Instead of offering a discount or stressing value on the order form try a 'money-off coupon' for the customer to enclose with their returned order. Again, it involves the reader and adds value

to the package received. Put 'offer limited to one voucher per household' on the coupon and you further increase its value.

- A reply envelope for the return of the order form.
- A quiz sheet or competition imparting further product details.
- Information from another company which sells non-competing products to the same market, and subsidises your marketing costs.
- Forthcoming related product information.

What to do with returns

Whether envelopes returned as undeliverable come to your firm or the mailing house will depend on which return address appears on the outer envelope. If they come to the mailing house ask them to batch up and send back to you at regular intervals.

Extract the contents, write the code from the order form on the envelope to show which list it came from, then delete the same code from the order form. You then have leaflets ready for re-use (exhibitions, insertions in other company post and so on) and envelopes ready to go back to the list owner. You should get a credit if the returns total more than 5 per cent of the list you rented, otherwise you will simply have contributed to cleaning the list. Don't forget a credit on list rental is a small element of your actual costs in mailing the addresses they provided; some firms may be willing to compensate further.

Card deck mailings

An increasingly popular format for business-to-business direct response advertising is the card deck mailing. In the business market this format offers the highest response rates. Typically this consists of around 30 small cards (7.5 × 12.5 cm) each featuring a different product, mailed like a pack of playing cards in a plastic envelope to an individual at a business address. A letter is usually wrapped around the pack, introducing the contents and highlighting several titles. On the reverse of each card is the return address and a space for ordering, usually on approval. An invoice is sent with the title ordered and becomes payable after the approval period has expired (usually 10 days).

The advantages of promoting this way

For the right book, inclusion in a card deck mailing is an effective way to gain sales. The simplicity and manageable size of the format appeal to the professionals they are mailed to. The recipients flick through the cards, extract those they are interested in, and may well pass on others relevant to their colleagues.

The card offers promotion for titles at a fraction of the cost of an individual mailing, and can be a very cost-effective way of undertaking market research before you are committed to an extensive (and expensive) print run.

Response comes back quickly. The professionals to whom decks are mailed are busy and tend to buy on impulse; each card provides enough information to make a quick decision on whether to purchase. There is no coupon clipping or hunt for an envelope to slow down replies and it is usual to expect 50 per cent of the response within four to five weeks of mailing. Some regular card deck users reckon to have 50 per cent within two to three weeks of receipt of the first card returned. But while the majority of the orders will come back quickly, cards will continue to trickle back months after mailing: some recipients obviously hoard them!

Sales will also come back through the trade: business booksellers receive orders from institutional libraries with deck cards stapled to them.

What kind of titles do well in card decks?

Having said it can be an effective form of promotion, the response rates tend to be low, with an average of around 1–2 per cent across the whole pack. At the same time the costs of producing and mailing the cards are not cheap, usually at least £750–£800 per title for a mailing of around 30 titles to 50,000 addresses.

It therefore follows that the type of book best promoted is of a price sufficiently high to bear the cost of promotion: at least £25 (unless you are promoting to gather new names in which case you would probably be satisfied with a break-even response rate). Even very expensive books or multi-volume sets can be effectively promoted through card decks, particularly if the card is treated as a way to gain leads: perhaps sending a prospectus to enquirers and following this up with a telephone call to close the sale. But however expensive the product, always provide the opportunity to order there and then; some people (in particular those who are familiar with the promotional format and the company sending it

150

10 days at your desk to decide

Yes! please send me the book overleaf at the price shown plus £2.95 towards post and packing (£3.95 for two or more books).

Guarantee: I have 10 days from delivery to decide. After that I can keep the book and pay the price (+p&p) shown or I can return it and owe nothing.

Signature _____

Name Mr/Mrs/Miss _____
BLOCK CAPITALS PLEASE

Position _____

Company _____

Address _____

_____

_____ Post Code _____

Tel No. _____ Fax No. _____
(in case of query)

VERY URGENT ORDERS	For several books please use an envelope or staple the cards together.
Telephone: 0353 665544	Remember to sign each one.
Have your credit card ready	Full details of offer in accompanying
Please quote ref: AK5	letter. Offer subject to acceptance. A B C D E F G H

TO:
Wyvern Business Library
FREEPOST CB 511
Ely
Cambs
CB7 4BR

If you prefer to use an envelope, just copy out this address – no stamp needed

No Stamp Needed

Figure 6.1 *A card such as this is included in card deck mailings. Reproduced by kind permission of Wyvern Business Library*

out) will part with large sums of money on the strength of the limited information, and each person who does so subsidises the cost of others who use the card to ask for more information.

'How to' books for which the recipient can perceive an instant need tend to do well; an easily understood title is crucial. Theoretical and complex titles for which more explanation is needed than is possible on a small card should be excluded, as should books of general appeal. There is a strong demand for new titles that offer current information and good value for money.

Card decks are a cost-effective way of promoting books that are poor performers through traditional direct marketing packages, as they can be supported by stronger titles in the pack.

Scientific, business, technical and professional publishers are all using card decks in many different subject areas: applied sciences; engineering; business; banking; investment; law; medicine and nursing.

What to say on the card

Experts estimate an average card receives one second of the recipient's attention, less as the format gets increasingly popular and more packs are sent.

Primarily, the copy should be appropriate to the audience; feature the benefits that are of most interest. The headline should contain the strongest benefit of all.

Most card mailers follow a headline with around 150 words of copy and usually a photograph of the title. They stress the currency of the information and the value for money that the book provides. Also very important is a guarantee of satisfaction should customers be less than happy with what they receive. The product can either be available on approval, or a full refund offered if it is returned in good condition within so many days of receipt. The fulfilment address goes on the back of the card, the orderer's details either beneath this or on the copy side of the card. Provide telephone and fax numbers for those who want to order straight away.

Some publishers provide a space for recipients to staple a business card on to the card, instead of filling in ordering details, thereby gaining still more information about their customers while inconveniencing them less.

Around 30–40 cards seem to be the standard number used for existing mailings; fewer, and the pack looks a bit thin by the time those of no interest have been weeded out; more, and it is too much effort to wade through. Many existing packs contain 32 cards which are as many as you can fit on to a machine sheet at one go.

Include a covering letter introducing the pack and highlighting several particular titles. Wyvern (see below) estimate that 'leading' a book in this way will approximately double a title's sales.

The very top card on the pack needs to have a space for the address label to be fixed to it and the PPI (postage paid impression) displayed so that the whole bundle does not need to be franked. In general, the packs get sent out second class; as they are light a lot can be mailed for the money. For the return address senders are increasingly not bothering to offer freepost or business reply addresses for business-to-business promotions; most orders will go out through the company postroom. Omitting the free stamp back also cuts down on the 'loony' replies – recipients who put the entire pack of cards in the post so that the sender pays for the receipt of each blank card or those who write abusive messages on cards they return.

Whose card deck to advertise in?

Wyvern Publications Ltd have 55,000 active bookbuyers on their list with a core of 35,000 who purchase most frequently. They mail roughly 500,000 packs of cards a year to small and medium-sized businesses. Wyvern monitor new and forthcoming titles in subject areas of interest to their buyers and will offer to produce a card and mail it in their decks for titles they reckon will sell, aiming to shift at least 1,500 copies a year. They usually buy 250–500 copies as a firm sale, but in return for handling all promotional costs ask for substantial discounts from publishers (75–80 per cent).

Other compilers of deck card mailings charge a flat flee for including a card on a particular title or titles. You provide camera-ready artwork and the orders come back straight to you. Most offer second and subsequent cards taken in the pack at a reduced rate, and charge a premium for a guaranteed position within the pack.

If you are planning to include a first card in someone else's mailing merely to test this medium, find out if you can:

- mail specific market sectors only;
- start with a test mailing to a small number of the total circulation only, eg 20%;
- pay for each enquiry received by the deck mailer for your product rather than for the card production. Some mailers will encourage this on the grounds that you may end up paying

more for your leads than outright payment for the card would have cost, and will be encouraged to advertise in future;
- appear within the first 10 cards in the pack.

Other hints for making your budget go further:

- Include two titles on the card, in the hope of improving both your response rate and the value of your orders. Obviously, both books must have self-explanatory titles and the benefits be even more strongly stressed, as the room for explanatory copy will be greatly reduced.
- Include a checklist of other relevant titles on the card. Ask recipients to circle those on which they wish to receive further information.
- Use the card to promote the offer of a copy of your current catalogue.
- In the US it is increasingly common for card decks to include mini-catalogues the same size as the cards, or double or triple cards which provide more room for copy and illustration.
- Can you include a card in someone else's card deck in return for their putting a loose insert in one of your mailings?
- If your efforts are successful, think about producing a pack of cards yourself, starting with a mailing to your previous purchasers. The start-up costs can be high: you will have to cover printing, design, photography, labelling and collating, inserting and mailing, polylopes (plastic envelopes), and postage. But if it works, the potential profits will be greater. You have the further option of subsidising your costs by including other publishers' or manufacturers' information in your own pack.

Other direct marketing formats

Advice on how to put together an effective card deck will be useful in considering how best to use other direct marketing formats. All the same conditions apply: limited space, the need to attract the recipient's attention quickly and the importance of mailing the right list. A variety of other formats have been developed. These include 'self-mailers' (the product information and order form are combined; recipients detach a reply device to return their order). Several types have emerged.

L-shaped cards

These are much used as loose inserts in consumer magazines. The main part of the copy is on the larger upright part of the 'L'; the 'foot' detaches, usually along a perforated strip, to form a reply card.

They can be cost-effective to produce, particularly if two Ls can be laid out as a jig-saw fit on the printing plate, making maximum use of the card. They work best for creating interest, eg stimulating requests for a catalogue or 'invoice me' type orders. Without the confidentiality of a reply envelope recipients would not be willing to note personal ordering information such as a credit card number on a postcard.

Roll fold sheets

A single sheet of paper, printed on two sides, with arrows and dotted lines indicating where the customer should fold and tuck the flaps in. This turns it into a reply device for which no envelope is needed.

'Bang tail' mailshots or one piece mailers

The most sophisticated sort of self-mailer. A long strip of paper folded several times, the outer end is stuck down to form an item suitable for mailing. When the mailing piece is opened and the information revealed, the other end of the sheet has been gummed to form a ready-made reply envelope, which the recipient has only to detach to use. Thus all the component parts of the mailshot are combined in one convenient and attractive mailshot. Such mailshots are expensive to produce, given the origami-standard of folding and finishing required, and provide much less space for explanation than a traditional mailshot. They tend to work well for products that are already familiar to the audience being addressed. For a further cost they can be fully personalised.

For other ideas on direct mail formats consult your letterbox, trade magazines, printers and designers involved in the medium, or visit the annual Direct Marketing Fair (organised by Reed).

A final checklist for mailshots

- Is the copy really strong on product benefits and reasons to buy?
- Would I buy from me? Is the copy strong enough?

- If you are writing about something you do not understand has the copy been checked by an expert: the editor or the author?
- Have you called the book by the same title each time?
- Have you used the title too often (boring)?
- Is it clear what the price is and how much should be added for postage and packing etc?
- Is it clear how to order and by when?
- Are the publisher's name, address, telephone and fax numbers and e-mail address on all the elements in the package?
- Are the contact details really large enough to find and read in a rush?
- What does the customer do if he or she is unclear about some aspect of your product; are you offering a telephone number for enquiries?
- Have you included an option for capturing non-buying prospects?
- Triple check the final proofs before you pass for press for consistency, grammatical errors etc. Once the job is with the printer you will pay very heavily for changes.
- How is the mailshot to be followed up: by your reps; by remailing; with teleselling etc?
- If you offer a slot for those who do not want to order now saying 'Please send me further information on ...' have you sorted out what you are going to send?
- Has everyone been warned in-house who needs to know that the mailing is about to go out: your reps; orders processing; the person manning the 'information line'; anyone else in your department who may answer your telephone?
- Is your address on the outer envelope so that undelivered shots can be returned?

Trial mailings

Direct marketing, as we are continually reminded, is a very testable medium: with teleselling you have feedback within days on whether your product is likely to be a success; with direct mail within weeks. All large-scale mailers test the market before they commit themselves to extensive campaigns. They test by mailing a selection of addresses from all the lists they are considering.

List rental companies can produce a trial list for you with an 'nth' selection from each possible list: perhaps every fifth or tenth name.

It is best if they 'dump' the entire list on to disk before the selection is made, otherwise there need be only one change to the master list in between your trial and your actual mailing and the 'nth' selection will be thrown out; you will end up mailing some people twice. For a substantial mailing (200,000 plus) most mailers would carry out a test of at least 10 per cent.

For publishers whose budgets are not so extensive as to permit large-scale test mailings the following may be considered.

- Comparing like with almost like. What is the track record of your company's promotion of related products to similar markets? Does this give you any useful hints on the selection of lists? You will see that accurate monitoring of your mailing results is crucial if you are to learn for the future.
- Try testing at the time of mailing: send two different sales letters to two halves of the same mailing list; try different subsidiary titles on the order form to see which produces the most orders. Code the coupons and watch the results.
- Don't over-complicate your job! If you don't want to end up being confused by your testing, and wasting money on pointless research, test only variables that can dramatically alter the results: product(s) offered; price; offer; time close and so on.

How to work out if your direct marketing is successful

One of the advantages of selling direct is that you can measure your results against costs, and so prove whether or not your marketing strategy is achieving satisfactory targets. The degree of accuracy with which you are able to do this depends on the kind of books you are promoting.

If a substantial proportion of the orders resulting from your mailings will come back through the book trade rather than direct (eg when approaching the schools market) the best way to see your results is to examine sales figures before and after a promotion goes out, and compare the total with the original estimates of market size and possible penetration (usually made when a title is commissioned). Other firms count inspection copy request cards returned after mailings to estimate success, or compare year-on-year sales figures.

On the other hand, if you are promoting to the business or industrial markets you may expect 70 per cent plus of your mailing response to come back direct. Although publishers are still not in a position to isolate and identify all the orders that result from a specific mailing, the attempt to establish the cost effectiveness of each campaign must be made.

To measure results against costs effectively you have to calculate the response rate of your mailing.

$$\text{The response rate} = \frac{\text{number of replies}}{\text{number mailed}} \times 100$$

No guarantees of what to expect can be made, and your criteria of what is successful will depend on the selling price of what you are offering and how many you have to sell to make a profit.

More important than the response rate is the *cost per order*, ie how much it is costing you to secure orders.

$$\text{Cost per order} = \frac{\text{costs of each mailshot} \times \text{numbered mailed}}{\text{numbers of orders received}}$$

Your costs of mailing will include all the various elements of the campaign: list rental; printing and design costs; copywriting if you have to pay for it; despatch and postage.

A quick comparison of your cost per order and the selling price of the product you are promoting will show whether your mailing is heading for profit or loss.

For more specific information on profitability you need to establish the *contribution per sale* for each title sold. To calculate this as well as production costs for the books promoted you need to know your company's policy on the allocation of overhead and other costs: your department's share of anything from bad debts and warehousing to staff costs and photocopying. A quick way of doing this is to establish a production and overhead cost for the main item you are selling (say 50 per cent of the sales price of the key title featured).

This enables you to calculate the *break-even response rate*: the minimum quantity of products your campaign must shift before it starts to justify the costs of the promotion and make money. The equation for working this out is as follows:

$$\frac{\text{Cost of each mailshot} \times \text{number mailed}}{\text{Cost of production for main title}}$$

(This formula is used as the basis for the break-even response rates in the example that follows.)

The equations get more complicated if a variety of lists is used for which rental values vary substantially (and so marketing costs differ for each mailing list addressed) or your order form features a variety of products. If responders order more than one product your total costs will be a smaller proportion of total revenues generated, and the economics of the whole mailing improved.

Your calculations will need to be recorded in a mailing analysis form which can be circulated to your colleagues. This is best done in tabular form; the example overleaf will give you an idea of how it may be laid out.

Notes
1. The publishing house's own list pulls best, followed by that of the company who provided the data for the book. The latter was provided as part of the agreement to publish.
2. Swaps with other publishers meet with varying success, but lists of known direct mail responders do better than subscriber lists.
3. Loose inserts tend to produce lower response rates than individual mailings, but this need not mean they should be avoided; they cost much less to arrange. Note that the response rates for lists 09 and 10 are practically the same although the cost per sale differs markedly.

A simpler way of recording results for a single priced product on which a very long-term view on marketing costs is being taken could be set out as follows:

Weekly sales report for new Encyclopaedia of Life Sciences

Week number (since mailing went out): 6

Date:

	Week total		Year to date	
	UK	overseas	UK	overseas
Academic libraries	1	8	17	17
Public libraries			11	1
Corporate libraries			3	10
Companies			1	2
Academics			3	7
Professional		1		9
Media			1	
Bookshops	1	1	27	16
Individuals		1		6
Total week sales:		13		
Total sales to date:			131	

Graham and Green monthly mailing report to 31 March 1999

Mailing and title	Code	Date mailed	Quantity mailed	Units main title	Units secondary title	Secondary units value	Total order value	% response	Cost per order
Mailing 99 – 4: NBL Financial Directory (price £95.00), 2 Secondary titles (prices £110 and £46.50)									
NBL own list	01	January	4,000	172	14	778,000	17,118.00	4.65	6.04
Directory entrants	02	January	10,000	91	–	–	8,645.00	0.91	30.88
G&G financial bookbuyers	03	January	1,500	68	4	266.50	6,460.00	4.80	5.85
List swap (another publisher)	04	January	1,500	30	2	220.00	3,070.00	2.13	13.17
List swap (another publisher)	05	January	2,300	18	2	156.50	1,966.50	0.86	32.31
List swap (another publisher)	06	January	5,000	42	–	–	3,990.00	0.84	33.45
List swap (another publisher)	07	January	4,300	22	3	139.50	2,229.50	0.58	48.33
Subscribers to Business Journal	08	January	3,500	27	4	186.00	2,751.00	0.88	31.72
Daily Tribune Business Information Subscribers	09	January	2,500	8	5	232.50	992.50	0.52	54.04
Total			34,600	478	34	1,979.00	42,222.50	1.48	18.99

Cost of mailing = £281.00 per 1000
Break-even for 34,600 = 205

Inserts:									
1.	10	December	5,000	20	3	33.00	2,230.00	0.46	24.60
2.	11	December	12,000	5	3	266.50	741.50	0.07	169.76
3.	12	January	10,000	18	5	232.50	1,942.50	0.23	49.20
Total			27,000	43	11	829.00	4,914.00	0.20	56.59

Cost of insert = £113.17 per 1000
Break-even for 27,000 = 64

Total sales to date:				677	58				
returns				5	2				

One final word of warning. Avoid including on your mailing analysis reports titles which receive a mixture of direct mail and general promotion through the trade. Many of your direct response orders will come back through bookshops and your cost per order will consequently look unreasonably high. For this type of title it is better to concentrate on sales totals and compare them with those of previous years or similar titles.

Making your direct marketing budget go further

- Try to cut down on changes and mistakes to the artwork. Printers estimate that at least 20% of their billing is for typographical changes, either to proofs, artwork or plates.
- Instead of individual mailings, try loose inserts or off-the-page advertising: these can sometimes offer better value for money, for although the response rate is reduced (on average 25% of mailed shots to the same list), costs are less.
- If a journal refuses to rent you a copy of their mailing list and does not accept loose inserts, can you provide ready filled envelopes for them to stick on subscriber address labels and post on your behalf? They maintain the security of their list and you are still able to mail. Alternatively, can you sell off-the-page by advertising in the journal?
- Can you join a co-operative mailing to the market you want to reach? These are organised by several firms to standard market sectors, eg schools and libraries.
- Can you co-operate with another publisher or a company selling a product to the same market and share the costs of mailing? Alternatively, can you put leaflets in each other's mailings? For example, pharmaceutical firms regularly mail doctors and so would be an ideal vehicle for sending publishers' information to the same market.
- Instead of paying for advertising/insert costs can you offer the relevant magazine a commission deal, paying them a certain amount for every sale you make? Alternatively, can you offer them advertising space in your own publications? Will they accept books for their institutional library instead?
- Is it worth making an initial offer which may not be cost effective in the attempt to gain long-term customers? Book clubs work on this principle: the first selection of titles is subsidised by members' subsequent orders.

- Can you improve your cash flow by getting orders in more quickly? Invoice and chase speedily; ask for money up front but offer a cast-iron guarantee to back up the offer. Consider offering other ways to pay if the market is likely to find these more convenient.
- Including other titles on the order form can improve the value of orders received.
- Offering incentives can encourage a higher value of order or get the orders in more quickly, eg 'classroom packs' which incorporate a discount; free draw for all orders received by a certain date; increased discounts or free postage and packing for orders over a certain value.
- Ask for referrals: the names of friends and colleagues to whom a copy of the mailing should also be sent.

Telemarketing

In the promotion of products direct to the customer the popularity of telemarketing is growing, both for creating sales and following up on other sorts of direct marketing initiatives such as mailshot campaigns. Selling over the phone is the natural extension of the personal contact for which direct mail strives, but by talking directly to the market much more comprehensive feedback can be obtained. Telemarketing is increasingly used for the promotion of goods to the consumer.

How much telemarketing is going on?

It is difficult to estimate the precise extent of telemarketing. Many firms offer a telephone number for the receipt of orders ('in bound' telemarketing) and involve their customer services staff in making 'out bound' calls but never calculate the costs of operating the systems independently; they get lost in overall company overheads. 'Out bound' work carried out by telemarketing bureaux can be estimated (the DMA Census 1998, gives the figure of £1,835.1 million which is greater than the estimated spend on direct mail), but some suggest that the work undertaken by bureaux represents no more than 5–10 per cent of the total telemarketing going on.

The advantages of teleselling

1. A highly effective means of selling; it produces orders.
2. Usually results in faster sales than other methods of marketing; better for company cash flow.

3. Immediate feedback on your product/company/offer/what-ever you are seeking to promote. Through first-hand contact with your market your company gains valuable and current sales information. Every call is an opportunity for research.
4. Improved customer relations. Telemarketing reinforces the reputation of your company for service by talking directly to your customers: everyone likes to be listened to.
5. By recording market reactions to your product and company telemarketing offers long-term leads as well as initial sales opportunities.
6. Very cost-effective. It is true that the cost per contact made is high in comparison with direct mail; that a mailing can cover more of the market for less money. But:
    ● Every contact yields information (compare this with a mail-shot yielding a 2% response; 98% of those contacted provide you with no feedback on why they did not order).
    ● You waste no further money on contacting those not inter-ested in your products.
    ● Responses are measurable on an hourly basis. You need to commit yourself only to a test marketing and decide to expand or cut back your efforts depending on the results.
    ● By using a telemarketing agency you can carry the number of staff working on your account without being responsible for the expensive fixed costs of staff hiring or training.

How to go about telemarketing

The introduction of telemarketing within your company will be most effective if the principles involved are adopted by the company as a whole rather than seen as the particular practices of a single department.

This means making it clear that telephone orders are welcome rather than a nuisance, encouraging the telephonist to return to those 'on hold' rather than leaving them to make their own decision on whether or not to hang up. To assess the situation, try ringing your own switchboard from home to find out what scope there is for improvement!

Second, telemarketing should not be seen as a separate marketing technique, but integrated into all your other marketing activities. Telemarketing can be used to follow up mailshots, make appoint-ments for reps or invite customers to preview evenings for your forthcoming list. The research you gain as a result should be central to how you plan to promote in the future.

Whom to ring

Another acronym for you. The prospect you are searching for is the:

M	A	N

(with the money) (and the Authority to purchase who) (has the Need).

The starting point should be your own list of past customers. Provided they were satisfied with what they bought, those who have purchased from you in the past are the prospects most likely to order from you in the future. If you make a few adaptions to your direct mail order forms you can start building your own teleselling lists for future campaigns. You should obviously ask for the telephone number (office and home), but other small additions will help you to build a database of future contacts. For example, before 'Name' write Mr/Mrs/Miss/Ms/title and record what comes back.

Firms that sell mailing lists are increasingly offering telemarketing lists too for an extra charge. Some job titles are much harder to reach than others. If you have selected managing directors you may find you are only reaching two every hour. Training and personnel managers are notoriously difficult to find: they are always running courses or interviewing. Marketing and financial managers are generally available. If you find a secretary persistently blocking access to a particular manager try ringing back during the lunch hour or after 5.00 pm. You usually get through.

If you are planning to mail a rented list and then follow up with a telephone campaign find out if there is a reduced list rental for the second copy of the list. It will not be offered unless you ask.

Examples of telemarketing usage

1.   Market research
Telemarketing is an effective way to test customer reaction to new products and ideas; to identify new market sectors and measure market attitudes; to find out who within an organisation should be targeted with sales information and how large their budget is, to test a price, offer or incentive.

2.   As part of a direct marketing campaign
Telemarketing is an excellent way to update mailing lists; to qualify (establish real interest from) sales leads generated; to follow up a mailshot and thus increase the response rate; to carry out post-

campaign research and analysis. The results of a telemarketing campaign can be set up as a database for future mailing of a market about which the company already knows a great deal.

3. Generating sales opportunities for reps

Telemarketing can be used to canvass sales leads and set appointments. This reduces the need for cold calls, establishes the prospect's interest in the company's products before the call is made and improves the effectiveness of the sales team.

4. Building customer relations

Telemarketing is a very good way to handle potential or actual problems such as customer enquiries or complaints, and to reactivate old contacts.

Who should do the ringing

Successful teleselling is a skilled art. The caller has to build a relationship with the prospect, all the while noting information passed on (whether directly or indirectly), preparing the next question and keeping the conversation going. In searching for the right people to do the ringing, you have four basic options:

1. Ring the contacts yourself.
2. Employ someone to do it in-house.
3. Pay a bureau to do it for you.
4. Pay someone to do it for you freelance at home.

1. Effective marketing requires a combination of two skills: product knowledge and an ability to communicate on the telephone. Whereas you may have all the requisite product knowledge, creating the time and the inclination to carry out teleselling in-house can be very difficult.
2. Another possibility is to find a freelance person to come in-house and carry out a telesales campaign on your behalf. Advertise in the local paper and provide a telephone number for those interested to ring you for more information, so you will hear them in action. Bureaux look for staff in the same way: the telephone manner should be confident and friendly and the voice clear.

    Remember, if you employ a freelance sales person in-house you must provide the secretarial back-up they need. Each call they make may require some follow-up: a confirmation of order; a letter to accompany a brochure that was requested. These are hot leads and must be dealt with straight away; they must never be allowed to sit at the bottom of an overworked (and probably resentful) secretary's in-tray for three or four days.

3. A dedicated telemarketing bureau probably offers the best way to test the water: having briefed them on your product, market and competitors, you benefit from their expertise on how best to target and time the approach. They are responsible for training the people who will work on your account, both in product knowledge and in selling skills.

    Most bureaux offer a basic package including the creation of a 'framework for calls' (never a 'script') based on a thorough understanding of product benefits, an initial number of telephone contracts and a report on the results. After this the client may decide either to abort the campaign, to make changes, or to carry on.

4. Employing a freelance person to work for you at home is possibly the least satisfactory option. Those making the calls (and the sales targets they achieve as a result) benefit from the competitive and supportive atmosphere of a telesales office. Faced with a difficult question a caller can seek advice immediately; with rudeness he or she can complain to colleagues rather than the walls. The actual time spent by those making calls from home can be difficult to monitor.

    It is usual to pay for telemarketing by the number of calls made and the time spent, not on the amount of goods sold. In the UK most telesales people are paid hourly rather than on commission, but with incentive bonus schemes.

Planning a telemarketing campaign

There should be detailed consideration of the objectives of the campaign together with an understanding of how far they are measurable by telemarketing. A framework for calls must be established; a basis for questions rather than a script to be read. For this you need to consider which of the selling benefits are most relevant to the market being contacted, whether an offer is appropriate, how the customer can pay, what further information is available should the prospect ask for more details; how the market research obtained as a result of the call is to be recorded for future use. If the product being sold is complicated it should be demonstrated to the people making the calls; if it is portable there should be one in the telesales office.

As an example of the kind of information-seeking ('open-ended') questions a telesales person should ask, here is a sample:

The product: *The Truck Driver's Handbook*. An annual publication featuring the key safety and legal requirements that must be complied with by lorries travelling within the EC and Europe generally. An individual copy is £12.50, a pack of 10 costs £100.

The list: the publisher's own list of previous purchasers of bulk copies.

To the switchboard:
Good am/pm, this is Ann Scott ringing from Overdrive Publishers. May I please speak to Mr/Ms (previous contact)?
Could you tell me what department that is please? Note (1). What job title? Note (1).
Could you put me through please?
   If the contact has left ask who has replaced, note the new name, initials and spelling and then ask to be put through.

To the contact:
Good am/pm, this is Ann Scott ringing from Overdrive Publishers. Do you have a couple of minutes to speak to me now? Note (2).
We publish the *Truck Driver's Handbook*, of which you bought x copies last year.
I presume that was for use by your drivers with some copies for head office?
If yes ask: How many drivers do you have now? Note.
If no ask: Who uses it? Note.
The reason for my call is that the 2000 edition will be available in two months' time. Do you know how many you will need this year? If you order now we can ensure copies are with your staff as soon as they are available.
   Listen to how many required. Note.
Is that enough for all your staff who need access to the book?
If you order over x quantity we are able to offer you a discount, and we will also cover the express delivery costs of getting the books to your offices.
   Explain discount structure.

The close.

So how many would you like to order? Note (3).

Thank you very much.

Our customer services department will invoice you for the books within the next few days.

Check the address of company, postcode etc, confirm spelling of name and any others terms you are unsure of.

Finally.

This is just one of a series of business handbooks that we publish. Would you like me to enclose a copy of our most recent catalogue with the invoice? Note (4).

Thank you and goodbye.

As well as the framework for the call, you need to provide your tele-sales people with the relevant information to deal with the possible objections/questions prospects may raise. This is probably best stored on a series of cards that the person making the call can refer to quickly without being 'thrown'. For the above product these 'objections' would most likely include:

It's too expensive.

> Yes £100 may sound a lot but this is information your staff need access to every working day; details that they are legally required to know and comply with, wherever they are. Note (5).
>
> Don't forget that the price of £100 gives you a £25 discount on copies for 10 staff members, and there is a further generous discount structure for customers buying bulk copies for their staff.

We did buy copies last year, but won't be doing so this year. It is company policy to buy copies only once every two years.

> Well, that is a way to keep costs down, but your staff will be referring to out-of-date information.
>
> Each year around 40 per cent of the information included in the book changes so by the end of two years they will be substantially out of date. And this is information they are legally required to know and comply with, wherever they are.
>
> Don't forget there is a generous discount structure for customers buying bulk copies for their staff, so you could perhaps afford to buy copies every year.
>
> Explain the discount structure.

We will get copies for the drivers but will make do with a couple of copies for head office this year; our staff can share.

> Well, yes, of course that is a way of keeping costs down, but in our experience we find those who regularly use the book need it on their desks, every day, to refer to when they are on the phone, or for instant access to information. You risk wasting expensive employee time as your staff hunt for the shared copy every time they need it.

It goes out of date so quickly.

> Of course the information in the edition does go out of date during the next year, but then it is accepted as the bible of the industry; it is what everyone else is using. And we offer an advice line all year round to those who buy on standing order from us.

We use online services.

> Online services are very valuable but we find they simply do not provide information as quickly as flicking through a desk copy or keeping a copy in the driver's cab at all times. Note (6).
> And of course, the costs of online services are substantially higher. Note (7).
> Don't forget that for those companies buying 10 or more copies on standing order we offer an advice line on current legislation all year round.

We let our drivers buy their own copies.

> Asking drivers to buy their own keeps your costs down, but when driving for your company, don't forget the legal responsibility is yours. Your firm must ensure each driver understands and adheres to local laws.

Does it include the recent changes in Albania?

> While I know it covers all the major political regimes in Europe, I'm afraid I can't tell you whether the recent changes in Albania are specifically included. I will call back and let you know. Note (8).

Notes

1. Gather all the information you can.
2. Depending on the level of contact you are calling it is important to establish permission for the call to proceed. As there are few things more annoying than having one's train of thought (or a meeting) interrupted by an unexpected and irrelevant call, be courteous. If you are polite enough to establish that it is an inconvenient time to call and you suggest that you ring back later, you will usually be offered a call back time.
3. This is called an assumptive close, a method of closing (or clinching) the sale. For this positive approach to be used the caller has to be sure the prospect wishes to order. Other possible techniques are:

   ● The alternative close:
   So would you like one pack at £100 or 10 packs at £750? (Either way is yes.)

   ● The incentive close:
   So if I take your order for the copies you need now you will save a further 5%. How many would you like to order on this basis?

4. This can be used whether or not you have made a sale.
5. Always agree with the caller then go on to explain your point of view.
6. Never knock the competition, it debases the whole tone of your conversation and makes a prospect sound stupid if they are already committed to the other option mentioned. Instead, if the competition is brought up by the prospect, make a positive comparison with your product by stating its benefits.
7. Arm yourself with any statistics you may need to refer to before any calls are made, for example the cost of online services; how long it takes to get information on screen compared with accessing information in a reference book. In this case it would be useful to make a few calls to people who regularly use the book before ringing any prospects.
8. If you don't know, never bluff. Say you will ring back and give the information the prospect asked for later.

How to keep track of calls

Information from the questions answered should be recorded on a ready-made telesales contact sheet. Notes should be made as the call proceeds or immediately afterwards. Once a few calls have been made all will blur into one another and the caller will not be able to remember who said what. A call sheet for the above product could be laid out as follows:

The Truck Driver's Handbook
Date called: _____ Caller: _____
Contact: Mr/Mrs/Miss/Ms Initials_____ Name _____
Company name: _____
_____
Address: _____
_____Postcode: _____
Telephone: _____Fax: _____
E-mail: _____
_____
New contact: yes/no
Department using book: _____
Number of staff in department:_____
Number of drivers they have on their books:_____
Copies bought last year: _____
Copies ordered this year: _____
Reasons: _____
_____
Requested catalogue?:_____
Action required: _____

Fax

The ubiquitous arrival of the fax machine in the late 1980s created a new opportunity for adding urgency to a sales message. This disadvantage to recipients was that they had to pay for the receipt of information they did not request, and receiving the message blocked incoming business calls.

Sending direct marketing material by fax is now illegal in several US states and legislation is under consideration in the EU. But where an established trading relationship between two companies exists, sending information by fax is an excellent way of communicating – for example to inform a client company about last minute availability of something they had requested.

Notes

1. Source: Direct Mail Information Service (DMIS), Consumer Direct Mail Trends 1998.
2. Source: DMIS, Business to Business Direct Mail Trends 1997.
3. Source: DMIS, Consumer Direct Mail Trends 1998.
4. Source: Questionnaire circulated in 1998 by DMIS through *Marketing Week* magazine. Information requested on the four most recent direct marketing campaigns.
5. The DMIS is run as an independent consultancy, although the Royal Mail makes a large contribution to the costs of research and publications.
6. Source: DMIS Letterbox Fact File 1998, Royal Mail Consumer Panel.

7

Using the Internet to sell[1]

In the past three years (in fact since the last edition of this book) there has been an explosion in the use of the Internet, and nowhere more so than in Britain.

The book trade has benefited from this expansion – books account for 30 per cent of online sales, and are one of the top five products being purchased over the Internet, along with computer hardware and software, CDs, videos and clothes.

Using the Internet offers several advantages to those promoting books. Firstly it allows small publishers to trade alongside much bigger players; a real problem when wholesalers or bookshops won't stock the output of small imprints.

> Any person with a phone line can become a town crier with a voice that resonates farther than it could from any soapbox. Through the use of Web pages, mail exploders and newsgroups, the same individual can become a pamphleteer.
>
> Justice Stevens, US Supreme Court Judge 1997

Internet bookshops are able to offer unlimited shelf space and consequently a much larger number of titles (average about 1.5 million) than even the largest physical bookshop (average 150,000). They can also do, all the time, what no physical bookshop can possibly achieve with similar consistency: organise; recommend and cross refer according to the tastes of the individual customer, with the added benefit of being open for business 24 hours a day, every day of the year. The returns rate from Internet bookshops is also very low (less than 4 per cent). Sales are dominated by backlist titles including reprints of out-of-print and difficult to obtain material, and hence are very high in the academic sector.

Most publishers now have a Web site for direct selling. They argue that the Internet is producing incremental sales rather than taking business from bookshops; in other words that Web sites are growing, rather than cannibalising, the market. In any case store-based booksellers too are selling this way. But in the longer term it is hard to see how Internet sales will not affect retail outlets. Certainly the advent of fully automated fulfilment services on the net means that selling even relatively low price books will become financially viable. In academic retailing the Internet could prove to be very serious competition to the specialist bookshop (see Chapter 12).

Every paper on the Internet starts with statistics to show the huge potential it offers as a means of direct selling. Here are some provided by Curtis Kopf, Director of Book Merchandising at amazon.co.uk, presented at the BML Annual Conference 17th March 1999.

- There are estimated to be 148 million Internet users worldwide, 70 million in the US and 33 million in Europe, 8 million in UK and 3 million in Germany.
- The growth rates in the UK are the fastest in Europe with an increase of 10–15% each month.
- Forecasts predict that there will be more than 300 million users worldwide by 2005.
- Early Internet users have tended to be affluent males aged 20 to 50 but demographics are changing as the medium becomes more widely used.
- Shopping is one of the four main activities. In 1998 it was estimated that more than $10 billion worth of business was carried out over the net, 30% personal and 70% business.
- Forecasts are that European online sales will be $425 million by the year 2000. By 2001, 25% of households in Britain will be on the Internet.
- The Internet gets heavily used for research prior to buying: it was estimated that in the last quarter of 1999, 48 million people will shop via the Internet in the US with 24 million purchasing online.

Observers predict that as well as becoming an extremely rich information resource the Web is becoming a dominant retailing environment, particularly as secure methods for credit-card transactions are becoming more widely available.

Marketing through the Web is a further stage in developing customer relations. Web pages can contain feedback devices of varying levels of sophistication. Even at their most basic these permit you to build databases of your customers and potential customers.

Habitual e-mail users respond to their e-mail before anything else and will often e-mail suppliers back to let them know products have arrived. The companies selling to them, by cutting out the middle person, can keep them directly informed of relevant special offers and share with them the substantial costs savings that this type of direct selling brings. What results is a series of stronger relationships between customer and service company.

What is the Internet?

The Internet is not a concrete entity but a set of software conventions – or protocols – that permit computers known as network servers to use the international telephone network to transmit and receive data in digital form.

Software called the Internet Protocol permits computers to link up over public telephone networks. This protocol is based on software originally developed by the US military to provide land-line communications in a nuclear war when radio would be useless. What has really driven the growth of this form of telecommunications is the progressive installation by BT, AT&T *et al* over the last 25 years of fibre optic cable as the backbone of international telephone trunk lines. This makes data communications hugely faster and therefore permits much richer forms of data to be transferred back and forth. You can now telephone almost anywhere in the world, but you can't communicate with them unless you share a common language. For computers, that language is the Internet Protocol (and its extensions).

How to set up a Web site to sell books

Objectives

First think about what your site is going to be used for. Is it for general company information, product and service information, customer support and feedback or online transactions? Bear in mind that if you are going to be accepting money online, the development time for your Web site must be multiplied by a factor of at least four. It's self-evident that the less interactive your Web site, the easier it is to get it up and running.

You also need to decide how much money you want to spend on your Web site. This will dictate the level of sophistication. In general, it costs a lot less than you think.

What to do first

To get access to the Internet you can either use a server belonging to a commercial service provider (an Internet Service Provider or ISP) or install your own server. Intense competition between providers is bringing about a rapid fall in subscription and connect-time prices.

When deciding whether to go it alone or use an ISP, you need to think about how big your site is going to be, what kind of support levels you need (how much do you know now about setting up a Web site?), how quickly you will need to change your information on the site and what the charges will be for doing so (beware very high update charges, the most essential point about an Web site is that it should be updated often).

Most ISPs start you off with about five megabytes of space on their server and will increase them in additional blocks. Look at the support levels they offer – ideally this should be 24 hours a day, 7 days a week. How flexible are they? Can they allow you to handle credit card transactions and capture customer details? If you want to link your database to your Web site it may be worth considering a leased line. This is more expensive, and will most probably entail an upgrade of your computer system, but will give you greater control and flexibility in the long run.

What will all this cost? Typically the costs for enrolling with an ISP are around £100 for set up, and then a running charge of £25 per month. If you have access to the web through a service provider, you'll probably get a mail account automatically (for an additional £15 a month), but some providers allow more than one per user, which can be useful in larger companies to 'pre-sort' incoming mail.

What are you going to call yourself?

The first thing to do is to register your domain (home site) name. Bear in mind that ISPs often include the cost of the domain name registration in set up costs.

Domain names have certain standard endings, depending on the kind of organisation you are. For example:

- Domains for international companies end in '.com'
- Domains for companies based in the UK end in '.co.uk'
- Domains for non-profit organisations end in '.org'

Registration costs around £100–200 for two years and you can search and register names with:

- http://www.internic.com
- http://www.nominet.co.uk

Bear in mind that you may have to think of an alternative name to your first choice, which may already have been taken by another organisation.

Planning and designing your Web site: how to attract people to your site

Exploiting the opportunities presented by the Internet raises the same difficulties as being a bookshop – you have to get people to visit your site and, once there, you have to get them to buy. You can be situated in a prime site at great expense (within the electronic shopping malls) or in the back street of a small market town (on your own pages with a little known server). You can pay thousands to have your shop fitted out stylishly (getting a Web consultant to create your pages for you with bespoke software for interactive communication and secure transactions) or you can fit your shop out yourself on a budget, having planned what you want and using a local carpenter (the building of Web pages is much easier than people think, and for as little as £150, if you already have a suitable computer, you can be up and running with an e-mail address and enough server space for a Web page or two).

If you decide to use an external Web designer company, you will need to evaluate their experience and decide whether it is relevant to your own needs. The typical costs for design and supply of five pages of graphics and one online form are around £1,000.

Establishing and maintaining Web pages is a great deal less costly than distributing material in printed form ... and the potential audience is millions. The word 'potential' is emphasised, however, because the Web's very popularity has made some sites very slow to access. The links around the world from server to server are now almost entirely fibre-optic cable, the backbone of international telephone trunk lines, but the final link from the service provider to user is still most usually an ordinary telephone line. As more and more sound and pictures are put on Web pages, the initial advantages of HTML, that most data was in the highly efficient form of ASCII, is being lost; the Web is becoming frustratingly slow for the average user. Of course developments in technology will eventually overcome such problems; signposting around the Web is getting consistently better.

The design of your site, both the look and feel of it, should not be resolved purely by your IT department but should include representatives from all parts of your company. When thinking about layout, try out the Web sites of your competitors and other organisations.

Maintaining your site

Maintenance is very important. Decide now who is to be responsible for maintaining content, developing and updating your Web site. The person selected should have an overview of the entire company's priorities and customers. The updating bit is crucial – it offers your customers a very bad impression if they call up your Web site and then find out that the information is stale or out of date.

This need not entail major changes but it does require alertness. Many Web sites declare the date they were last updated. Simply making sure that the date is not more than a week old is often all that is necessary. You can even link your pages to a company database so that changes in your product profiles, price or availability can be updated automatically.

Marketing your Web site

Offline

- Consider producing postcards, mouse-mats, mugs, sticky labels for your stationery and so on.
- Print your URL (Uniform Resource Locator, or the Web page address) on all your promotional material, stationery, business cards, invoices, etc.

Online

Registration
You are able to list your URL and keywords in all the appropriate Internet directories, catalogues and search engines in order to increase both your Web site ranking and traffic going to your Web

sites. This can either be done through individual registration and submission or professional Web marketing products and services. Some of these are free; others have to be paid for.

Linkage

This involves seeding the Net with links to your Web site. This is carried out informally through e-mails rather than submission forms and sites will not link unless they are compatible. This is therefore more time-consuming, but in the long term likely to be more beneficial, as you are directing traffic to your Web site from other relevant sites.

E-mails

These provide a cheap, instantaneous and unobtrusive method of contacting a vast number of people personally. There are several different avenues to explore:

- Press releases
- Discussion groups and external e-mail lists
- Search engine and service provider forums
- Company contact database
- All corporate external e-mails, which often list URL and current positions of key executives.

Online advertising

This offers great potential for targeting the precise online audience you want to attract. For example, you can try banner advertising (thin boxes with a message that flash at the reader) on selected Web sites or against certain keywords on search engines, where 1,000 banners can cost £15–150.

Testing and launching the site

Testing is essential prior to launch and every time changes are made to the site. You will usually be able to work on an administrative site and view changes on a pre-live Web site.

Once the site is launched you need to concentrate on the marketing of your site and attracting the relevant audience. Thorough analysis of traffic through your site will allow you to develop the future content and structure and address any complaints, problems or suggestions you may have received.

Running a site after launch

It is vital to ensure that your site not only attracts first time visitors but also offers something to entice them back on a continual basis. Consider the following promotional ideas:

- Display blurb and jacket for all major titles
- Feature major titles permanently, adding in new reviews/press snippets
- Run special promotions such as competitions and special offers for bulk orders
- Feature your press releases
- Provide articles on authors
- Provide sample chapters
- Give useful URLs
- Give details on forthcoming conferences
- Provide information on how to submit new product ideas.

Above all, be sure that company information, promotional copy, contact details and so on are all kept up to date.

Online bookshops

Most publishers today are aiming to increase their sales via online promotions through links, partnerships and electronic catalogue transfers with Internet bookshops and key customers' Web sites.

You need to decide in-house who is going to be responsible for research into online bookshops, how information is sent to them, and who will deal with the commercial aspects such as agreeing terms and discounts.

The main online bookshops are listed in Table 7.1. You should visit the sites for information on what kind of details to supply and how, as well as costs and timing issues.

E-mail

E-mail provides us with a particularly valuable marketing tool. It is quicker for the recipient than reading a mailshot and non-intrusive (unlike telemarketing). It also offers much lower costs of delivery

Table 7.1

Bookshop	URL
Alphabetstreet	www.alphatstreet.co.uk
Amadeus	www.globes.co.il/Amadeus
Amazon	www.amazon.co.uk
	www.amazon.com
Barnes & Noble	www.barnesandnoble.com
Blackwells	www.bookshop.blackwell.co.uk
BOL	www.bol.com
BookPl@ce	www.bookplace.co.uk
Books Online	www.booksonline.co.uk
Internet Bookshop	www.bookshop.co.uk
Virgin	www.virgin.net
Waterstones	www.waterstones.co.uk

than other direct marketing methods, with often much higher responses.

You should be aiming to increase sales via e-mail promotions to your customers and secondly to develop mailing lists through the collection of names and e-mail addresses. E-mail also provides a very valuable method of market research via direct customer contact and sophisticated statistics reporting.

An effective e-mail should be targeted to the appropriate audience, be short and entice a reply. The goal should be to start a relationship with the recipient and encourage them to request more information. Think what you have to send – sample chapter, author information, press release, suggest a visit to the Web site and so on.

You can also use e-mails to send press releases, highlight forthcoming events and distribute flyers and leaflets.

It is advisable to use a multi-e-mailing facility software package such as Campaign or MailKing, and a contact database as a storage solution for collecting e-mails and maintaining lists. This allows you to mail lots of people individually at the same time (without the entire circulation list appearing at the top of the message).

What an e-mail looks like

- **Branding** To successfully convey your brand without a logo use a simple header at the start of your e-mail, eg:

  Alison Baverstock
  e-mail: baverstockjam@mcmail.com

- **Subject line**   Keep it short (no more than 55 characters). Use BCC (blind carbon copy) for multiple mailings.
- **Address field**   Put yourself in the 'TO' field. Use BCC or individual addressing depending on the number of e-mails being sent.
- **Body copy**   Keep it short, inviting and certainly no more than a screenful. Avoid using attachments.
- **Formatting your message**   The look of the message is determined by the user's software so it is difficult to predict how it will be received. Problems occur with spelling, truncated messages, and non-standard characters such as quote marks, bullet points, apostrophes, asterisks and underscoring. It is advisable to use a line length of no more than 50 characters so that the whole width of the message is visible on screen at the same time. Use underscores or asterisks to convey emphasis as using capital letters is regarded as shouting.
- **Signature**   These need to be standardised company-wide and include all contact details and your URL.
- **Disclaimer**   Many companies now add a disclaimer to the end of all external e-mails. This can be reassuring to individuals who are often more protective of their e-mail address than their terrestrial one. You can cover who the message is meant for and the use to which you plan to put their data, eg 'we will keep your details on file to keep you up to date with our publishing programme but will never pass your e-mail address on to a third party'. Provide the chance to 'unsubscribe' for those who wish to do so.

Where to find your audience of e-mail users

Firstly send press releases with your URL to your media list; hopefully information requests will come back. You should also place alert/announcement e-mails in appropriate Internet discussion groups and forums. You can locate appropriate groups/lists through your authors, editors, search engines, service providers and Supersites, eg:

- www.mailbase.ac.uk
- www.lizst.com
- www.webcom.com/impulse/list
- www.listtool.com
- http://sunsite.unc.edi/usenet-i/search

- http://usenet-adresses.mit.edu
- www.lsoft.com

Before you start posting messages, it would be a good idea to do some market research. Study group/list guidelines, legal messages and existing e-mails to understand the audience for each channel. Check the relevance of their announcement and the style of message to be used. Bear in mind that the majority of groups and forums are now moderated, so it is a good idea to find out who does this or who cultivated the audiences and develop a good working relationship with them.

Notes

1. I am indebted to Victoria Nash of Macmillan and Nicholas Jones of Strathmore Publishing for invaluable assistance with this chapter.

8

'Free' Advertising

Publishers of books and journals are lucky in that they have access to a wealth of free promotional space, in all kinds of media. Free feature and review opportunities are available to no other manufacturers on such an extensive scale.

News coverage or a feature in an influential newspaper can help your message reach a much wider audience. Presented as editorial material (rather than as an advertisement) you have the chance to inform public opinion and re-orientate popular debate, or simply to spread information by word of mouth.

Similarly, getting an author on to a chat show can make a tremendous difference to their public image. When media coverage is harnessed (as it always should be) to information on title availability, you should achieve the real aim: larger sales.

Features and reviews of books in the media are one of the most influential ways of shaping reading habits. They are important to almost every kind of reader, from academics noting reviews in a journal they respect to general readers in a bookshop, turning to the back cover of a paperback to see which newspapers or columnists have endorsed it. For some books it is not even important that the coverage is favourable; getting a book banned can do tremendous things for its sales potential. As a Hollywood starlet once said: 'There's no such thing as bad publicity.'

Getting this kind of coverage is often known as 'free advertising', although, done well, it takes an immense amount of time and effort. This chapter is devoted to telling you how to go about it.

Who liaises with the media?

The large general publishing houses usually have a specialist press officer or publicist who liaises with the media on behalf of a variety of lists. More frequently, the job falls to the marketing department.

What you need to succeed in dealing with the media

1. Determination
2. Persuasiveness
3. Knowledge of and belief in your products
4. Imagination
5. A voice and personality that comes over well on the telephone
6. A good memory
7. Persistence.

When to start pursuing coverage

The best time for thinking about media coverage is early in a title's development. Author tours, radio and television appearances, competitions, entry for literary prizes and so on are best thought about well in advance as they take a lot of planning. If you are liaising with authors you will have their long-term commitments to consider too.

Planning press coverage is easiest if you have an existing network of media contacts with whom you are in touch on a regular basis. It is a good idea to make a list of all the journals and programmes likely to be significant to your list and find out the name of the features or news editor. Ring up and introduce yourself; confirm that they are the right person to send information to; check the address and spelling of their name. Ask if you can take the most important contacts out to lunch: it will be easier selling ideas if your face is already known.

Don't just pursue contacts in the media that you read or watch yourself. Try to get into the habit of buying a variety of different papers to see the kind of opportunities for coverage that they offer; watch and listen to broadcast programmes of all kinds. Similarly, don't forget to send copies of your press information to Reuters and the Press Association – they may feed it to many different regional papers. The local papers or radio station in an author's home town will almost certainly want to do a feature too.

Then, armed with a list of contacts, work at feeding the right people with the right information at the right time and in the way that they are most likely to use.

Recording the names of your contacts

A campaign for coverage usually starts with the sending of a press release to a mailing list of journalists, this being followed by telephone calls to secure definite features.

Whatever system you decide on for the management of your lists (in-house or out-of-house) do keep a basic point of reference on your desk, or PC, ready to refer to at all times. Be very methodical about recording ideas that particular contacts have responded well or badly to in the past, their days off, the best times to contact and so on.

If you are starting from scratch, a good way to build up press information is to subscribe to the services of a media agency such as PIMS London. For an annual subscription you will receive a manual (and updates) which lists all the press names you might need; you can order them on sticky labels whenever you want to send out a press release.

How to write an effective press release

If you are charged with preparing a press release, what should it say? Make it enticing but short. You are trying to assail the overworked and overwhelmed journalist with the news or feature value of your particular story. Make it short, pithy and interesting. Remember that thousands land on most editors' desks every day. It should make the recipient want to know more, but provide sufficient coherent information for inclusion should they decide to use it straightaway. My brother, a sports journalist, tells me that, to be honest, it's the 'freebies' on press releases that attract his attention first. Here are some of the maxims of the late John Junor, journalist and newspaper editor.

> An ounce of emotion is worth a ton of fact.
> Everybody is interested in sex and money.
> When in search of a subject, turn to the royal family.

The first couple of paragraphs should tell the basic story (the who, what, when, where and why). Sub-editors, especially those on regional papers or local radio, may have gaps to fill and be looking for copy. If your information is succinct and sufficiently interesting it may get used whole. Follow the initial explanation with an expansion of your arguments, illustrating with examples from what you are promoting. Tell enough of the story to make the journalist want to know more, but not so much that there is no angle left to discover. (Never include information in quotation marks: it implies the story has already been covered and is therefore stale.) Provide relevant information on the author to prompt the journalist to want an interview. Suggest the kind of feature that might be written.

If there are very few names on your contact list, tailor what you send to each. 'Special to...' at the top of the release may well increase the likelihood of your information being used. Ring and discuss the prospect of a special feature with your editorial contact beforehand. If there is definite interest you could consider offering an 'exclusive'. A telephone call can establish how a particular journal wants information presented and suggest the angle from which your title will be looked at. The easier it is for a paper's staff to assimilate your material into their format, the more likely it is to be used.

Remember that, as with any other written format, long blocks of justified copy put the reader off. Illustrations, particularly cartoons, attract attention. Provide clear information about what the recipients should do next: whom they should ring to arrange interviews, how to obtain a review copy and so on.

Adding an embargo date to the bottom of your release means every journalist has the same chance to prepare the story before publication; no one should print the information before that date and 'scoop' their rivals (very important if you have sold the serial rights!).

Ensure that you add to your press release all the essential information you would wish to see included should it get used whole: publication date, price, availability and so on.

Ensure what you send is relevant. Don't devalue the impact of your press releases by producing them too often or sending them to the wrong homes. If you send information 'just in case', the journalist will almost certainly take a similarly marginal view. The danger is that they may then devalue what you send in future.

It always pays to follow up a press release with phone calls to those journalists you particularly wish to take up the story. Whether or not you get coverage is often not due just to the interesting nature of the story you present but the surrounding package of ideas you offer. You are trying to tempt the journalist to cover your story to the exclusion of all the others he has competing for his attention, so do be imaginative!

HODDER BUYS HEAVENLY PLEASURE ...

When Araminta Whitley first read Adam Williams' debut novel, THE PALACE OF HEAVENLY PLEASURE, she knew within the first few pages that she'd found something unique and exciting. Epic in scale, complex in characterisation and plot, with a wonderfully romantic and adventurous sweep, it is as compelling a piece of storytelling as you could hope for. And when she then sent the novel out, on a Friday afternoon, it was clear by nine o'clock on Monday morning that others agreed. Nearly everyone who received it abandoned their weekend, and finished the 1100-page story, set in China at the turn of the nineteenth century in the midst of the Boxer Rebellion.

After a hotly-contested auction, Carolyn Mays of Hodder was the delighted victor with a six-figure deal.

'I couldn't let the story go until I'd finished it', she says, 'and I had to be the publisher. We have a book that is wonderfully evocative of China at the time of the Boxer Rebellion, and an incredible story, rich in intrigue, romance, faith – and a rare understanding of two cultures and their opposing views.'

After the excitement of the auction, the sale of the book to Carolyn then prompted a flurry of overseas sales – to St Martin's Press in the US, Belfond in France, Droemer in Germany, Longanesi in Italy, and Luitingh in Holland.

Adam lives in Beijing and currently heads up the China operation of a major Far East multinational. He has lived in China for the past eighteen years, but his family's connections go back much further. 'They were living in China during the Boxer Rebellion,' he says, 'and the stories I was told as a child, are the material that shaped the plot of this book. The names and places have changed, but most of it happened somewhere to somebody.' Adam also has a deep admiration for Chinese culture. Deep rooted as it is in pragmatism, he believes that the contradictions between Chinese and western ways provide for endless philosophical debate, and are an excellent source of drama.

When Carolyn won the auction, Adam flew over from China to meet the team at Hodder and was soon enthusing about his own adventures. He has searched for the lost cities of the Silk Road on a camel expedition into the Taklamakan Desert, competed in the East African 'Rhino Charge' rally and the 2000 London to Peking Marathon, and made a number of Central Asian explorations. He is a wonderful and unusual mixture of suave international business man, and boys' own adventurer.

FOR FURTHER INFORMATION
PLEASE CONTACT
Kerry Hood
at Hodder & Stoughton
on 020 7873 6173

Figure 8.1 *Getting coverage for a new book is doubly difficult if no one has heard of the author. Here Hodder attract attention for a new author with a sheet giving information on how the title came to be commissioned. The headline is slightly suggestive and the attractive lettering and eye-catching Chinese letters draw attention to the book – in the original they are in red. What is more, the release is printed on special thick cream paper and is a pleasure to hold. Most significantly however, by telling the story of the book's acquisition, rather than simply announcing that it is to be published, the reader is drawn in. It was accompanied by a more conventional release giving information on plot and author. Much press interest followed*

When is the best time to contact journalists?

The best time seems to be after about 10.30 until about 12.45; then from about 2.45 until 4.30. It isn't that those are the only times they work, just that those times provide the best opportunities of catching them at their desks.

Arranging features

Suggest ideas that sound appealing – locations, people, vehicles – perhaps in unusual combinations. Features do not have to be written by the paper in question. If you can arrange for an author to write an article for a particular magazine, he or she may receive a fee and the book a valuable push (publication details should be mentioned at the end of the piece). Similarly, can you persuade *The Times Educational Supplement* or *Education Guardian* to accept an article by a teacher on how your new reading scheme works in practice; or one by a mother for *Practical Parenting* on how her son has at last learnt to read using it? Often the personal stamp on this kind of feature gives it more authority and makes it more interesting to readers, who in these two examples would consist mostly of other teachers and other mothers.

Author interviews – on the air and in print

As well as considering the setting up of interviews in newspapers and magazines, would your author come over well on the radio or television? Are there specific programmes that would be interested in recording their point of view? Local radio stations offer lots of opportunities for coverage. If the author is unavailable, could you do the interview yourself? Alternatively, offer a different author from your list for interview and you may still secure coverage for your house's titles ('switch selling').

If you set up interviews, be meticulous in confirming all the details to everyone concerned, even if you are planning to accompany the author. Write down the name of the programme and interviewer, and where the author should be when. Brief the author on your contact at the programme's reaction to the press release you sent. This may give hints of the type of question to be asked. When it's all over, and if it went well, consider sending a postcard of thanks to the relevant journalist/producer, or even a small memento (you have a warehouse full of suitable items). You may want to be in touch again.

Speaking effectively on radio and television

How you or your author prepare for a presentation on the air will depend on the attitude of the interviewer: whether it is likely to be 'hard' (eg Jeremy Paxman) or 'soft' (eg the majority of local radio interviewers). Think carefully about your aim(s) in accepting an interview. What points must you get across?

Politicians react to a hard interviewer by 'spring-boarding', using each question as a possible launch pad for conveying what they have decided they want to say – the essential points they wish to get over ('I'm glad you asked me that, but of course we must not lose sight of the really important issue which is...').

The 'hard' interviewer resists tangents and puts forward difficult questions that demand real answers not waffle. A 'soft' interviewer, on the other hand, will allow the interviewee to shape the discussion, guiding or prompting with questions to ensure an interesting programme, or to change the subject (about four minutes per topic is considered sufficient to satisfy the attention span of the audience to popular radio).

If you are doing the interview immerse yourself in all the information you can find and practise answering questions in your head on the way there. Don't over-rehearse; you will sound wooden and unconvincing. Talking from memory enables you to concentrate fully on the questions being asked. Keep one or two key statistics to hand that you think you may need, but remember that figures are hard to absorb at first hearing. Don't use too many; alternatively, can you restate them as fractions? Whatever you do, don't read out prepared statements; not only does this sound very impersonal but, if it is information already in your press release, the interviewer will probably have used it to introduce you.

Live interviews need not be daunting; the knowledge that it is for real (not for editing later) can help you to marshal your thoughts. It is easy to forget how many million listeners there are when you are actually talking to just one.

Selling ideas by phone

How successful you are in setting up the kind of coverage suggested in this chapter will depend on the kind of books you look after and the way you target and present information on them. But equally important will be your own personal contribution: how persuasive you are when talking to journalists on the telephone. Here is some basic advice on how to sell ideas over the phone.

1.   Prepare yourself

Try to find somewhere quiet to do your ringing. Even if this proves impossible, still put yourself in the right frame of mind. Concentrate on the job in hand and work out what you are going to say so that you are coherent but not word-perfect.

After a few phone calls you will find a pattern to the calls emerges and that this affects your presentation. Ring the really big prospects third or fourth, once you have ironed out your presentational style but before you start to sound too smooth. Don't make too many phone calls on the trot; you may begin to get casual.

2.   How to start and what to say

Once you have said who you are and why you are calling, start by asking if now is a convenient time to talk. If it is not you will almost always be offered a time to call back and speak to your contact directly later on.

Involve the person you are speaking to. Ask basic questions. If the paper has covered the author before, jog the journalist's memory about the story that appeared last time, and say how this one differs. If you are talking about a well-known author provide some little known details to perk up their interest. Talk about basic trends in society that your product highlights.

Ensure you are being listened to by putting your points clearly and asking for a response (open-ended questions). Don't talk too fast or be afraid to hesitate. If you listen to some of the best radio inter-viewers – Sue Lawley on *Desert Island Discs* or Jenni Murray on *Woman's Hour* – you will hear how they repeatedly rephrase their questions, and use 'um' and 'ah' to ease the impact of hard-hitting questions. It is all designed to involve the interviewee and coax them into answering responsively. You have no body language at your disposal; no chance to see from eye contact whether attention is wavering. Your voice has to do it all.

Try not to be too complicated. Use words that are readily under-stood and that you won't stumble over. At the same time, don't overwhelm the listener with information. A brief description of the story on offer followed by two or three good reasons why the journal you are ringing should cover it is plenty. Suggest the kind of feature you think would work best: an author interview, a visit to a school to see a major new scheme in progress or a new angle on an existing news story which information in your book provides.

3.   Be methodical

Write down who said what immediately (you may think you will remember but after an hour of phoning you won't be sure which call was which). If you are following up a press release be sure to have by your side copies of whatever it was you sent; many of those you call will say they have either not received or can no longer find it. Fax or send more. Do this straight away so that the new copy of your release is received while your conversation is still in their minds. Attach a compliments slip referring to your call and your offer/suggestion for coverage.

If the correspondent you want to speak to is not available, by all means leave your name. But if an assistant offers to return your call don't expect it will happen; it practically never will. You are the salesperson and the journalist will expect you to ring back with your story.

If an interview or visit is promised confirm everything in writing, ringing up the day before to make a final check on the arrangements. Make friends with the secretary/production assistant who is more likely to spot double bookings.

Track the coverage you get. Scan the papers you circulated for what subsequently appears or employ an agency to do this for you. Stick a copy of each item of coverage in the title file so it can be incorporated in publicity or used on the jacket of a new edition.

4.   Let others know what you have set up

Don't forget to let your reps know about forthcoming coverage; anything that is likely to increase demand can encourage booksellers to take more stock. Let the *Bookseller* know for their 'On the air' column; inform *Books in the Media*.

5.   Lastly, don't give up

Getting a journalist to come along to hear at first hand the story you are pushing is not the end of the matter: you then have to hope that the promised feature appears. Someone may well turn up from the right paper and make notes, but this only serves to increase your anxiety as the days go by before the story finally appears in print.

Is there anything more frustrating than your carefully nurtured feature being squeezed out at the last minute by something much more up-to-date, with the added annoyance of having to start all over again with a now rather dated story? Or offering a scoop, only to have it turned down at the eleventh hour when it is too late to fix up an alternative?

In conclusion, it may be disheartening when no one wants to cover the story that you have convinced yourself is a winner. It is worth remembering that you would have scant respect for a newspaper that printed everything it was offered. In dealing with the press, a very large part of your success will depend on the skills you develop in matching your expectations to journalists' ability to deliver. Like so many other parts of marketing, it can be both utterly frustrating as well as absolutely exhilarating.

Ensuring press coverage for very specialised products

If you are responsible for promoting a list of academic or highly specialised books, the kinds of coverage for which you should be striving are reviews and specific features, perhaps backed up, where appropriate, by news items in the right journals. Achieving general 'publicity' is a waste of time better spent elsewhere.

Target the right person. Find out the name of the gardening and bridge correspondents, as well as the literary editor. Similarly, you can get worthwhile coverage for high-level topics by developing good relations with particular correspondents on papers in which you wish to be featured, especially if you feed them stories on an exclusive basis. Very specialised titles too can provide the subject matter for interesting features with a little imagination. For example, when Macmillan published *Faraday Rediscovered*, a collection of papers on different aspects of the physicist's immense importance to the history of science, one of the book's two editors was working at the Royal Institution where Faraday's laboratory was still preserved. We held a launch party cum demonstration, and invited all present to watch him demonstrate two of Faraday's major discoveries. It was a novel way of engaging press attention.

Book reviews

The theory is as follows. New and revised books are reviewed in the media, the reviews are read/heard by the market, who are consequently motivated to buy. Such coverage is highly influential in all markets as it offers objective analysis of the product.

You will be required to put together a review list for almost every title you publish, and the prospect sounds enticingly simple. Be warned, achieving review coverage is not as simple as it sounds.

Building up and maintaining intelligent relationships with review editors requires immense attention to detail and a great deal of time. And the sheer volume of books being sent for review in the small media space and time available means securing coverage can be very hard work. It also often takes a long time to see results.

National dailies may be able to offer a relatively quick turnaround from receipt of book to appearance of review, but in academic journals it can take months, during which the author too is impatiently waiting to see the title featured.

The role of the literary editor

Most magazines and newspapers have a literary editor who organises the coverage of books. It is to this person that you will probably be sending review copies of titles you are working on.

Accept right now that the literary editor is a crucial ally. It is their job to find interesting copy on books; it follows that they are the only people you can truly count on to be interested in your products. They may also open the gates to other people within the magazine; getting personal satisfaction from seeing book features on pages other than the literary section. Paula Johnson, until recently Literary Editor of *The Mail on Sunday*, told me that every Friday she would put together a list of book-based snippets; forward topics that were capable of exploitation by other journalists on the paper – perhaps the news editors or the gardening correspondent. To this list she would append photocopies of all the relevant press releases sent in by publishing houses.

So, even if you do decide to send your review copy and press release to the news or sports desk, it is almost always worth sending one to the literary editor too.

Particular hints when putting together press releases for literary editors

- Do you really need a press release? Would a phone call to a key contact work best, bearing in mind that this would be an exclusive offer? If you do decide to send one, consider how this press release will fit in within your company's PR as a whole; will it detract or add impact?

- Bear in mind the environment in which your material will be received. A literary editor on a national paper will get 40 to 70 book packages a week, into an office already overflowing with other titles, press releases and people. Titles are shelved by the month in which they are scheduled for publication, but additional piles of books soon build up wherever there is floor space. It follows that information that is clearly laid out and quick to digest is best.

- Put the press releases inside the book you are sending so they don't get separated on opening.

- If you use quotes keep them crisp, short and relevant. A long list of quotes looks boring and implies that every angle has already been thought of.

- Cover the basics: date of publication, author information, publisher and contact details (phone, fax and e-mail). Ensure the date includes year of publication in case the book gets put to one side for use later. Correct information saves the journalist time and makes it more likely that your material will be used.

- Get the name of the literary editor you are sending it to right.

- It's absolutely unforgivable to send a literary editor English with grammatical errors in it.

- Be sure to mark paperback originals as such; they will be given special treatment as they have not been reviewed as hardbacks. If you fail to make this clear they are likely to appear in the 'new in paperback' feature with much less space accorded.

- Don't put copy that is on the book jacket in the press release that accompanies it. Very boring and insulting to the literary editor's intelligence.

- Ensure it is photocopiable.

- Keep freebies relevant. Literary editors tend to feel very strongly about making their own mind up and are inclined to take a dim view of 'bribes' or facetious additional enclosures. The book should stand on its own merit; it follows that anything additional should be tasteful and pertinent.

- Find out when their 'copy day' (ie when material is sent to press) is and target material accordingly. For example, for a Sunday paper, Friday is a very good day for material to arrive.
- As with all promotional formats, the conventional can bore, whereas the attitudinal soundbite or quirky approach may attract attention.
- If you have a really important project signed up, ring your contacts and let them know. This may spark them into asking your author to write or review something, giving valuable pre-publicity.
- Don't ring and remind the literary editor if they haven't yet covered a book – most really hate it! Instead, consider sending a note with details of really key titles not yet covered, hoping that they will not be forgotten.

Printed review lists

Many marketing departments have a printed review list. It may be a fairly extensive document divided into different subject areas or perhaps consist of a series of different sheets, each one listing specialised media in specific areas. The fact that this list is printed should make you suspicious. Magazines change their readership and formats extremely quickly these days: new ones are launched, old ones go out of business. A printed form means it has been around for a long time and probably no one has got around to updating it. Use such a form as the basis for your review list and you will end up opting for journal and magazine titles because they sound right: about as sensible as voting for people because their names are nice.

Find out if anyone bothers to update the address list when magazines and newspapers move or die; this is even more unlikely if several departments are using the same system as everyone will assume it is someone else's responsibility. And things do change. PIMS reckon that each new monthly issue of their media contacts directory includes over 2,000 changes. Worst of all, ticking a list and sending it off for central despatch deprives you of the chance to add a personal message, and, unless your mailing list is very up-to-date, address it to the relevant review editors by name.

How to compile your review list

Keep an on-going reference point for review editors you have worked with in the past and those that represent journals that are important to you. Keep it on your desk at all times and update it as you go along.

Search the book's title file for suggestions of where to send review copies; locate the author's publicity form; have a think. Look through the latest editions of PIMS and BRAD. Use your common sense; ask any friends you have who work or are interested in the relevant area which journals and magazines they read. Ask the title's editor.

If this throws up some important journals where you have no contact, excellent. Ring up and find out who the review editor is. Introduce yourself. Mention the book in question and ask if they are interested. Better still, if it is a journal likely to be useful to your area of responsibility in the future, suggest you meet up. You can use the opportunity to guide the review editor through your company's publishing programme for the next six months, and perhaps offer page proofs of forthcoming titles before other journals as a 'scoop'. Ask about their reviewing policy (time taken, where to send, the kind of books they like to see, etc). Write it all down.

Then, prompted by the information you have secured, remain in touch. Tell the review editors about the books you want to send; suggest how they could feature them; gently remind them they have not yet reviewed what you last sent (perhaps with a third party post-card which sounds less like a telling-off than a reminder phone call). Such contacts often enable you to speed up coverage: can the book be sent directly to the reviewer, to the editor at home or to their new feature writer?

When not to give books away

If you have a limited number of copies available for review (and, if the print run is low, giving away five more than you need can make the whole project uneconomic), send out a press release to the journals you think may feature the title and ask the various review editors to contact you if they would like a copy.

Similarly, bear in mind that today it isn't just the marketing department and magazine staff who know the meaning of the term 'review copy'; you will receive many requests for free copies of the titles you are responsible for promoting. Don't erode your basic market.

What to send out with review copies

It is essential that review copies do not go out unannounced. It is surprising how many publishers forget to enclose a 'review slip' giving title and author details, ISBN and publication date and how much it will cost (price is not always shown on the jacket). Provide a name, address and telephone number from where more information can be obtained and to where copies of any review should be sent.

In addition, send any other information you think may secure the interest of the review editor: a press release, a copy of the book's promotional leaflet if you have it already, a photograph of the author or copy of an illustration from the book, and a hand-written note from you saying why you think coverage of this title will appeal to their readership – anything to encourage them to select for review the title you send in preference to all the others received the same morning.

Sending out very expensive/desirable books for review

What happens to all these books once they have been considered for review? In general those doing the reviewing regard the books as a perk. They are usually sold on to specialist bookshops; the prices paid depend on how recent they are. A difficulty arises here for the publisher of very desirable or expensive books: are requests for review copies really genuine or a 'nice little earner' for the review editor? Send out a large pile of books to a comprehensive list and you will still get calls from editors on the list to say that they have not yet received their copy.

One solution adopted by a fine art publisher from central London was to send out review copies by taxi and ask for a receipt from each magazine before handing the book over. Publishers of very expensive works such as encyclopaedias may send out review copies with an invoice which they cancel once the set is returned. Alternatively, they may offer to sell the work at a trade discount to the reviewer.

Free copies for minimal coverage

The recommended reading lists produced by academics and teachers feature only the briefest of book details (author and title, and if you are lucky, the name of the publisher) but inclusion is vital. Most educational publishers offer 'inspection copies' for this market, sending unconditional free copies to particularly influential figures. See Chapter 12 for further information.

The relationship between editorial and advertising on magazines

The relationship between editorial and advertising is a tricky one, particularly because you are getting involved in the internal politics of other companies. If you try to point out that a connection between editorial and advertising sales exists you will be met by a haughty indifference (from editorial) or a jocular denial (from advertising). Nevertheless in most cases the one pays for the other and it is common practice for the advertising department to sell space around forthcoming editorial features.

If your advertising budget makes you a major supporter of a magazine you have a right to have your books looked at seriously. Undoubtedly the best way is to avoid the issue arising in the first place by making friends with the review editor and keeping in touch about anything you send in. No contact followed by an accusation of no coverage is a bad way to begin.

9

Paid Advertisements and Organising Promotions

There used to be a sharp distinction in marketing terminology between advertising that was paid for and promotions that were negotiated to be mutually beneficial to participating parties. Commonly referred to as 'above the line' (space advertising in the press or through the broadcast media) and 'below the line' (promotions) marketing, the line in question was that at the bottom of the invoice which showed how much was owing.

Today the understanding is very different; things are not nearly so clear-cut. There has been an explosion of opportunities for marketing and the emergence of a wide variety of selling vehicles. For example, there is now a wide range of new media such as new magazines, commercial radio and television stations. At the same time promotions, once seen as very down-market activities which while they might engage the consumer's passing interest, did not support and build the brand, have lost their tacky image and become much more mainstream. The old sharp distinction between above and below the line marketing has blurred. Promotions are advertised in the press; firms placing space advertisements use the opportunity to make special offers directly to their market. Significantly, there are now marketing service companies offering 'through the line' services.

Publishers too have been affected by the changes. Traditionally, the book trade spent little on advertising (too expensive) other than in the pages of the *Bookseller*. They did not take part in many promotions due to the restrictions imposed by the Net Book Agreement. But as books have had to compete more and more with other products for the same office budget or 'leisure spend' the techniques employed to sell to those markets have *had* to become more professional and mainstream. Today it is relatively commonplace to see books advertised on the sides of buses, on the tube (in the carriages, on the platforms and beside the escalators) as well as on 'adshels' (poster sites protected by perspex covers on bus shelters or on pavement sites). At the same time, books are now commonly the subject of promotional campaigns. For example, promotions have featured books on the back of cereal packets, available free to those who collect coupons; book and toy packs produced as incentives for certain stores and books as the subject of editorial 'features' and 'reader-offers' that magazines and newspapers consider likely to appeal to their readership.

This chapter will look at both paid-for advertising and promotions in further detail. These two areas are deliberately linked.

Straightforward space or broadcast advertising on its own is not a particularly effective method of persuading people to buy books. It is very difficult to isolate the sales that result, and for publishers with a large stable of different titles each with a small budget, hard to make it pay. For academic and specialized titles, advertising can be particularly hard to justify. What is more, there are often cheaper ways of reaching the same market than simply taking space in a publication (loose inserts, bind-in cards, test mailing a small section of the subscriber list and so on).

Publishers are increasingly finding that it is much more effective to link space advertising into a promotional campaign. For example, taking the message that is being put over in the ad and reinforcing its understanding as part of a competition, or offering readers a special price that is redeemable through a cooperating bookshop, with all parties sharing the advertising cost.

Where to advertise?

Trade advertising

Mass-market publishers announce high-profile advertising campaigns to the trade as part of their new title information – look through a recent edition of the *Bookseller* and see how the copy for major new titles stresses how much is being spent on space advertising. The publisher's aim is to isolate a main title in the bookseller's mind, in the hope that they will respond by stocking in quantities appropriate to the promotion budget. It should be pointed out that not all the activities announced actually get executed.

Advertising to the end user

Deciding where to advertise is a matter of successfully identifying the market for a particular product, and then the media that the market reads/listens to and respects.

Which magazines does your target market read? Which radio programmes do they listen to? Look at the author's publicity form for suggestions; talk to editorial and marketing staff; use your imagination. Make a short list, consult BRAD for the relevant advertising rates and timings. If they are within your budget ring the advertising manager of each publication and ask for a sample copy as well as details of the audience profile (useful ammunition when you start to be pestered for a booking).

Cost

Your first reaction should be that advertising is not cheap. While you should never accept that the first rate you are quoted will be the total you eventually pay (see Chapter 11 on negotiating) the cost of advertising does not end with buying the space/time. For example, for a space ad, in addition you have a range of other associated costs including:

- the writing of the message (your time or freelance help)
- design of the advertisement and layout
- photography
- final film, whether supplied on disc or conventionally
- motorbike/courier despatch – ads often seem to happen in a hurry.

For a broadcast ad you have to pay for studio time and most likely for the voices to be used for the recording.

Many regular advertisers book space through a media buying agent who handles bookings for a variety of different clients. Because they are booking time and space on a large scale such agents get much greater discounts than are available to individual publishing companies. The arrangement between agent and client is usually based on splitting the discount/commission they receive (on a pre-arranged basis), so it can end up costing clients *nothing* to use their services.

Having decided where to advertise, study the media

If you have decided to advertise in a particular publication or station get to know the audience by studying what they see/hear. Copy works best when it is personal, so when you start writing you should be aiming your message at one typical individual. Can you picture them? If you can't then your copy is unlikely to be convincing.

For example, in a magazine or journal, look at the job advertisements – this should tell you clearly who is reading the magazine. Read the letters page; look at the editorial; examine the spaces taken by other advertisers. You want your advertisement to be sympathetic to the style and format of the magazine and yet remain sufficiently different to attract attention. If you are taking a series of advertisements ask if you can be added to the free circulation list, to which advertising sales reps usually have the power to add names.

Where to appear

When you read magazines look out for those advertisements you notice and observe their position. In most publications you can specify a definite position, in more specialised media or in return for discounted advertising rates you may only be able to express a preference; 'run of paper' (ie at the discretion of the person handling the page make-up) may be the cheapest option.

Certain pages may be more expensive than others: a news page will generally cost more than a book review page. It may pay to take the more expensive slot if in return you reach people interested in the subject matter who do not read book reviews. Consider specifying a position next to a regular feature: the crossword; winning lottery numbers or cartoon.

The range of prices available to those booking broadcast media slots varies enormously depending on audience figures at specific times of the day.

What to say

How much you write depends on four factors:

1. how much there is to say about the product
2. how much the market needs to know before deciding to buy

3. how much time and inclination the market has to read
4. what you want the market to do as a result of reading your ad (order direct or rush to the nearest bookshop).

For the advertisement of a new general fiction title to the trade it may be sufficient to include publication and promotion information in an eye-catching format; conveying the atmosphere of the book and your promotional theme through arresting illustration. Bear in mind that the fact that the product is a book and that it comes from your publishing house may be the least interesting things you can tell the market – author reputation (or notoriety) and subject matter will almost certainly be much more significant.

If you are writing to the trade to remind them that your new novel is top of the best-seller lists, don't make the mistake of assuming everyone is convinced of its saleability. Provide all the information the bookseller needs before making a decision to restock: the sales patterns of the author's previous books; details of promotional highlights to come that will further support demand; proof that strong sales will be a *continuing* trend.

For books that have a more exact application, for example academic and business books, additional information will be required. You will almost certainly find you have less space than you need, so make the best use of it: emphasise all the key benefits to the market; be clear and specific. Get on with your sales message straight away and don't waste space on general statements. Omit words you don't need, for example instead of

This book provides …

start with:

Provides …

which has much more impact.

If the title is expensive make sure you stress the customer's guarantee of satisfaction.

Limited space is the more usual problem, but if your market has the time and opportunity to read long copy, do provide it. For example, on the tube in London, it has been estimated that 85 per cent of travellers do not carry anything to read, or cannot get access to their reading material because the trains are so crowded. Given the choice, wouldn't you rather stand opposite an advert that provided you with plenty to read?

A checklist of information to include in your advertising copy

- An eye-catching headline *(not just the title)*
- Publication details: title; author; extent; price; ISBN; publication date
- Key market benefits
- Briefly what the book is about
- Contents
- The offer if there is one
- Statement on value for money
- Author and qualifications (writer of ten previous standard works or a leading name in astrophysics research)
- For what kind of reader (mass market fiction; management; research etc)
- In what (new) way it meets market needs (concentrate on this rather than knocking your competitors; in the limited space available this can be confusing)
- New features/highlights if a new edition
- Format (without jargon, eg hardcover not HC)
- Related titles you publish (relevant new and backlist; part of a series or house reputation?)
- Relevant testimonials or review quotes
- Information on how to order (if it is available on free inspection say how and where from)
- A guarantee of satisfaction.

The number of items from the above list you can include will depend on the kind of title being promoted. For mass-market fiction the name of the author and the new title may be enough; for an educational or academic monograph more justification for purchase will be needed.

For ideas on how to present the copy see Chapters 3 and 4; for information on how to ensure eye-catching design and legibility see Chapter 5.

How to order

Any form of marketing material should entice readers to buy the product or service described. When planning an advertising campaign the marketing manager has to decide the most efficient and most likely way of getting the customer to respond.

Is a campaign to the trade best followed up with a visit from your rep or a telesales campaign? If your market is unlikely to use a coupon for ordering (eg you are writing to libraries) make it clear how the product is available, if possible providing an information telephone number for queries. If the product you are selling is very highly priced, provide the means of progressing to the next stage in the buying process (for example a catalogue or prospectus containing further information) but always provide the opportunity to purchase straight away. If it is very cheap, direct marketing would not be cost-effective, and orders are best routed through retail outlets. It follows that it is essential that your reps know of any advertising campaigns, so they can persuade stockists to take more.

The despatch of an inspection copy precedes most large-scale adoptions of academic and educational texts so provide a coupon for that purpose; don't just quote your address and leave it to readers to draw one up themselves – most won't bother. Always provide telephone or fax numbers for direct ordering. Consider turning the whole advertising space into one large order form – provide a box to tick beside every title detailed and an address panel for the orderer to fill in at the foot of the page. For further information on making order forms easy see Chapter 4.

When using the broadcast media, simple products can be explained and the viewers/listeners urged to purchase. For products that require a longer explanation than time permits, a telephone number can be given for just such an opportunity – 'To hear more please ring …'.

Space advertising for specialist publishers

With much smaller budgets and very specific markets, specialised publishers might well assume that advertising is not an area of marketing relevant to them.

Not necessarily. Even if you accept that space advertising is not always the most effective way to gain outright sales, there are still many reasons for continuing to advertise. Most require the taking of a long-term view of selling to specific markets rather than short-term coupon counting. Consider the following.

Advertising is just one element in your marketing mix

The message you provide in your advertising reinforces other stimuli to purchase: mailshots; advance notices; reviews and word of mouth. Collectively, they boost your profile and lead to sales.

Advertising can be used to update your sales message; remind the market of catalogues now available; pass on good reviews or sales figures; refer to topical events that make your publications particularly relevant. One small independent publisher found that taking a weekly slot in the *Bookseller* with witty and informal information about themselves paid real dividends: they had their best ever year.

Maintaining the public profile of your list and publishing house

Both your market and your authors need to know that you are actively publishing and selling titles, even if the announcement in the media results in no direct sales. For example, it is commonplace for advertising sales departments to sell space around editorial features. And if *The Times Educational Supplement* runs a special feature on a subject that is of central importance to your house you probably need to be seen advertising there. Similarly, if you are a children's publisher about to set out for the Bologna Book Fair, you need to advertise you presence in the special fair edition of the *Bookseller*, this edition will form a checklist of key children's publishers long after the fair is over.

Even if your list of titles in a particular area is small, if you advertise alongside your major competitors you rank yourselves with them. Advertising can thus provide a boost to your whole list as well as the possibility of attracting new authors.

A cost-effective way of reaching your market

For a magazine with a highly targeted readership, and a product relevant to that market, space advertising can be a very cost-effective way of spreading sales information. Bear in mind too that many very specific journals have a high pass-on factor, so the readership is much higher than the circulation figures alone imply. Per head of the market reached, space advertising usually compares very favourably with the costs of circulating a mailshot or employing a rep (but compare this with the cost per response). For some less specific books (eg women's reads), on-page ads in the right magazines can be the *only* way to reach the market, or some of it.

Backing up the sales efforts of your reps

Their ability to point to space advertising as a visible sign of promotional commitment increases their credibility with those they sell to. An occasional 'big splash' can impress both trade and end market.

To support a publication you want your books to be reviewed in

A large proportion of the revenue of magazine and journal publishers comes from advertising sales. If you don't provide advertising revenue would readers be prepared to pay the higher cover price that might result? Is there a danger that without advertising revenue an important publication might fold and the outlet for reaching an influential market be lost?

To carry on a winning trend

Even if your product is the market leader, you need to carry on reminding potential purchasers of its success rather than assume saturation point has been reached. Previous purchasers still read advertisements for products they already own. The sales copy confirms their good judgment and, if they are satisfied with their purchase, they are interested to read about new developments.

It is worth noting here that many magazines are becoming conscious of the need to offer improved value for money spent on advertising to their customers. In a bid to improve the advertiser's feedback several now include reader-response cards or tick-box coupons to request further information from those advertising.

Organising promotions

Promotion means putting together building blocks of awareness.

Walter F Parkes, head of Steven Spielberg's DreamWorks Studio

As already discussed, more and more publishers are trying out promotions, sometimes arranged on their own, sometimes in conjunction with promotions agencies which specialise in setting up mutually beneficial arrangements between non-competing organisations approaching the same target market.

For the remainder of this chapter 'promotion' is used in the widest sense, meaning pushing or promoting to a higher position.

The ideas that follow assume a broad market; there are specific sector references to be found in Chapter 12.

Features, reader-offers and mock reviews

With limited formal review space available, many publishers are now concentrating their efforts on promotional campaigns that achieve a similar effect. For example, magazines that see a particular publisher's products as appealing strongly to their own readership may be keen to set up special features, perhaps supplemented by reader-offers of varying complexity. By presentation as media feature rather than space advertisement, all such gambits offer editorial endorsement which impresses the market.

Competitions and contests

A competition is a very good way of getting people involved with your product, whether in-house (bottle of champagne for best slogan for our new campaign) or out-house (how many words can your class make from the title of our new school dictionary?).

Competitions are also an effective means of securing news and feature coverage in the media, particularly through local papers. There has to be some basic explanation of the book or product being promoted before the prizes and rules can be described. The competition is then trailed, takes place and the results are announced – it's a lot of coverage for relatively little effort (much of which will be done for you by the paper's promotions department). You can get substantially increased exposure if you tie a competition into an advertising package.

If you want a large response, keep the questions simple (tie-breakers tend to put people off) and ask the audience to write or ring in with the answers. If you are using a competition to 'qualify' prospects, to find out whether they are really interested in buying what you have to offer, you may want to ask more difficult questions and get a smaller, quality list of potential customers.

What should you offer as a prize? In general, if you are promoting a book or other published product, your prizes can be copies of the product(s), or perhaps the winner's choice from your whole list. In this way the cost to you of providing the prizes will be substantially less than their value to the winners. If you are using a competition to build a database of people interested in your product, for example for a high priced multi-volume reference work, the prize should always be the product itself (otherwise you will be building a list of people attracted by a free holiday – or whatever else it is you are offering).

The prizes *need not be enormous*. Listen to local radio and you will find that small rewards are supplemented by the great pleasure of winning and being mentioned on the air. You could consider pursuing sponsorship if you want to offer bigger prizes, but this can be very time-consuming and the resulting media coverage will have to be shared.

A few ideas for competitions

- When organising local radio interviews to boost author tours try offering a few copies of the book as prizes for correct answers to a quick competition. Not only do you get a good idea of how many people are listening (and it's usually very encouraging), you prolong the author's time on the air.
- If you are promoting a book that lends itself to a quiz, mention on your press release that prizes are available if the media use the book's content as the basis for a competition. Consider supplying a page of sample questions.
- Offer a prize to booksellers for the best window or in-store display for forthcoming major titles/promotions.
- Schools are short of money and keen to increase their resources by taking part in competitions to win books. Class project or quiz sheets that fill up small slots of teaching time are always popular and can encourage teachers to purchase more copies of your materials, or to fully appreciate their benefits by using them in new ways.
- Even if you get only a few entries, celebrate the prize-winners. Get your nearest rep to present prizes and ask the local paper to cover the ceremony: most will be pleased to feature a good local story.

Sponsorship

The pursuit of sponsorship is a vast subject in its own right, and can be an excellent way to get your firm or product's name in front of a specific audience. The key to really effective sponsorship arrangements is ensuring compatibility between the the interests of all parties involved.

Consider both outgoing and incoming sponsorship. Supporting an event of interest to a market you want to reach (eg a children's publisher backing a children's theatre) is outgoing sponsorship. Accepting money or help in kind in return for promoting a sponsor's name in addition to your own product (eg books sponsored by supermarkets) is an example of incoming sponsorship.

Give careful consideration to what both parties expect out of the sponsorship deal and put it in writing. Sponsors have become accustomed to receiving requests for support from all sides, and expect more than a straight exchange of logo for cash. Most want to work together to capitalize on joint markets, media coverage and potential image building. A great many sponsors are also attracted by possible opportunities for corporate entertaining.

Offering incentives

Some publishers offer incentives to purchase with expensive products, for example free calculators with business books or a free set of CDs with a music encyclopaedia. Such offers can encourage the order to come more quickly if a 'sell-by' date is added. Giving the reader a choice of offers can be particularly effective; the reader's attention is directed towards making a decision between several items they would like to own; the actual decision to purchase is assumed.

Others use an offer to boost the size of order, for example a free item (or perhaps free postage and packing) if the order value is over a certain size.

Getting your product adopted as an incentive in a promotion

Regular incentive fairs are held where those producing products likely for selection as incentives in promotional campaigns can display their wares. It is worth attending just to see the kind of promotional deals that are set up.

Interestingly, promotional companies like using books as they imply quality and have a high perceived value (discounting of books is a relatively recent phenomenon). When choosing an incentive to promote sales of a magazine, nothing apparently out-pulls a free book plastic-wrapped on to the front cover. Publishers can offer either old stock or, if the print run of the magazine is sufficiently extensive and the promotional opportunity seen as valuable enough, produce a special edition.

Along similar lines, try offering training institutions bulk copies of books that are relevant to the courses they run. They may decide to incorporate a copy of your product into the course fee, thus enabling them to sell an added value package to their customers. Bulk sales of key reference materials can similarly be made to organisations who might distribute them to their workforce or customers, perhaps offering the opportunity to have their own logo printed on the spine (for more information on bulk sales see Chapter 1).

Produce free material

When the 20p coin came out I was working for an educational publisher. We sent (with our regular schools mailing) free worksheets by the authors of our best-selling maths scheme to every primary and middle school in the UK. The material showed how to incorporate the coin into giving change, receiving pocket-money, purchasing and so on, and was very popular with schools. We were convinced it encouraged brand loyalty.

Produce a news sheet

Again, excellent for customer loyalty. Even editorially outstanding or best-selling products can become boring to the market. So tell customers about the progress of further products from the same stable, report on how others are using your material, provide feedback on problems familiar to the market, include 'human interest' stories. Have you noticed how many of the new out-of-town superstores are producing customer magazines? Perhaps they are trying to challenge a view of them as impersonal supermarkets which offer no warmth or advice.

Allow the reader to try your publication out

Fiction publishers produce early 'reading copies' for bookshops in the hope that they will generate excitement about forthcoming titles. Similarly, booklets containing extracts from new novels are made available to customers by the till-point: a good way of gaining market research on what is likely to sell, as well as promoting the next season's list. For the same reason, the sale of serial rights to magazines and newspapers is an excellent way to arouse interest and tempt readers to want the whole volume.

'Home interest' magazines find that printing recipes boosts their readership. If you are promoting a new cookery book try featuring a sample recipe in your advertisements. A promotion organised by Sainsbury's for Delia Smith's recipes had a huge impact on sales of the items listed. There was a national shortage of liquid glycerin as a direct result!

Stunts

From poetry reading on Waterloo station, to balloon releasing from the top of the Scott Memorial, it's up to you and your imagination. Two cautionary notes:

1. Make sure the stunts you arrange really are relevant to the main aim of press coverage ie selling more stock. The punters should remember both the event and the product.
2. Do target stunts at the right people. Chocolate cakes sent to feature editors to announce publication of a new cookbook may be very much appreciated; if booksellers get to hear of it they may just conclude you have too much money to spend and demand more discount.

10

Organising Events: Sales Conferences, Launch Parties, Press Conferences and Exhibitions

Sales Conferences

Most publishing houses brief their reps at regular sales conferences. New titles are presented; feedback on previous promotions is sought; information on company sales passed on and a friendly, 'we're all part of the same team' atmosphere encouraged.

When they are held depends on the kind of list being promoted. Educational publishing houses may hold one in the school holidays before the start of each term, or perhaps one before the autumn selling cycle and another in the spring. A general publishing house will usually tie the conferences into the major selling and catalogue seasons: one in the summer to launch the autumn/winter list, another at Christmas for the spring/summer titles.

At first you will probably be required only to sit and listen to those presenting. There is much you can learn for when your own turn to do this comes around, both from your reactions to spending the majority of the day listening and the presentational style of those you hear.

If the organisation of a sales conference falls to you, do remember what the real purpose is. While a sales conference offers a valuable opportunity for marketing and editorial staff to get together, and everyone enjoys a day out of the office, the real function is to brief the reps. These occasions give them the chance to tap the brains of those who commissioned and authorised the books they will try to sell over the next few months and to find out all they can about them.

Checklist for a successful sales conference

1. Establish exactly who needs to come and to which sessions. Be firm about who should be there, and for which sessions. You should consider (tactfully) excluding some people. For example, will the presence of the managing director and chairman inhibit reps from asking question they really want answered? Very large groups can jeopardise both the presenter's ease of delivery and the audience's willingness to respond out loud.

    If political necessities mean the entire hierarchy is present for the formal presentation, consider organising an informal get-together afterwards for questions. Alternatively, can you divide into two smaller groups (perhaps home and export staff) and present different subjects in different locations at the same time? Harder work for the staff presenting titles, but worth the effort if improved recall results.

2. The venue. Ensure that the space is adequate for the numbers attending. Is there somewhere for participants to get a breather between sessions?

    Find out about building renovation programmes in advance; they are very noisy. What is more, they never run to schedule, so if you are assured they will be over by the time you arrive, have it confirmed in writing. Is there air conditioning; how loud is it? If not, will opening the windows make it impossible to hear the speakers over the roar of passing traffic? Check that all the bulbs in key lights are working (in particular note the speaker's reading light for use when the room is darkened for slides). Negotiate with the venue's manager about the rates you are offered: never accept the printed price list as absolute.

3. Provide the delegates with a folder containing copies of advance notices, leaflets and covers for all the titles to be presented at the conference. They can make notes on these as they listen.

4. Keep the sessions short and vary the presenters (two short presentations are preferable to one long one by the same speaker). If the conference lasts over several days, try to avoid a long session on a Friday afternoon. Don't offer alcohol at lunchtime. Drinking after the evening meal is an established ritual; try to supplement it with something more stimulating, perhaps an after-dinner talk provided it is amusing and not too heavy. Are there any sports facilities available nearby: tennis courts; a swimming pool?

How to present effectively at a sales conference

1. If it is up to you, think about how you want the room arranged: as a conventional boardroom or without any desk? Do you need a lectern?

2. What equipment do you need? Does it exist in-house/in the hotel? Does it work? Be different: if everyone else is using PowerPoint, should you talk from a flipchart or commission some cartoons?

3. Provide yourself with a list of key points to mention for each title and practise talking around them. Mark times on your notes, eg 'point I should have reached after 5 minutes'). Speak slowly, particularly at the beginning. You don't have to be word perfect; this may encourage you to speak too quickly. Hesitations and occasional repetitions help to get the message across. Time yourself. Never read from a script or, worse still, from the file of advance notices that the reps too have in front of them.

4. Wear something comfortable; be particularly careful what shoes you choose. Stand on both feet. Resist the temptation to fiddle with your tie or hair. Smile.

5. Make eye contact, not just with those you know are sympathetic – allow your gaze to move around the room.

6. The rep wants to know the major selling points of the books being presented. Pass on anything that is likely to be of use when the title comes to be subscribed to the trade: anecdotes about the author or the project, feedback from market research, comparisons with the competition and so on. Choose three or four main themes, then shut up.

7. Use props. Hold up book jackets and covers; turn the pages of flipcharts you have prepared in advance.

8. Involve the audience. Ask questions and announce competitions, incentives and games for anything from slogans to future sales.

9. Don't distribute samples of the hot-off-the-press promotional materials until you have finished speaking.

10. It sometimes helps to make sure that you are the last one in the room. It can be terrifying to sit at the front and watch your audience building up in front of you!

11. Don't be afraid to ignore persistent or difficult questioners. They are probably annoying everyone else in the room too. Suggest you discuss their difficulties after the general session has finished.

Promotional parties and book launches

The following checklist will help you to organise such an event for the first time.

What are you seeking to get out of it?

The aim of a promotional party or book launch is usually media coverage leading to more sales. You provide the opportunity for journalists and gossip columnists to meet the author and hear more about the book. They report it, the public read what they say and flock to buy the title. Even if the party does not result in specific features or news coverage, you can promote gossip and word of mouth and keep the author's profile high. At other times such a party is organised as a celebration, or to boost the company name. Sometimes the arrangement is purely political: to keep the author happy.

When to hold

Monday is a bad day if you want coverage in the Sunday papers; most Sunday journalists get the day off. Tuesday is too early in the week for them to be interested in covering for the following Sunday. Friday evening is best avoided as POETS day (push off early tomorrow's Saturday). As regards timing, after work is convenient, say around 6.30 pm. Alternatively, try lunchtime.

Whom to invite

Ask enough of the author's friends and relations to make them feel comfortable and prevent the room from looking empty. Ask all the relevant journalists and 'media people' you want to cover the book. Try to ensure the event is not a re-staging of the last office party as everyone who is working late comes along for a free drink.

Who else is interested in the book's subject matter? Members of Parliament; captains of industry; 'television personalities' – all can be invited. If there are well-known names who can't be there but are fully committed to the subject, ask them if they can provide a message of support which you can read out.

Send out the invitations three to four weeks ahead accompanied by a press release giving more information on the title being launched. Provide your name and telephone number for rsvps and make a list of all those invited/expected in alphabetical order by surname. On the day sit by the entrance and ask the names of all who arrive, tick them off and hand out pre-prepared name badges (if appropriate). If possible get someone experienced to stand next to you so you don't ask the company chairman for his or her name.

All members of the home team should carry a badge saying who they are; it has the added advantage of deterring them from talking to one another.

If you are expecting a VIP or main guest ensure that someone is ready to receive and host for the rest of the evening. 'Big name' or not, they will probably still be nervous.

Book a photographer to take pictures of (preferably recognisable) guests enjoying themselves. Brief them on the combinations of people you want recorded. You can circulate the results afterwards to members of the press who failed to turn up and still secure coverage in their papers. Try offering a picture to one paper as a scoop first, in return for a guarantee that it will be featured in a prominent place. Newspapers are much more aware of the artistic and intrinsic merits of the camera than they used to be. No longer do all photographs have to appear as illustrations to the text; a good photograph and caption can form a feature on their own.

When circulating a photograph, always stick a good caption on the back: it can make the difference between the shot being featured and being ignored. Ensure you repeat the caption on the accompanying press release. If the photo is to be used, it will go off to be processed and production people do not always take notice of stickers on the back of images they receive. Only when the picture is put on the page will somebody remember about the caption!

The venue

The location should be relevant to the title being launched. If your subject matter is of interest to a particular section of the press choose a location that is easy for them to get to, eg city venues for financial books. If the venue is very special but difficult to reach either lay on transport (eg a bus will collect from a particular place at a particular time, and run a shuttle service back) or forget it.

When to expect the guests

If you put 6.30 on the invitation, most will arrive around 7.00 and stay (depending on how good the party is) for about an hour. You can influence how long they stay by the timing of the welcome speeches: most will wait until they are over.

What to provide

Make the drinks as simple as possible. In general more white than red wine will be drunk, and many people will ask for soft drinks: the commonest mistake is not to provide enough. Guests are usually given a drink as they come though the door into the reception; thereafter glasses are most easily replenished by waiters (or staff) walking around with bottles and topping up. If you decide to provide more exotic drinks (eg cocktails or spirits) have them ready mixed on trays; waiters can circulate and offer to exchange empty for full glasses. If you have a principal guest let them know what you are proposing to provide and ask if they have any special requirements.

As regards food, for early evening receptions most organisers work on the assumption that the guests will be going elsewhere to eat and so lay on cocktail party nibbles. This usually means providing things that can be eaten with the fingers. Do be imaginative, but combine this with practicality. Be aware of hot items that spurt butter or burn the tongue, or fall apart on impact. Dips are popular as are chicken pieces, sausages, small sandwiches and so on. Most people prefer to help themselves from passing trays rather than load a plate which they then have to juggle with a wine glass and risk looking greedy.

For lunchtime launches, something more substantial may be needed. Offer a couple of choices (one vegetarian) but choose dishes that can be eaten with a fork, standing up.

When selecting the menu ask freelance cooks for their suggestions and the associated costs. A hotel will give you a price list. Don't be ashamed to negotiate on price (perhaps by asking if they have anything simpler on offer), particularly if you are offering a hotel a booking at a time when it would otherwise be empty.

Speeches

After the party has been in full swing for about half an hour someone should thank everyone for coming and the author(s) for providing the occasion for the party, welcome any key guests and reporters and make a few pleasant remarks. The author may reply.

You may find some resistance to formal speeches, but it is very important to concentrate people's minds on why they are there; to provide a focal point to the event. However, do ensure that the speeches are neither too long nor too many.

What to have to hand

Even though you have already sent out press releases with the invitations keep a pile of any written materials to hand. There will almost certainly be journalists who want to go away and write the story up straight away but have forgotten to bring the necessary information. Copies of what is being promoted should be on display. They are very likely to be removed by guests, so if the material is valuable the number available needs to be carefully controlled.

What to do afterwards

Follow up journalists who did not attend and offer them a photograph and a story. Make sure those who said they would feature the book do so (for hints on getting media coverage for press conferences see Chapter 8).

Did the venue provide all they said they would; did all go smoothly? If not, negotiate.

Press conferences

A press conference calls together key members of the relevant press to impart a story/version of events. These should only be called if you have definite news to impart. If you call a press conference and there is no news story you will make journalists wary of accepting your invitation the next time you ask them.

You will need someone to chair the event: to coordinate questions and ensure that all the news points get raised. The book's editor or author may be the ideal person. Alternatively, consider asking someone with related interests who may be a 'name' in their own right. If chairing your press conference links their name with a cause they support they may do a particularly good job for you.

Author tours and signing sessions

A promotional tour during which a popular or newsworthy author gives a series of talks, or perhaps signs copies of a new book, requires an immense amount of planning. There are many reasons why it may be well worth organising:

- resultant media coverage
- accelerated word of mouth about the title/author
- the chance for the public to meet a particular author
- attracts the public into bookshops
- raises the profile of books in general and your house's list in particular.

All of these should lead to increased exposure and more sales. What is more, stock signed by the author cannot be returned to the publisher's warehouse if it subsequently fails to sell.

Interestingly, from the purchaser's point of view, there does not seem to be any evidence that, in the medium term, signed copies are worth more: signed and unsigned often sell for the same price in second-hand bookshops (the exception to this rule is the science fiction market where a signature can add a great deal to a copy's value).

Such events are often organised in conjunction with a local book-shop which orders extra stock to meet anticipated demand. Be sure the event is well publicised by yourself or the bookshop in advance. It is common practice for the shop and the publisher to share the cost of some preliminary space advertising, but be aware that the costs of advertising in London papers such as the *Evening Standard* can be five times what you would pay outside the capital.

On the day, a few shop staff should be available to crowd around the signing desk and get things off to a good start: nothing attracts punters like seeing a crowd. The yachtsman Alec Rose created a record by signing 1,250 copies of his book in Hatchards in Piccadilly. In the same shop, Twiggy was overcome by the crowds and signed just four of hers.

Exhibitions

- Putting up the display. Some firms instruct reps or have mobile exhibition teams who will provide everything needed if you inform them in good time of the nature of the exhibition and the stock required.

- If you have to mount the display yourself, find out what will be available on site (screens, tables, chairs, platforms and so on) and from what time the exhibition room is available for assembly. Take enough additional promotional material to make your stand look interesting (posters, showcards and so on). A large cover for the table looks better than bare wood – a few yards of a crease-resistant polyester from local department store is as good as anything. Whatever your company colours, if it is black it won't start to look grubby. Everyone who is to help run the stand needs a name badge to identify them as part of the company.

- Never underestimate how many people you need to help run an exhibition stand. It is far better to have several people taking stints than assign one poor soul for the whole day: by the end of it they will be incapable of selling a cold drink to a thirsty man.

- Don't look too casual and never smoke on the stand (very off-putting to customers). Similarly, although you may be delighted to have some company from fellow employees, never stand in clusters. It is very difficult for the potential customer who wants to ask a question to have to break up your conversation first.

- Have a means of recording potential interest to hand. This needs not be a lengthy form – it is impossible to keep a conversation going and fill out such a document at the same time. Instead, arm yourself with a pile of index cards (stiff enough to write on without requiring something to lean on) and a stapler for attaching the enquirer's business card. With this information you can contact each prospect after the exhibition to discuss their interests in further detail and move on to talk to the next potential customer. (Obviously, if your stand is not busy or the enquirer is particularly interested you can talk for longer and in more depth.)

- You should have stock of your brochures and catalogues ready to hand out, but what you want to ensure is that they re-emerge from the ubiquitous exhibition carrier bag handed out to visitors as they enter. Can you mark the products you discussed with a highlighter pen? Staple your own business card to the front of the brochure to make recall more likely.

Award ceremonies and literary prizes

Literary prizes attract more attention today – the award of the annual Booker prize is featured on the news pages (not in the book section) of the national dailies. Prizes offer both short-listed and winning titles the promise of substantial extra sales. The publication of many novels is scheduled for what is seen as the most advantageous time for getting on to the short list for a particular prize.

If one of your titles is a front runner for a forthcoming prize you will be required to put together a plan of action to support and sustain media interest, and further capitalise on it if the books wins. For example you may have to produce (overnight) stickers to go on book jackets for circulation to booksellers saying 'Winner of X' and prepare attractive point of sale material.

For details of which prizes are run, when, and how to enter them see the booklet produced by Book Trust. For details of the Whitbread Prize, contact the Booksellers Association.

11

Profit or Loss: 'The Bottom Line'

Marketing costs money. Even if you concentrate on the 'free' promotional techniques listed in Chapter 8 you will incur costs: your time; the telephone bill; the production cost of free copies given away for review or feature and not recoverable through sales. While most of these activities will be paid for out of the general company overheads, when it comes to drawing up a budget for the active promotion of a title, a firm decision must be taken on how much can be spent. A glance at the title file of a forthcoming book should show you how many it has been estimated can be sold in the first year(s) after publication. The marketing budget will be designed to produce these sales and so generate enough revenue to:

a) *pay for the outlay on the book*: production; promotion costs and so on
b) *produce a profit* which first makes a contribution to company overheads such as staff and telephone, and second produces an outright profit to invest in new publishing enterprises and remunerate shareholders.

Where do marketing budgets come from?

The budget assigned to the marketing department will be just one of a whole series of payments which senior managers of a publishing house have to allocate. For example, house overheads have to be provided for – both those that are attributable to specific departments (staff and freelance hours) as well as those which come from the company as a whole (audit fees, personnel department costs and the post room). The marketing department may see their need for a decent budget as paramount but the level of spending cannot

reasonably be substantially increased unless there is a strong proba-
bility of extra sales resulting. The marketing budget is but one
element in the financial equation of the publishing business, as the
following examples show.

New general hardback title, print run: 3,000

	%	Amount £	Balance £
Published price			25.00
Less discount to book trade	45	11.25	13.75
Less production costs (origination, artwork, paper, binding, etc)	18	4.50	9.25
Less royalties to author	9	2.25	7.00
Less marketing budget	6	1.50	5.50
Less publisher overheads and expenses (storage, despatch, representation and staff)	20	5.00	0.50 (2% of list price)
Potential profit on print run of 3,000			£1,500

Subsequent mass market paperback edition of same title, print run:
30,000

	%	Amount £	Balance £
Published price			6.99
Less discount to book trade	50	3.50	3.49
Less production costs (origination, artwork, paper, binding, etc)	10	0.70	2.79
Less royalties to author	7	0.49	2.30
Less marketing budget	5	0.35	1.95
Less publisher overheads and expenses (storage, despatch, representation and staff)	20	1.40	0.55 (7.9% of list price)
Potential profit on print run of 30,000			£16,500

NB To make ends meet on the above kind of project, publishers are increasingly marketing a 'C format' version (hardback edition size and type of paper, limp binding) in between hardback and paperback editions.

New educational textbook, heavily illustrated, print run: 5,000, limp binding

	%	Amount £	Balance £
Published price			9.95
Less discount to book trade on 50%★	17.5	0.87	9.08
Less production costs (origination, artwork, paper, binding, etc)	30	2.99	6.09
Less royalties to author	5	0.50	5.59
Less marketing budget	15	1.49	4.50
Less publisher overheads and expenses (storage, despatch, representation and staff)	20	1.99	2.51 (25.2% of list price)
Potential profit on print run of 5,000 ★assuming 50% sale direct to schools			12,550

New academic monograph, print run: 500, hardback

	%	Amount £	Balance £
Published price			40.00
Less discount to book trade	25	10.00	30.00
Less production costs (origination, artwork, paper, binding, etc)	22	8.80	21.20
Less royalties to author	10	4.00	17.20
Less marketing budget	5	2.00	15.20
Less publisher overheads and expenses (storage, despatch, representation and staff)	20	8.00	7.20 (18% of list price)
Potential profit on print run of 500			£3,600

Professional or reference book being sold through the mail, print run: 2,000, lots of statistical tables, hardback

	%	Amount £	Balance £
Published price			49.95
Less discount to book trade on 30% of sales	10	1.49	48.46
Less production costs (origination, artwork, paper, binding, etc)	23	11.49	36.97
Less royalties to author	10	5.00	31.97
Less marketing budget	20	9.99	21.98
Less publisher overheads and expenses (storage, despatch, representation and staff)	20	9.99	11.99 (24% list price)
Potential profit on print run of 2,000			£23,980

Notes

1. These figures are not designed to show that any one type of publishing is intrinsically more profitable than any other; the amounts quoted as potential profit obviously depend on selling all the print run. For subsequent reprints some titles would show much healthier margins, once the basic origination, permissions, illustrations and marketing costs had been paid for.
2. The figures show that the increased cover price of a hardback book in comparison with a paperback is not due solely to increased production costs (as is generally believed), but the lower print runs and hence higher unit costs for each book printed, as well as a higher royalty rate.
3. The levels of discount given to different accounts will vary hugely according to a number of factors such as quantity taken; terms (firm sale or sale or return) and overall level of business between the two parties.

These examples show the complicated financial structure of publishing. Each title is in effect a separate business for which costs must be calculated, the marketing allowance being just one part of that equation. If it is thought essential to award a larger than average marketing budget, or indeed to assign more money to any of the above costs (eg give more discount to the UK book trade, or spend more on production) then either the unit sales must be greater to justify the increase or another variable must be altered. Options here include increasing the unit price, printing fewer copies, lowering the quality of materials and hence the production costs, paying reduced royalties, or looking for a co-publishing deal which makes production costs more favourable and eases cash flow.

Marketing budgets cannot be seen in isolation.

Drawing up a budget

A budget is a plan of activities expressed in money terms. Successful management of a budget means delivering, at an acceptable cost, *all* the promotional strategies detailed in the budget. It is not just a question of keeping promotional expenditure within the prescribed limit irrespective of how many of the planned activities are achieved.

The amount allocated to the marketing budget (and to other departmental budgets) is usually based on a percentage of the firm's (or section's) projected turnover for that year: ie what you can spend is dictated by what you will be receiving.

For each forthcoming title the marketing manager will estimate market size and the percentage likely to buy. Anticipated future income from new titles is added to other sources of revenue such as reprints, rights sales and investment income. Projected turnover for both the year ahead, and probably for the next three- or five-year period, is planned at high level management meetings. Expectations are subsequently monitored against actual performance, usually on a monthly and annual basis. Comparisons are then made with previous years and long-term plans are updated.

The manager calculates what it will cost to reach potential buyers; aiming to reach as many as possible with the budget allocated; deciding where the available resources will have the most impact. Some companies have tried to improve sales by substantially increasing their level of promotional expenditure, but if it costs proportionally more to achieve the resulting extra sales the outcome can be financial ruin. Decisions to overspend on marketing may still be made, and sometimes the risks pay off, but it should not be forgotten that monitoring a budget is an essential part of drawing one up and people do lose their jobs or firms go out of business for failing to implement what they have agreed to.

How much is spent

If the overall marketing budget is based on a percentage of antici-pated turnover (different amounts being allocated to various titles according to need and ease of reaching the market) what kind of percentages are we talking about?

The question depends entirely on the sort of list the house produces. On high price reference works selling mainly through the mail to specialist markets, on which little discount is given to the book trade, marketing budgets may be as high as 20 per cent of anticipated turnover, perhaps more to launch a major book in the first year after publication. If, on the other hand, the firm is selling educational titles with much lower prices through bookshops and wholesalers there is less room for spending large amounts; budgets will probably average 6 to 8 per cent of forecast turnover. On acad-emic or very specialised reference titles the percentage spent on marketing may be no more than 5 per cent.

It used to be the case that publishers would try to recover promo-tional costs on the first edition of a new book; today they are frequently forced to take a longer-term view. Higher advances and increasing competition from large corporate publishing outfits, interest payments to finance production and overhead costs before any sales revenue is received, have ensured that sometimes a hard-back is only made profitable through the subsequent publication of a paperback edition, or even the same author's second or third book with the house (hence the popularity of two- and three-book deals).

Other types of book require heavy spending on promotion at the time of publication: if sales do not take off well then they will be flops in the long term however much money is subsequently allo-cated. Directories (whether in hard or soft format) are a good example of a type of title needing a large initial promotion budget, perhaps for two or three years, until the sales strategy can become chiefly one of encouraging renewals. The same goes for a new series launched by an educational publisher with a view to getting large scale adoptions. Once the adoptions have been made and the scheme is being used in schools, less intensive selling will be needed. When promoting a new journal it may be cost-effective to spend the whole of the first year's individual subscription revenue on acquiring a subscriber; once their subscription is recorded they should stay for a number of years to make the venture profitable.

Remember that even if you give identical budgets to all your titles, some will always outperform the others. If sales for one title disappoint and you have extra resources to spend, it is usually better to spend the additional funds on titles that are doing well than on trying to recover the position of the poorer sellers: it's better to back the winners.

How the budget is divided up

Four main categories of expenditure exist, in decreasing order of importance.

Core marketing costs

These are the regular marketing activities which are essential to the selling cycles of the publishing industry. I include here catalogues, advance notices and new book/stock lists. The total sum required for these items is usually deducted from the marketing budget before further allocations are made. These should only be cut as a very last resort.

Plans for individual titles

New titles or series, or perhaps works that are already published but need actively promoting should have specific amounts of money allocated to their marketing. The allocation is not always made exactly in proportion to the anticipated revenue: some markets may be easier to reach than others and need less extensive budgets.

If it is your responsibility to draw up these preliminary allocations, decide on which titles or series the money could most usefully be spent and then look at actual costs of reaching the market. How many people are in it? How much would it cost to reach them? If you have the information, how much did it cost to reach them last year? Look at last year's actual costs and then add a percentage to cover inflation. Alternatively, ask the same suppliers to requote. What response do you need from the market to justify the sum you are proposing to ask for? Is this attainable? What backlist titles in the same subject area can be listed on promotional material to increase the possible chance or size of order?

Budgets for 'smaller' titles

Next comes the allocation of money to titles needing (or receiving) smaller budgets. This may mean you will only be able to promote them actively if you pool the budget with that of other titles and do a co-operative leaflet or 'piggy back' mailing. This is not necessarily an unwelcome compromise. Boosting a range of related titles together encourages an awareness of your publishing house as a particular type of publisher and may attract both new purchasers and new authors. In the same way most editors have a responsibility for building a particular list. Co-operative promotions back up and give authority to your main title strategies and can provide a useful push for the backlist books included.

Contingency

Last of all may come a contingency amount to be used at the marketing department's discretion on any title or group of titles as good ideas come up. It does not always reach the final budget: during the process of reconciling how much the marketing department would like to spend with how much is available, sacrifices are looked for. The contingency budget is often a casualty.

The sum of these four areas of spending is usually based on (or at least compared with) the percentage of the firm's anticipated turnover as discussed above. By drawing up a budget in this way the interdependence of all the titles in a list can be seen. If one title fails to achieve what it is budgeted to do, all the other titles in the list will have to work harder if the firm is to survive or profit margins to be maintained.

Reasons for failure may vary: production time may be longer than anticipated; an author may produce the manuscript late or produce a text that needs substantial and time-consuming reworking before it can be published; copyright clearance can take up to six months. Until a title is actually released for publication, recorded dues cannot be added to the sales figures. If this happens at a financial year end, sales will be lost from the year's figures. If the manuscript cannot be remedied the sales will be lost altogether, a serious situation if money has already been spent on promotion.

When to spend it

Once a basic marketing sum has been allocated the next step is to budget for when it should be spent during the year. There are external constraints on you.

1.   When the market wants to be told about new books

Promotion is usually a seasonal business; timings will vary according to the type of book being promoted and the market being approached.

Roughly 40 per cent of the year's general sales in bookshops take place between the middle of October and 24 December. Most publishers for this market therefore time their main selling season so that the books are on the stockists' shelves ready to meet this bonanza. In the same way educational publishers promote titles to the schools market at the times when teachers are considering how to spend their budgets (usually September, January and March), and academic publishers aim to reach their market when reading lists for students are being compiled (usually early spring onwards, with more notice for really important titles).

2.   When the books themselves are scheduled

The production department will produce a list giving scheduled release (when stock goes out from the warehouse to the trade) and publication dates (when bookshops can start selling). Promotion schedules should be planned around these dates; with some types of book timing is particularly important. Year-books and directories must be promoted early because they age and get harder to sell as the new edition approaches. Academic monographs too must be promoted ahead of publication: as much as 60 per cent of first year sales can occur in the month of publication. If promotion plans have not been carried out and the dues recorded by the time of release, sales may never recover.

The need to promote early should be balanced against the risk of peaking too far ahead of publication date, with the danger that the effects will be lost. The fault may not be yours: the author may deliver the manuscript late; production can take longer than anticipated.

3. When you have time to market them

Obviously, promotions that are not related to publication dates (for example re-launching old series or organising a thematic push for the backlist) can be scheduled for less busy periods in the calendar, but again market acceptability must be considered.

Publishing is most often a seasonal business and you cannot really avoid this, just accept that you will be busier at certain times of the year.

How to monitor your budget

Once the budget is established, stick to it – or only depart from it in a conscious fashion, with permission! In most houses once invoices have been passed by the person who commissioned the work (ie they check them against the quote) they are sent to the person in the accounts department who deals with promotion expenditure. In return monthly reports are provided on spending levels. Even if you have this service, the figures you receive will be several weeks behind your actual expenditure and I would recommend keeping a record yourself, with a running balance of how much has been spent (or committed but not yet billed) and what still remains from the title's budget.

It may be helpful to decide at the beginning of the year the percentages of the individual title budgets to be spent on print, design, copy, despatch and other key elements. That does not mean the proportions cannot be changed. I once printed 50,000 copies of a cheap flyer for a single title instead of the more usual 10,000 because the author had arranged lots of mailings and insertions that were to cost little or nothing. I therefore spent most of the despatch budget on printing.

I find it useful to look at costs per thousand for leaflet production lists and mailing charges. Unit prices for print reduce as numbers increase, mailing lists and despatch charges in general do not (or not by very much). Harness your promotion expenditure to your marketing responses and you start to get very sophisticated market information. If you compare the costs of producing a catalogue with the orders received directly from it (or perhaps received during the period over which it was being actively used for ordering) you can compile a figure for orders per page and an accurate indication of how profitable your endeavours have been. This is the way the rest of the retail trade is run (floor space:revenue).

Money-saving techniques – or how to make your budget go further

1.   Take your budget personally

If you do this you are more likely to be efficient in its use. Circulate mailing results; analyse the progress of each promotion; record sales figures before and after promotions; make recommendations on how they could have been improved/why they were so good.

2.   Be ever mindful of opportunities for marketing

Mailing lists may be yours to use if you ask; secondary markets may exist and prove highly profitable if you think of targeting them. Watch what your competitors are doing – one very effective way of doing this is to give each member of staff in the marketing department a competitor to 'adopt'. They then become responsible for watching out for their marketing and plans. Pool the information at a meeting and you can have a very helpful overall survey of your market.

Learn from other industries by developing a general interest in advertising and marketing. Above all, be interested in your products and who buys them.

3.   Get better value for money

- If you are sending your information to standard outlets (eg bookshops and libraries) use co-operative mailings rather than bearing all the despatch costs yourself. In surveys most libraries, academics and schools say they don't care whether promotional material reaches them on its own or in company; it is the content that counts. If commercial opportunities do not exist then consider forming partnerships with non-competing firms to share costs. Can you take exhibition space in partnership too?
- Try different ways of reaching the same market: loose inserts; inserts in delegates' packs at conferences; displaying material on exhibition stands. They may attract slightly lower levels of response than individual mailings but the cost of sales will also be substantially reduced. Can you reach more people for less money?
- Make as much use as possible of the promotional material you produce. If you prepare a central stock list or standard order form, run on extra copies and use in mailings, include in parcels

235

or send to exhibitions. If you use a new book supplement in your catalogue (perhaps inserted in the centre fold) can this too be reprinted for use in mailings?

Think laterally. Why not send all academics a catalogue request form in case they are interested in other areas for which you publish? There are certain well-known combinations of interest and profession (many academics like opera and lots of politicians seem to be interested in bird watching); if you have books on your list likely to appeal, try them out.

- Instead of sophisticated design, concentrate your attention on effective copy and buying reasons that speak directly to the market. Remember that over-complicated design can get in the way of effective communication.

- Sometimes you may not need a brochure at all. A sales letter with a coupon for return along the bottom can be a very efficient way of soliciting orders. (The opposite does not apply, by the way; brochures always need a letter to go with them.) Update your information not by reprinting but by sending out accompanying photocopied pages of reviews or features that have appeared.

- If your catalogue is designed as a series of double page spreads, could these be turned into leaflets later on? With this in mind, if you are working in more than one colour, ensure that anything you may want to delete later on (such as page numbers) appears in black only, which is the cheapest plate to change.

- Can full-colour material be reprinted for a second mailing in two colours rather than four?

- Use the author's contacts. Supply authors with advance information sheets and leaflets; ask if they are members of societies that would circulate a flyer on a forthcoming book with its journal. The same goes for publishing deals that involve learned societies or other specialised organisations: how can they help you promote the resulting title?

4. Use free publicity to the maximum possible extent

The pursuit of free publicity should not replace your standard promotional tools, rather, it should back them up. But don't end up paying for advertising space if the magazine would have printed a feature with a little persuasion. Many magazines are willing to make 'reader offers' – an editorial mention in return for free copies to give out. Nor should you offer to pay for a loose insert if your author is on the editorial board and could have arranged for it to be circulated for nothing.

5. Negotiate as a matter of course

Always ask for discounts. There is a standard publisher's discount of 10 per cent in booking advertising space. Sometimes more can be squeezed for sending camera-ready copy (although they won't be expecting anything else), the fact that it's the first time you have advertised with them, or simply that the rate they quote is too expensive for your budget. If you have the time, use it – the advertising sales representative will probably come back to you with a reduced price. Particularly good deals can be obtained just before a magazine goes to print – once it has gone to the printers the space has no value at all. If you go for a series of adverts you should get an additional discount; likewise if you book a year's requirements in one go.

Do you have someone in the department who has previously worked in advertising sales? If so ask them to handle negotiations for you and you will almost certainly reduce your anticipated costs further still. Consider going on a negotiating skills course.

One final tip on dealing with discounted offers: decide where you want to advertise and then negotiate on price. If you allow yourself to get used to responding to the special offers available from magazines you are less than committed to appearing in (ie you would not have paid the full price), your marketing becomes much less targeted and you run the risk of seriously overspending. Remember that space costs are only one part of the total outlay. Use the continual saying of no as an exercise designed to find out just how much can be negotiated off the list price.

6. Try to get money in more quickly

Books may be sent to trade outlets on a variety of different terms, some more beneficial to the publisher than others. Encouraging the trade to 'buy firm' rather than on 'sale or return' prevents unexpected returns which reduce sales and the overall profitability of particular titles.

Provide every opportunity for customers buying through the post to pay early, and in the most cost-efficient way for you. Some credit cards charge a higher percentage of the sales invoice than others for the use of their facilities.

Asking individuals for payment with order rather than the chance to pay later with an invoice will depress the order response slightly, but improve your finances. Can you compensate by offering a cast-iron guarantee of satisfaction or their money back?

Institutions such as schools, colleges and libraries will need an invoice to pay against but can they be encouraged to pay sooner rather than later? State your credit terms on the order form. For serial publications, directories and journals offer customers the chance to complete a standing order. In return offer to hold the price for a second year or perhaps a discount.

Don't regard the wording on your company order forms to date as 'standard'. Study those you receive from other industries, appropriate the best ideas, experiment with different formats and styles, all with the intention of making yours as user-friendly and easy to understand as possible. Get someone not connected with a promotion to fill in the order form before you pass it for press.

7.   Apply for all the free help you can get

Can your authors arrange for you to attend relevant meetings and run book exhibitions? Does your firm belong to any professional associations from whose collected wisdom you can benefit? For example, most publishers promoting by direct mail belong to the Direct Marketing Association but the number of marketing department staff regularly attending meetings is much lower. Find out about the special interest publishing groups that are part of the Publishers Association and get copies of the reports they publish; when you are more experienced it may be worth trying to attend. The Royal Mail offer a range of services and discounts to bulk mailers (see Chapter 6).

Hanging on to a reasonable budget

Finally, having said that the marketing department budget is just one of many financial responsibilities of the company, it is certainly true that when times get hard, cutting the marketing budget is often considered the easiest way to reduce expenditure.

The best plan is to combat difficulties with information so you know why titles are selling badly and are making changes to market them more efficiently. Compare sales patterns of annual publications with the same period last year. Are any market changes responsible for the differences you see? If you are promoting through the post did any individual list perform badly? By mailing a new selection of different names you may be able to remedy the situation (although having had to mail twice to achieve your basic orders the gross margin will still be reduced). Telesales can tell you a great deal. Talk to the reps and customer services. Are products being returned because they do not meet the expectations of those they were marketed to? Is the offer unconvincing? Try another, or better still test one against another before you start and pick the best.

If cuts are the only option, the key skill is knowing which elements to axe while doing the least possible damage to sales. Understanding the reasons why particular promotions have either failed or succeeded will help you decide what to avoid in future, and how to plan better for next year. The very last elements you should cut are the regular tools of the trade: the advance information sheets and the catalogues on which so much of the publishing sales cycle depends.

12

Approaching Specific Interest Markets

I Selling books to public libraries

Few people realise the amount of time and attention public librarians devote to promoting books: from careful consideration of which fiction to buy to tracking down obscure non-fiction material that can be purloined from other branches. And they are devoted to maintaining these services. When county councils cut the book-purchasing budget or there are fresh rumours of plans to impose charges for loans, whereas the general public reacts for the most part with apathy, it is librarians who are vociferous in opposing any suggestion of cuts in public services.

The importance of librarians to publishing

Libraries spent £93 million on books in 1997–98. Although this is down from £112 million in 1994–95, it still represents around 5 per cent of UK publishers' home sales. Sales of some types of books are 60–80 per cent to public libraries (eg hardback fiction), almost 100 per cent in the case of large print titles. What is more, librarians undertake a wide range of book promotional activities, all designed to encourage people to read more books. Many publishers still know little about such initiatives. Here are a few examples.

- Bookstart was the 1982 brain child of Wendy Cooling of Children's Book Foundation at Book Trust. Set up as a scheme to introduce very young children to books, it is now operating nationally and has had extremely impressive results. Once they start school, children with early access to books do better in every subject and the sharing of books with adults plays an important part in their social development. Libraries were involved in this scheme from the very beginning: the pilot scheme in the Birmingham area benefited from an alliance of local library services and health visitors. Parents were presented with a free book, a poetry card, an invitation to join the local library and information about sharing books with babies. Sainsbury's are now major sponsors of this scheme.

- Hampshire run a fiction reading scheme whereby all first novels are read by teams of volunteer staff from County Library Headquarters in their spare time. The reader's comments are inserted in the front of the book ready for inspection by local branch librarians when they come to HQ in Winchester for their regular viewing of potential new stock. If they decide to take copies of titles that have been recommended by HQ in their libraries the books will be paid for centrally by headquarters, rather than coming out of their individual library new book budgets. In this way branch librarians are encouraged to stock unheard-of authors and to tempt their readers to try them; a terrific service to both the budding authors and their publishers.

- Every library authority in Britain and all 227 Asda stores took part in the Big Read promotion which was staged in May 1999 as part of the National Year of Reading. More than 1,000 Asda staff and librarians were trained to run reading events for families in branch libraries, stores and 120 mobile libraries stationed in Asda car parks. This was the biggest ever partnership between public libraries and the commercial sector, with the main aim of promoting books and reading.

- Ask in your local reference library for articles published on a specific topic and you may well be offered an online search through national databases to see what is available. You then have the chance to read them through the inter-library loan system. (Some libraries make a small charge for this service.)

- Children's librarians encourage younger members to acquire the habit of reading. Many offer a regular storytelling session for pre-school children and organise activities and quizzes during half-terms and school holidays. The children's borrowing sections are made as attractive as possible. Books are displayed too with an awareness of the readers' sensitivities: the cover design is apparently vital. Whereas girls will read a book that shows either boys or girls on the cover, boys like to see boys illustrated. School librarians spend most of their time promoting books and reading in schools.

- Fiction promotion in libraries is becoming increasingly widespread. Whereas at one time the only form of recommendation to readers was the 'just returned' shelving system, today libraries are actively promoting particular titles to readers. For example, Hampshire, Dorset and West Sussex, backed by the regional arts association Southern Arts, have been running a co-operative fiction promotion scheme called *Well Worth Reading* since 1988. The project takes a thematic look at fiction. Leaflets combine reviews of around 25 titles in a particular subject area, some by authors who are already well known, to create a sense of security, others by less familiar names. The promotions are immensely popular with the public and (as is evinced through co-operation with local booksellers) definitely result in extra bookshop sales. The scheme now finances itself by selling substantial amounts of promotional materials to other library authorities world-wide, and has received sponsorship from Waterstone's, The Arts Council, Virgin and many other organisations.
- It is now relatively commonplace for individual library authorities run book festivals and promote books through booklists on specific subject areas.

What gets borrowed

Here are the subject totals provided by the Library and Information Statistics Unit at the University of Loughborough. If you are involved in selling to the libraries market these are very interesting.

Table 12.1

	Percentage
Children's fiction	22.3
Children's non fiction	6.0
General fiction	21.0
General non fiction	21.3
Short stories, horror and humour	1.1
Historical fiction	3.1
War	1.2
Mystery and detective	12.8
Science fiction	0.1
Light romance	10.4
Westerns	0.7
Total	100.00

Falling loans

In recent years library loans have been falling. UK loans in 1997–98 were 501.2 million, down from 650 million in 1981; in 1994 they consisted of 55 per cent adult fiction and 20 per cent children's books. Loans per head of the population are running at 8.5 nationally, down from 11+ a decade ago, but loans in the UK are still high compared with many other European countries.

The possible reasons for the decline in loans are interesting. More accessible bookshops occupying prime retail sites (eg Waterstone's and Dillons) and publishers' initiatives to make books purchasable wherever the public has time and the inclination to spend (eg garage forecourts, garden centres and so on) have surely had an impact on the public's willingness to buy rather than borrow. Cuts in the book purchasing funds for libraries have also had an effect – readers can lose interest if new books by their favourite authors stop appearing on the shelves. Finally, perhaps the public has less time for reading these days due to the vast range of alternative distractions on offer that were not (widely) available 10 years ago, for example the Internet, interactive CD systems, the wide availability of videos and so on. With these competing attractions the meaning of words has also, significantly I feel, changed. I heard a parent in a playground recently suggesting to their child that they visit the library on the way home – it turned out they meant a video rental shop.

Librarians will tell you that among their regular users there is a preponderance of those who are at home for a part of the day: the retired, the unemployed and mothers with small children. Cuts in opening days and hours enforced by central budgetary restrictions have had an effect on the borrowing of these groups.

There are however some very interesting groups that spend *more* time in libraries. The National Centre for Research in Children's Reading has revealed that children from ethnic minorities, and in particular girls, make vastly more use of local and school libraries; ethnic minority girls are the largest group of borrowers from libraries (78.4 per cent of the sample borrowed very often or often, as against 45.6 per cent of the full 1996 survey).[1]

Librarians point out that their customers are today using libraries in new ways: local businesses as a wide-ranging resource for market information, job-seekers for the well stocked periodical collections, local historians for the specialist services available. All these activities result in active use of the library's resources but record no corresponding loans. A report on the future of libraries in 1995[2] made many exciting suggestions for the development of the library service but did not discuss in detail how it was all to be paid for. Without new funding many initiatives are doomed.

A further political development that has affected the libraries has been the reorganisation of local government. The removal of certain key centres of population from county responsibility and their establishment as independent 'unitary authorities' from April 1996 has made many of the purchasing authorities smaller. Thus Portsmouth and Southampton are now independent purchasing authorities rather than coming under Hampshire. This has undoubtedly reduced the scale of purchasing and consequent discounting, meant that more of the money destined for books is eaten up in duplicated administration costs, which leads to fewer titles being bought.

How big is the library market?

In the past publishers have known relatively little about the library world. There are very few job moves between the two professions and publishers have tended to take library sale for granted. But with budgets being cut and publishers struggling to sell, their mutual interests are undeniable.

Mailing list availability reveals the diminishing size of the market. IBIS (part of Mardev) provides the following in the UK and Eire, and the figures are for 1996 and 1999 and reveal how many libraries, and particularly the smaller ones, have already closed.

Table 12.2

	1996	1999
Major libraries (more than 200,000 volumes)	286	273
Medium public libraries (100,000–199,999 volumes)	390	370
Small public libraries (less than 100,000 volumes)	2926	2743

Another way to establish the main spenders is to look at the published statistics. Public libraries are buying books out of public money and so are accountable. The amount each local authority spends each year can be found in the annually published CIPFA statistics (see Appendix 4 for address).

Libraries used to be part of the Department of Education and Science. The responsibility for them then moved to the Department of National Heritage and now falls to the Department of Culture,

Media and Sport (DCMS). Many librarians speculate on how interested the DCMS is in libraries compared with high-profile initiatives such as dishing out lottery money and football.

Where do library budgets come from?

By Christmas each year most library authorities have drawn up the budget they require for the following year. How much is actually awarded to them to start spending the following April can depend on both demographic factors and the party in power: Conservative-controlled councils tend to spend less than Labour, Liberal and SNP.

The overall budget is subdivided into amounts to be spent on salaries and overheads, audio-visual requirements, online services and so on. Roughly a fifth goes to form the book fund, and this is further subdivided into amounts for reference books and for lending stock. Of the book fund the estimated allocation for the different types of stock purchased for one library authority[3] is as follows:

Table 12.3

	Percentage
Fiction	30
Lending non fiction	35
Children's	14
Reference (non-lending)	15

This is then further divided into amounts for the different libraries in the area, depending on the socio-economic profile of the region served and the type and rate of borrowing.

How librarians decide what to buy

There are a number of different information sources on new books and new authors to which librarians have access.

- They all read the *Bookseller* and rely heavily on the spring and autumn export editions. They read the library and literary press and know which authors have forthcoming titles. Reviews tend to come out too late to stimulate the initial ordering of new titles but can promote reordering, or mean a favourably reviewed author's subsequent title is well stocked.

- Library suppliers and the local bookshops from whom librarians buy books keep them in touch with forthcoming titles. Each week new books are sent to the county, borough or 'unitary authority' library headquarters by specialist library suppliers: these are known as 'approvals collections'. Different kinds of material come from different suppliers and the displays usually remain for around six weeks while local branch librarians view them and put in bids for the titles they would like to stock. The final order is amalgamated and placed by the area Acquisitions Officer (sometimes also called the Bibliographical Services Manager) with a variety of national and local suppliers.

  Rather than allocating specific titles to individual libraries a few authorities have adopted a policy of circulating area stock. Books are bought on the basis of an 'area structured fund' and all libraries in a particular region have access to them.

  Although the Acquisitions Officer will brief library suppliers on what the approvals collection should contain (for example, fiction from particular publishers, price not above or below certain amounts, specific titles requested) it is the library suppliers who put it all together; all at their own risk and thereby tying up a tremendous amount of capital. Since the demise of the Net Book Agreement libraries have been demanding greater discounts on the titles they order, in particular (and not unreasonably) on titles they see heavily discounted in the high street. This means there is less margin available to support services such as the approvals collection and today there is strong pressure by suppliers to offer libraries advance information on CD ROM instead. The CD ROM can not only give full bibliographical information but can often show the cover and sample pages in full colour.

- Librarians know what their readers want to borrow. This is based on both informal observation and statistical analysis. Any casual observer in a library will see that romantic fiction is very popular (roughly one eighth of all library loans[4]). It doesn't matter whether you group these titles alphabetically or by genre, avid readers look for the familiar format and titles they have not yet read. On the other hand, computerised issue systems, request schemes whereby readers can order titles from other libraries or put their name on a waiting list, and official monitoring such as PLR and published surveys by Book Marketing Limited (BML) which publishers and libraries can subscribe to, have provided accurate information on what readers want to borrow.

- Marketing material. Publishers who sell books to the library market circulate their seasonal catalogues and leaflets; some library suppliers compile their own catalogues. Once viewed, these are usually kept on file at library headquarters. Several publishers are now displaying attractive point of sale material in libraries.

How to present information to libraries

The one publication that the entire library profession reads is the *Bookseller*. *The Library Association Record* and *Public Library Journal* are widely seen too. Direct mail and catalogues are probably best addressed to the Acquisitions Officers in each of the different regional authorities (their names and addresses can be found in the annual *Directory of Acquisitions Officers*, a copy of which should be in your local reference library or library headquarters.) These are the people who are in a position to structure the composition of the approvals collection from which branch librarians chose their books. Librarians of small libraries simply do not have the time to read publishers' catalogues and rely on what is available to view.

Information to include in the copy

You should include all the main reasons for librarians to stock particular titles such as author reputation (reviews of previous titles), subject matter and readership, but it is vitally important that all this is backed up by the appropriate bibliographical information:

- Publication date
- Price
- Extent
- Size
- Format
- ISBN
- Series
- ISSN
- Illustrations, diagrams and tables: colour; black and white
- Is it a new or re-issued title?
- Binding: is the paper acid free and sewn?

- Is there an index?
- The time span for publishing part works.

An article by Paul Moorbath, in the *National Acquisitions Group Newsletter* in January 1990 confirmed librarians' reliance on the information publishers send out and the need for the details listed above.

Asked to rank selection aids in order of importance, the librarians put publishers' catalogues at the top of the list, ahead of review coverage and the availability of *British Books in Print*. Lack of price, accurate publication date and details of the intended audience were their chief grouses for individual title entries; several complained of catalogues lacking an index.

Public Lending Right

The concept behind the Public Lending Right Act of 1979 is simple. Authors earn their living through royalties on books sold, copies sold to libraries may have many readers but only one sale. PLR compensates the writer for these multiple borrowings. The funding comes from the public purse.

To receive payments authors must be registered on the PLR computer in Stockton on Tees. No author who died before 1982 is registered (hence no payments to Enid Blyton or Agatha Christie) but the estates of those registered authors who have died since then may still be credited. The money available is not large – £5 million in 1998–99 – and before any of it is distributed the cost of running the computerised sampling system on which the borrowing figures are calculated is deducted (13 per cent in 1998–99), although the costs of a new computer system were supported in 1998 through additional funding from the Secretary of State for Culture, Media and Sport. The balance is divided among the authors on the basis of an annually calculated rate per loan. This was 2.07p per loan in 1998–99 up to a maximum of £6,000 (this has been the maximum since 1989, received by 100 authors in 1998–99). The scheme does not apply in academic libraries and so authors of key texts that are so popular that they are only allowed out to readers within the building for a couple of hours at a time, are heavily disadvantaged. Nor does the scheme apply to the reference sections of public libraries, so many extensively used 'core stock' items such as books on local history are excluded from its research.

While no authors would pretend it has made them rich, it has made many feel valued – over 17,000 authors had their books lent out sufficiently often by libraries to generate a PLR payment in 1998–99.

> PLR is a life saver in a career of ups and downs – a continued source of satisfaction through some dark days.
>
> Nicola Thorne, romantic novelist

PLR has also provided a good deal of information on borrowing patterns. The feedback provided by the PLR team is extensively used in public libraries. This includes subject breakdowns, 'classic' authors lists, and comparisons of local, regional and national trends.

PLR – Most borrowed authors in UK public libraries, based on sample loans July 1997–June 1998

1. Catherine Cookson (12 of the top 20 most borrowed titles were hers)
2. Danielle Steel
3. Dick Francis
4. Josephine Cox
5. Ruth Rendell
6. Jack Higgins
7. Agatha Christie
8. Emma Blair
9. Terry Pratchett
10. Barbara Taylor Bradford
11. Virginia Andrews
12. Dean R Koontz
13. Rosamunde Pilcher
14. Maeve Binchy
15. Harry Bowling
16. Audrey Howard
17. Bernard Cornwell
18. Ellis Peters
19. Wilbur Smith
20. Mary Higgins Clarke

II Promoting academic and scientific titles

There has been a quiet revolution going on in British universities in recent years. If you are tasked with promoting to this market, it is important that you understand what has happened.

1. A huge increase in student numbers

Britain is now moving towards a continental model of mass education at higher level. The government wants a higher proportion of 18-year-olds in university education and the increase in student numbers is remarkable.

Table 12.4

Student:Staff Ratios

	1985–86	1995–96	Percentage increase '85–'95
Full and part-time students	592,000	1,291,595	+118
Full and part-time staff	69,900	109,082	+56
Students:staff ratio	8.47:1	11.84:1	+39.8

Source: Association of University Teachers, Paper and Pay Review 29.5.99 (www.aut.org).

The vast majority of students are now emerging with university degrees since the removal of the 'binary divide' (between universities and polytechnics).

2. The main job priority for academics is now research not teaching

As the above chart shows, the increase in student numbers has not been adequately compensated for by an increase in academic teaching time; indeed, the emphasis placed on teaching has never been lower. These days academics still give lectures but are encouraged to spend as much time as possible on their own research; tutoring is largely done by done by research assistants and postgraduate students. The overall result has been a sharp decline in academic mentoring, a reduction in the depth of undergraduate degrees and an increase in significance of MA/MSc.

In order to win promotion academics must publish their research. Lecturers with a lot of published research win points for the institutions they work for and higher funding as centres of excellence. This has led to the emergence of a premier league of universities with a strong research departments which are thus well placed to win further research funding.

3. Sharp decline in academics' standard of living and corresponding rise in resentment

Derisory pay; intolerable demands to teach, research and administrate all at the same time; students who cannot be failed, for fear of litigation.

Nigel Spivey reviewing *The University in Ruins* by Bill Readings,
Financial Times

The Dearing Report into higher education[5] recommended the appointment of an independent pay review committee to look into academic pay. That committee concluded that the remuneration of academic and academic-related staff had declined substantially in relation to comparable professions and recommended an increase of 20 per cent (in real terms) in salaries over the next few years. They were subsequently offered three per cent. There is great resentment within academic communities at the lack of value placed on their contribution, and at the time of writing their union is engaged in industrial action.

At the same time their job security has become increasingly fragile. Most new appointments are made on the basis of a rolling contract that must be reviewed after three or five years. If the university (or a particular course) is not paying its way, then staff can be laid off. Research assistants and research fellows seldom have any job security at all, and no identifiable career path. Over the past few years there has been a strong trend towards the 'casualisation' of the academic work force; today almost half are on part-time contracts.

What is more, departments are now required to bring income *into* the university, through carrying out research for industry and other parties willing to pay. There has been a massive growth in external income over the period (35.6 per cent of total income in 1985–86 to 46.9 per cent in 1995–96). Academics get no personal share of this external revenue (although they can often use a proportion in pursuit of their own research interests). Over the same period administrative demands on staff have grown substantially, often through governmental increases in workload, for example teaching quality assessment and the research assessment exercise.

> I left academia because I didn't fancy earning half of what a tube driver earns. But the career structure didn't really appeal to me either. I'd studied a fairly unusual subject – theoretical physics – which is at the cutting edge of science and attracts a lot of people who are very good. You would find 100 of the brightest people chasing just one or two academic jobs.
>
> Dr Jon Underwood, interview in *Guardian Higher*, 18 May 1999

4. Universities are not the top educational priority

Academics have lost the battle to persuade the government that additional spending on education should be directed their way. Governmental educational priorities are currently primary schools (notably the reduction of infant class sizes) and further education (post-16).

Academics lack the budget, both institutional and personal, to buy the equipment they need. Book purchasing by libraries has been cut back to the extent that only titles deemed absolutely essential by the course lecturers are bought (it follows that the librarian's role in selecting titles has been greatly reduced). Many departmental libraries rely on buying back student copies of key texts at the end of the academic year. Budgets for information technology can be particularly poor (for example £100 a year for an archaeology department of six staff).

When it comes to personal purchasing, as one lecturer put it:

> Book-buying is beginning to feel like a luxury. I have to be very, very sure that I want a personal copy of a book before I buy it. If I can, I review it for a journal and thereby get a free copy. If I can't get a review copy , but I can't justify £50 of my own money, I will see if I can get the library to buy it. And if that's not appropriate, I just do without – as often as not it will replicate what the author has written elsewhere and represents a search for HEFCE[6] points.

The same academic's annual travel allowance was £350, when one trip to London for an early meeting by train costs £81.

5. Students' indebtedness is now established

The student grant has gone; students now rely on loans to be repaid once their post-study remuneration reaches 85 per cent of average earnings (£17,784 up to 31 August 1999). This is having a knock-on effect on applications. Students are in general opting to stay closer to the parental washing machine and support base and there is a move away from the London colleges where accommodation is so expensive. There is very little money around for book buying.

This difficult position certainly offers publishers both opportunities as well as threats. The opportunities are:

- Because academics are keen for those on their courses to pass (the future of courses with low student numbers/poor pass rates is dodgy), a notable trend is the emergence of the single-book course. For the publishers who commission the right book from the right author, in a popular subject area, there is great deal of money to be made.
- While academics suspect there has been a reduction in applications from those from a background of low 'cultural capital' (ie generally low regard for education), and notably from 'returners' (those whose education was interrupted early, most usually to have a family) it is certainly true that students who do achieve places are the better resourced, with increased levels of financial support from parents. Such parents usually place a high emphasis on book purchase.
- Academics need to be published to get on. This creates a supply of authors eager to write and then to promote the titles they produce.

Where to start

Faced with the challenge of selling specialists something on their own discipline, about which you know next to nothing, publishers often try to couch their information in an elevated tone, sympathetic to lofty academia. Remember:

1. You don't have to develop a special way of writing

Academics get quite enough worthy prose from their students, and your information is best presented as simply as possible. When promoting to every other special interest group the essential requirement is to provide quick access to relevant information; academics should be treated in the same way.

So, avoid long sentences and paragraphs and complicated syntax. Never reprint a lengthy and highly complex advance notice drafted by the author or book's editor, assuming that once it reaches the right market, it will be understood. Remember that your title information will also be read by a range of other people who are not subject specialists: booksellers, reps, librarians and those standing in for academics on leave of absence or maternity leave. One further point, remember that English may not be the recipient's first language.

2.   Academics value the information they receive

Apart from receiving details of titles relating to their own research interests, academics prepare new courses and lectures for students. They draw up core and further reading lists for those taking them, balancing preference (what the students should buy to get the most out of the course) with realism (what they can realistically be expected to afford). In addition many have responsibilities for recommending titles to be purchased by college libraries and discussing student requirements with local bookshops.

All this means that they are very interested to know what is being published in their subject, and that they value what you send. This has been confirmed by several studies of academics to the promotional material they receive through the post.[7]

The ordering of academic titles through the Internet

Studies of academic ordering patterns repeatedly found that although academics found direct marketing a very useful way of acquiring information, they still preferred to order titles through a bookshop. In other words, academics used direct marketing as a medium for amassing information but not necessarily as an ordering facility.

Since then, there has been an explosion in Internet access and it seems that academics have embraced the new technology with particular enthusiasm – most get free access through university facilities. This has had a dramatic effect on their buying and browsing habits. Ross Beadle, Marketing Director of the Internet Bookshop (owned by W H Smith) estimates that at least 50 per cent of their sales are of academic books, whereas the academic market is around 7 per cent of the total book market. To date they have sold around 900,000 different titles not stocked by the big wholesalers, thus functioning for the academic community as a vast special order facility.

This constitutes a serious threat to academic bookshops. If academics have become used to ordering hard-to-find titles that are seldom stocked by college bookshops through the Internet rather than via their local bookshop, and receiving them quickly and at a discount, it will surely not be long before they start ordering textbooks in the same way, and encouraging their students to do the same.

And the more rarefied the academic subject (with low print runs and high prices), or the more expensive the titles in that area (eg legal textbooks costing up to £100 each), the greater will be the incentive to buy through the Internet and receive a discount

The real danger for academic bookshops is that although academics have the power to recommend, it is students that constitute the bulk of the market. To date student access to the Internet has been quite difficult, the low availability of credit cards to the students being the main obstacle. But as the stigma associated with indebtedness for students has now gone, and parents are having to guarantee their student offsprings' spending, it will surely not be long before more students have credit cards. Once wider student Internet access is achieved, the sale of textbooks through this medium will deprive academic bookshops of the main revenue that supported their stocking of marginal titles with very low sales potential.

Academic publishers are now in many cases actively promoting titles to academics via their own Web sites and finding that response rates are very high.

What kind of books do academics buy?

In general academic purchases fall into several types:

- Books they use for teaching and recommend to students for purchase, ie textbooks.
- Summary books and study aids.
- Books they recommend for further reading through the library or use for their own research ie academic monographs.

- Journals. For advice on how to promote journals and periodicals see section iv of this chapter. But note right now that one of the most pressing reasons for academics subscribing to new journals is the opportunity they offer to be published themselves.

1. Textbooks

Textbooks are promoted to academics teaching at universities, and colleges in the hope that they will be adopted, ie appear on the reading list that accompanies each course as an essential manual and be purchased in large numbers by both the students taking the course and the libraries serving them.

Promotions of textbooks are generally geared to getting a sample (or 'inspection') copy of the new book into the academic's hand. Each new academic year the local bookshops that serve college populations ask academics for details of what they will be recommending to students and the numbers likely to be taking the courses. They then stock copies according to their experience of what will sell: what the libraries will take, how many students will share a copy, and how many will have the motivation or cash to buy a copy of their own. These are stocked ready for the start of term.

If the title is adopted and quantities duly bought through the bookshop the academic may usually keep the sample sent.

When is the best time to mail academics in order to get adoptions?
Mailing the academic market is less time-specific now that different institutions organise their time in different ways. For example, there are traditional three-term years, three-term/two-semester years and two-semester years. You should send advance information on forth-coming titles with an inspection copy request card as soon as you have it, but always back this up with a realistic idea of when the title will be published. There is nothing more annoying for the academic than planning to change the key course book only to be told it is not available until half way through the first teaching term. If this has been their experience of your house, they will be wary of adopting your titles in future.

Be aware that most academic departments encompass a very wide range of individual subject interests. If budget restrictions mean you are mailing the head of department only (rather than all lecturers) your information should motivate the head to pass it on to the right person or circulate to all possibly interested. Try putting a circula-tion list box on the front of the leaflet.

Distribution of free copies

You may decide it is worth distributing a number of copies of a new textbook free to key academics without requiring them to recommend it or show how many copies have been bought as a result. Likely recipients include heads of department where particularly large numbers of students may buy the book, or key respected academics within the book's subject area who may respond with a favourable quotation that you can use in your publicity material.

Some academics are well aware of their key role in the profitability of textbook publishing. If you look after a stand at an exhibition or conference you may have several soliciting free copies on the basis of the large student numbers they have it in their power to recommend to. To provide every university department with a free copy in the hope of securing sales would erode a book's basic profit margin, so be careful with your largesse.

2. Summary books and study aids

Sales of these titles have become particularly strong in recent years, to the detriment of the standard (and it has to be said generally longer) course texts and background reading.

These titles are a guide to passing exams. They are revision books that list, in summary form, all the key information candidates must have at their fingertips to pass. With students desperate to pass in order to stay on the course, and academics equally keen to maintain student numbers to keep the course running and themselves in a job, such books have a widening market.

3. Research monographs

The scholarly monographs promoted to academics are often the result of a PhD or other long-term research project. Markets for these titles are necessarily small and most of the sales will be single copy; to interested individuals or libraries. Print runs and promotion budgets therefore tend to be small too.

Although these titles may also end up on reading lists, they will usually be listed as 'further reading'. As multiple sales are unlikely, inspection copies are not offered; rather, they are generally available 'on approval'. After a period for examination they must either be returned in good condition or paid for.

Although marketing budgets are small (around £700–£1,000 per title is fairly average) markets are highly specific and easy to target;

extensive and costly mailing campaigns are in general not required. It also pays to capitalise on all additional paths to the potential market: with a print run of 500, sales of 200–300 can recover the costs; selling a further 50–100 gets a good margin and profits on sales above that can be very substantial.

How to get the best value out of a small budget

- Get your timing right. As much as 60% of the first year sales for an academic monograph can occur in the month of publication. If you are late promoting the title, sales may never recover.
- The standard in-house procedures for book promotion are particularly important: ensure the title is listed in catalogues for the season in which it is due to be published and make sure that the advance notice is ready to appear at the right time containing up-to-date information.
- Similarly, deploy all possible 'silent salesmen': make sure the book is featured in *Books in Print* (Whitakers), the export editions of the *Bookseller* and individual booksellers' catalogues, and that the British Council have information for relevant exhibitions that they mount overseas.
- The best use of the marketing budget is probably the circulation of a small leaflet or flyer (one-third A4 is about the cheapest you can produce). Don't spend too much on production of the leaflet itself. Instead, concentrate on targeting the market, through mailing appropriate lists of academics, distributing a loose insert to the subscribers of relevant journals, circulating at specialist meetings and so on.
- Costs of producing small leaflets need not be great (see the hints in Chapter 5 on design and print). You can make the possible size of orders even larger if you list a couple of related titles on the back (journals too if you publish in the same area). The Internet provides an inexpensive means of disseminating information. Ensure your leaflets cross refer academics to your Web site – and of course make sure your Web site includes information on all forthcoming projects. E-mail academics to tell them about new publications of interest (see Chapter 7).
- Co-operative promotions. Wherever possible pool budgets for several related titles and mount a thematic promotion to more of the market. Send your material out in shared mailings when you can (for example to libraries). Is it worth organising co-operative advertising for all the titles in your list; perhaps taking a page in

The Times Higher Educational Supplement twice a year to detail all the books that are forthcoming for that season? Most academic monographs have self-explanatory titles and authors well known in their field, so interest can be aroused at a glance from those reading.

- Make maximum use of free publicity: reviews, feature articles and so on.
- Help the author to gain personal sales: provide copies of the advance notice for circulation to colleagues and ask for details of forthcoming conferences at which leaflets could be inserted in delegates' packs. Is a co-operative bookstall or exhibition being organised? If not, does the topic or relevance of the conference warrant you organising one yourself?
- Are there any specific interest groups that offer the possibility for 'special sales': learned and professional societies and associations who may promote to their members?

Writing promotional copy for books you don't understand

It is not uncommon to find employees with an arts background facing the seemingly insuperable challenge of promoting lists of high-level science and medicine to experts in these fields.

So how do you prepare copy for leaflets? Before you try to decipher an incomprehensible blurb provided by your editorial department, think about what the market needs to know about the book you are promoting.

Academics are more interested in the treatment of a subject and the up-to-dateness of the content than either publisher reputation or the speed of supply. Asked to rank other information needed in order of importance, repeated surveys have confirmed the following list (in order), and this shows what your priorities should be.

- List of contents
- Brief summary of the main features
- Detailed description of the contents
- Designated readership and level
- Information on the author
- Extracts from review coverage
- Sample pages
- Photograph of the cover.

Table 12.5 *Example of how to get good value for money from a small budget*

New title on Ophthalmology, hardback price £42.50
print run 500, marketing budget c.5 per cent of sales: £1,050
rights: worldwide excluding North America

	Quantity UK	ROW	Price (£)
Loose insert in relevant journal one	150	650	80.00
Loose insert in relevant journal two	100	240	54.00
Loose insert in relevant journal three	116	609	116.88
Loose insert in relevant journal four	133	513	100.00
Mailing lists of:			
UK academics coded for ophthalmology	376		
UK libraries with a section on ophthalmology	640		
Stock of leaflet for author	200		
Stock of leaflet for exhibition use	200		
Reps and other in house use	200		
Total leaflets required	4,085		
Print	4,100		
Copy provided to designer on disk, design and artwork for 2pp A5 flyer			120.00
Printing single colour on 100gsm opaque paper			96.00
Instant print for 1,000 letters 2pp A4			45.00
List rental			132.00
Postage @ 19p			193.04
Labels			16.30
Fulfilment			30.50
Envelopes			30.00
Total expenditure			1,013.72
Balance to spend/save			36.28

The last item always scores low – I suspect few professionals would admit to being influenced by the look of the jacket – but I still try to feature a book-shot if budget permits. Academics are book lovers and a well-produced item will always win admirers (and possibly new authors). What is more, if it is a substantial tome that you are promoting, a picture conveys both value for money and the impressiveness of the publication.

You should check and double check first that the information in the following list is there and second that it is correct:

- Author
- Title
- Series
- Publisher
- Publication date
- Page extent
- Illustrations
- ISBN
- Binding
- Size.

Disentangle long and difficult blurbs

If the first information you receive on a forthcoming academic title is a long and complicated essay by the book's editor or author, the temptation to reproduce it whole in your leaflet rather than try to simplify it can be enormous, particularly if you have no inkling of the subject matter and are short of time. Remember:

- Most academics can tell by looking at the title and contents whether or not a title is relevant to them, so a detailed list of the contents is always preferable to a long description.
- *The more you become familiar with the difficult blurb, the more you will come to think you too know what it means.* Your first reaction is the one to hang on to. Remember there will be many other non-specialists who need to understand the key selling benefits too (librarians, booksellers, your own reps and so on).

Where to start? Read the text, looking out for main verbs and key clauses. Try dividing up long sentences, lifting out the main features and highlighting them as bullet points. Divide up long paragraphs so the copy looks more readable. Explain to the editor (or author) what you are trying to do and ask them to check your results.

Avoid starting your copy with a general sentence or paragraph: they are usually more concerned with demonstrating your under-standing of the subject matter than the academic's need to know. If it helps you to get started by all means write one, but delete it once you have finished; your arguments should hold water without it.

Try to answer the following questions:

- If it is a new edition, what has changed since the previous one? Do you have factual information on the number of items in the index and the number of chapters completely rewritten?
- If it is a textbook what course is it for? For what level of students?
- Who has reviewed or endorsed it and in what? Your own opinion will carry far less weight than that of the academic's peer group.
- Who is it by? Include qualifications, current position, special areas of research that are relevant to the subject and book.
- Have you made it clear whether the book is a collection of the writings of several authors or an entirely new book? Make sure you distinguish conference proceedings as just that.
- How does the recipient get in touch with the publisher? Is there a reply card for requesting inspection copies; a telephone or fax number or e-mail address for ordering?
- How will the recipient who wants to order pay for the title? Is an institutional sale more likely than one to an individual?
- What payment facilities and what guarantees do you need to offer?
- Is your copy too 'hard sell'? It is a practice best avoided: it will not be convincing and probably makes the recipient suspicious.

Get rid of all academic 'publishingese' – words that are familiar within the industry but sound bland and unconvincing to the rest of the world. Particular words to look out for are 'prestigious', 'unique' and 'completely comprehensive'. Instead, try defining these terms and explaining precisely how they apply to the product you are promoting, and you will find your description is far more convincing. The following example of academic publishing jargon ironically describes an updated textbook on communications:

> It is written in a clear and accessible style by well known authors who have used a new streamlined organisation and a fresh teaching style.

Academic jargon is more problematic. There may be certain words that you have to include (eg 'postmodern'), as a flag to show that the book deals with current issues!

As a final check, have the editor, or author, check what you produce.

An example of unscrambled copy

The following copy reached me in a publisher's catalogue. The author details have been changed.

Cultures of Consumption
Commerce, Masculinities and Social Space in Late Twentieth Century Britain
Geoff Deade
Cultures of Consumption examines the construction of images of masculinity and the effect they have on identity, sexuality and sexual politics. It opens with the public face of male sexuality in consumerism, as represented in the street fashions of hip-hop, rap and house, which encourage men to see themselves sexually. This is followed by an exploration of a range of influences from black and white culture, where men are recreated in the postmodern landscape of the city.

Geoff Deade captures the energy and intertextuality of urban, postmodern culture and those who create its subcultures. He explores the ironies of class, colour and sexuality which he sees represented in it.

March 1999, hardback £45, paperback £15

This is a wonderful example of academic jargon; using words that will be familiar to subject specialists but could arouse no more than 'switch off' from those not similarly enlightened, but who nevertheless make buying decisions about the book.

I would certainly recommend a more readily understood title or subtitle – the book's major concern seems to be masculinity and that is hardly evident from these. Starting the book blurb with a repetition of the book title is both repetitive and boring; it's far more engaging to begin with a question. Here is my suggested rewrite:

Cultures of Consumption
How men are seen in late 20th century Britain
Geoff Deade
Where does today's popular image of men come from? And how does it affect both how men see themselves, and relations between the sexes?

This radical new book begins with an examination of the male image in advertising and how this has encouraged men to see themselves sexually. An exploration of a whole range of influences follows, from both black and white culture, drawing out issues of class, colour and sexuality. The result is a crucial study that reflects the ever-changing face of urban culture and sub-culture.

'An exploration of postmodern issues that is both subtle and dynamic. Fascinating.' David Evans, Silversmiths College, London

March 1999, hardback £45, paperback £15

Notes

This is a title that would feature on the recommended reading part of a book list; it is not a textbook. The copywriter thus must try really hard to get the title noticed. A quotation is a particularly good ploy for attracting attention. Pre-publication, there will be no reviews to quote, so your best option is to find an academic teaching in a department well known for courses/research in this area. In this case, the title is one of a series, and so the series editor could usefully be asked to provide an overview of the title's significance.

Sending information to academic librarians

You probably won't be able to afford the preparation of different types of information for different recipients but it is worth bearing in mind their different priorities and the best means to reach them.

Academic librarians rely heavily on written sources for information about new books – compared with academics they have less opportunity to browse in bookshops or see books at conferences. For set texts and background reading they rely almost entirely on the recommendations of the academics. For journals, purchasing decisions are generally made by a committee, because different departments' needs must be traded against each other. Some academic departments hold formal regular library stocking meetings; others bump into each other in the corridor and discuss. Some departments allow individual academics to recommend titles according to their share of the overall departmental budget. The great majority of university and college libraries buy through library suppliers and other wholesalers.

The self-study market

Lastly, don't forget the adult education market for academic books: students who either study in their spare time or combine learning with full-time jobs or even holidays (there has been a huge growth in holidays that combine free time with some form of studying in recent years). These students tend to be highly motivated and have larger disposable incomes to spend on books. Their spending can also go on over a number of years: studying part-time, it usually takes at least six years to get an Open University degree.

Reaching them can be problematic. Adult education centres are reluctant to pass on names and addresses of their teaching staff. Some of the teachers are full- or part-time school staff, others are retired professionals. It may be worth your arranging for the delivery of copies of your catalogues to larger adult education centres, asking your reps for local feedback or perhaps trying to contact the teachers through space advertising in relevant publications.

There are a variety of initiatives to build up mailing lists of potential book buyers from the ranks of those who are studying whilst working, a very profitable sector of which are those studying for an MBA while holding down a full-time job: they have the money to buy and the motivation to get on and complete the qualification.

III *Selling to educational markets*

Educational publishers produce materials for sale to schools: courses and textbooks; background reading and teachers' notes; and audio-tapes, video, computer software and other teaching aids.

Most publishers concentrate on producing texts and course materials for the major curricular areas. The long-term investment needed for this means that the major players in the educational market tend to be specialist publishing divisions within larger companies who can provide the funding necessary (eg Heinemann is part of Reed International; HarperCollins is part of Rupert Murdoch's News International). Smaller companies tend to specialise in specific market areas.

Getting a title widely adopted in schools can take a long time. Teachers need to evaluate sample copies of new material, perhaps to try them out in the classroom and discuss the results with their colleagues, headteacher or local school advisers. Once the selection has been made and the material adopted they will not be able to afford to change horses. But for the publisher who can invest time and money in promoting texts for adoption, the long term rewards can be substantial: a profitable course of reprinting, new editions and the publication of related materials can be embarked upon.

How big is the market? Figures for the number of schools are as follows:

Table 12.6

Nursery	1,685
Primary	23,213
Secondary	4,435
Independent	2,501
Special	1,518
Pupil referral units	333

Source: Department for Education and Employment, published in Education and Training Statistics for the UK, 1998 edition, £14.95 from HMSO

There are nearly 10 million pupils in full- or part-time schooling (public and private sector, ages 2–19).[8] Each year around 2,000 new titles come out but much of the educational market value is in the sale of reprints and new editions.

As a percentage of the 1997 market, the schools sector consisted of 18 per cent (as compared with consumer sector 75 per cent and academic and professional sector 7 per cent). The overall value of the school and ELT book market was £210 million in 1997.[9]

Recent changes in the educational market

In recent years there has been a huge change in the priorities and responsibilities of government education policy and a great deal of consequent restructuring.

The National Curriculum (NC), first introduced by the Education Reform Act of 1988, was piloted in 1990 and fully implemented in schools by 1995. Broadly speaking, the idea behind the NC is that children all over the country of the same age should be learning the same things. The parameters of learning are set out for teachers and parents, making teachers more accountable to their pupils and giving interested parents a clearer idea of the academic level their child should be at. Children are fully monitored by their teachers and there is a comprehensive formal testing system to gauge pupils' progress. Parents have access to all written records of the child's performance. At the same time, all schools are now subject to a thorough review by Ofsted every four years and teachers themselves have regular assessments of their own performance.

Teaching is centred on three core areas of the curriculum (maths, English and science) supported by the study of foundation subjects (history, geography, French, art, music, design and technology, and physical education). A cross-curricular approach encourages the teaching of the same topics from different subject viewpoints, so the child's general understanding is enhanced.

The main complaint about the NC has been from those required to deliver it: the logistical burden involved. The administrative tasks imposed on teachers are onerous and some would say detrimental to good teaching; a plan must be produced for every 15 minutes of 'contact' (teaching) time and there has been little guidance on the practicalities of what to do with the other 34 children whilst the 35th is being assessed. Class sizes have continued to rise over the period, although the Labour government has made the reduction of infant classes to 30 children a priority. Many teachers complain that the huge increase in record keeping is of dubious relevance and that the tests did not teach them anything they did not know already. The league tables that resulted from the assessments were over-simplistic (there was no weighting for local socio-economic conditions) and have, in any case, have become a political football.

But as time goes by, a new generation of teachers is coming into the profession and the percentage of those who remember life before the NC will inevitably decline.

The second major change in education has been the implementation of Local Management of Schools (LMS), whereby headteachers receive from their local education authorities the responsibility for managing an annual budget to fund everything – staff, books, stationery and other costs. How much they receive depends on complicated equations based on the number of children in the school. How much they actually spend, and on what, is decided after discussion between the head and the school governors (an enormous increase in the latter's powers). A further option has been introduced for schools to become, in effect, independent state schools, receiving their funding direct from the Department for Education and Employment.

How does all this affect book publishers?

While the curriculum is laid down by the government, UK schools are free to choose from the range of commercially published material available; there is no 'centrally approved list' of texts. Publishers have had to develop new materials in response to government-inspired curriculum changes and competition to have their particular materials adopted is fierce. What most publishers are observing is more demand for books from schools but less money to buy them.

While there has been substantial extra money from the new Labour government (in 1998 and 1999 special aid to schools has amounted to almost £140 million, an increase in expenditure of over 70 per cent) the vast majority has gone to primary schools to fund materials for the literacy programme. Is this enough? A recent research study for the Educational Publishers Council by publishing consultant Keith Nettle contends that funds needed for books to support the literacy hour in a primary school with two form entry might run to four times the figure allocated. The Numeracy Strategy launched in March 1999 will need an additional £8,000 per primary school to provide pupils with the books they need.

Further up the school age, textbooks continue to be underfunded. A recent survey from Keele University found that half of secondary school students have to share books in class and that two thirds of them cannot take books home for homework. 'Class sets' now routinely comprise one between two and a Head of English commented:

> Some schools have to buy the £1 edition of a play that gives you the words and very little else. Some schools can't even afford that and download Shakespearean texts from the Internet and exist on photocopying.

What is more, the book spend is no longer ring-fenced; LMS allows funds freer movement within schools' budgets according to individual priorities. So book acquisitions is one budgetary area available for cutting when contingency planning leads to increased stringency. For example, it is common to hear of schools attempting to save teachers' jobs by cutting back on maintenance and teaching materials.

Yet part of an Ofsted inspection involves a report on available books, materials and resources for learning. It would require a change in the law in the UK to make books chargeable to parents, but there are plenty of precedents for this in other European countries. For example in Ireland textbooks are bought almost exclusively by parents. (On the other hand, where books are bought by parents, a thriving second-hand market also exists, and this can result in strong parental pressure on schools not to change texts; which in turn means publishers find it hard to introduce new books.)

Computer materials

Whilst the average expenditure on pupils in the UK is just £13 per primary pupil and £20 per secondary pupil, the picture for software publishers is more encouraging:

> Today's politicians tend to be bewitched by the magic of the new information technology. It is much easier to persuade them of the need for computers than for books.[10]

In recent years a number of government initiatives have been established to get computers into schools with funding earmarked for that purpose. The Labour Government has allocated £100 million over the next three years for electronic content for the National Grid for Learning. Maintenance costs for the hardware eat into other areas of the budget and there is the ongoing need for software. The Internet is already being tapped for texts in some schools, and there are reports from teachers of a growing band of parents who use it to help their children with their homework.

How teachers decide to spend their money

The good news for book publishers is that teachers continue to see books as the main agents of the school curriculum. What is more, they are for the most part very diligent in determining which published materials will be best for their school, trialing their hunches in the classroom before major capital expenditure is made.

Headteachers and departmental heads may talk to the local advisory staff and their colleagues in other schools. In most schools or departments, areas of priority for spending are outlined, perhaps at the end of a school year. Publishers' catalogues are rigorously checked for price comparisons of both installing new materials and the renewable costs of replacing items that can only be used once, such as workbooks. Discussions – and lobbying – over what to buy take place in staff meetings. There is an increased concern with getting value for money and teachers respond to the possibility of saving money on what they need as they would to any consumer offer – with interest.

Some schools have very well organised PTAs (Parent–Teacher Associations) who organise fundraising. Although this can raise valuable sums to eke out the annual budget, PTA money tends to be spent on more high-profile projects than the provision of textbooks, for example school trips, swimming pools or resources for the computer room. This view may change as book provision becomes demonstrably poorer – interestingly in Ireland recently a substantial sum of money was given for school library books from the National Lottery.

How publishers keep in touch with the market

Good educational publishers need to keep up-to-date with a lot of different trends in education: governmental educational initiatives, predictions of future demographic developments, and new practices and fashions in teaching. They frequently employ editorial and subject advisers to scout developments and spot good teacher-produced materials being used in schools (the genesis of many a good textbook). They talk to local education authority subject advisers, school inspectors, examiners and lecturers in teacher training colleges, and attend exhibitions and meetings. They also keep in touch with their sales managers and visit schools with the reps to hear at first hand how their materials are being received. They know exactly what their competition is producing, and can estimate market share.

If all this information is being brought in-house, find out how much you can get access to. Start reading the educational press. Most of the quality daily papers have an education feature once a week and you should be aware too of how the tabloids report educational issues. It is worth subscribing to *The Times Educational Supplement* as well as association journals for teachers of specific subjects that are particularly relevant to you (for example *The School Science Review*, published by the Association for Science Education, is essential reading for science publishers). It is also worth keeping in touch with the relevant union and teacher association publications.

How materials are ordered by schools

More and more schools are ordering their materials direct from publishers. The latter have been approaching them with special offers, often made at specific presentations to teachers. LMS has made schools determined to get the best possible value for money from their budgets.

Schools may prefer a more individual service from booksellers but low trade discounts (average 10 per cent on textbooks) can make servicing these orders uneconomic. The wholesale market for school book supply has been going through a very difficult period and for many such firms book sales are now negligible; they supply a whole range of other goods. (For further information see Chapter 1.)

How to reach the market

There are a number of well established methods for promoting to educational markets:

- Mailings – to schools, advisers and so on
- Representation within schools
- Despatch of inspection, approval and free copies
- Web sites and e-mailings
- Mounting displays at exhibitions and conferences
- Promotion through teachers' centres
- Promotion to school advisers
- Space advertising
- Free publicity
- Sales overseas.

Mailings

When to mail? State schools receive their annual budgets at the start of the new financial year on April 1st. Educational publishers therefore tend to send their main information (usually their catalogues) at the start of the calendar year when teachers are considering how to spend the next year's budget.

This can be followed up with mailings at other times of the year, usually March (just before the budget arrives) and September (to coincide with the new school year ahead). Have a look at the list of dates for co-operative mailings to schools offered by any mailing house and you will see when publishers like to contact schools.

What to send?

Primary publishers usually produce an annual catalogue in full colour, and follow this up with specific leaflets on major courses and materials mailed during the course of the year. Most secondary publishers produce a series of individual subject catalogues, one for each curricular area in which they publish and a complete catalogue listing everything they produce. Again, these are followed up with specific promotions on major works. Extra stock of everything produced should be sent to the reps visiting schools for them to hand out as required.

Whom to send to?

Primary publishers usually send their material to the headteacher or head of subject (all available by name from list rental companies specialising in this market).

Post addressed to the headteacher is routinely opened by the school secretary and passed over. After a quick look through – and perhaps a short note to the subject coordinator involved if something looks particularly interesting – the catalogue will be stored along with the material from other publishers in the staff room or the head's office until the time comes for deciding how much to spend and on what.

In secondary schools the overall budget is divided between the various departments and it is the departmental heads who have responsibility for spending. Specific mailings can be addressed directly to them (again names are available from list rental companies), but for the general despatch of catalogues in January publishers often send a package consisting of separately marked items for different departmental heads to the school secretary, together with a letter asking her to divide up the contents as appropriate. This is obviously considerably cheaper.

When targeting information you have to bear in mind the different needs and priorities of those within schools who will benefit from your materials, and who may, or may not, be involved in the decision to purchase. The financial responsibility may be that of the headteacher or head of department, but it is the classroom teachers who have to make the material work. You do not know how much consultation will be involved so your material should stress all the benefits you offer to the various interested parties. For example, a new maths course available to primary schools could offer the headteacher the benefits of cost effectiveness, efficiency, longevity, satisfied teachers and classes. The class teacher meanwhile may appreciate the practical benefits of your material working well with mixed ability classes so that all children can be occupied on the same material at the same time, leaving the teacher free to concentrate on individual needs and problems.

You have the choice whether to send your material yourself (bearing all the costs of postage and despatch) or to join with others and mail co-operatively (which is cheaper). Schools tend to say they don't care how the promotional material arrives, but if a catalogue reaches the school on its own it is perhaps more likely that a teacher will sit down and browse through straight away. Most people would be daunted by the simultaneous arrival of four – or more – catalogues and put off looking through them until later. On the other hand, the fact that all publishers tend to send their material at the same times of year could adversely affect this theory. If you do decide on a co-operative mailing:

- Find out who else is to be included in the pack. There are bound to be certain of your major competitors with whom you do not wish to join hands as you arrive in schools.
- Do specify a position within the pack. If the mailing house is using plastic envelopes find out if your catalogue can go on the outer edge.
- Don't forget other potentially interested parties, for example teacher training colleges, subject advisers, school suppliers who may stock and promote your titles, teachers centres and so on. You can either rent the lists or build your own.

Preparing your promotional material for sending to schools
What are teachers interested in? From my research, three major factors emerged:

1. National Curriculum (NC) relevance. Appropriate and attractive material, developed by teachers for real teaching needs will always attract attention.
2. Value for money. Schools are short of money and there are long discussions at staff meetings over what to buy, concentration improved by the knowledge that whatever is selected prevents further spending in that subject area for a number of years. Special offers and money-saving gambits on quality materials undoubtedly attract attention.

It follows that you should highlight all the special offers and promotions that you are making available to schools: library packs that incorporate a discount, starter packs for courses or an inspection copy system that can provide teachers with free copies of books. Similarly, lay out complete information on pricing and availability in a clear and consistent way. If you are promoting a scheme and the cost of installing yours is less than that of your competitors provide installation and running costs. (Your reps may appreciate an expanded version of this with item by item comparisons for use when they are discussing prices in schools.)

3. Teacher support materials. Whereas the NC laid down *what* should be taught, it largely did not lay down *how* (schools have to set out their own policies on how each subject is going to be taught based on NC policy). Back-up materials for teachers who spend increasing amounts of their time recording and assessing, and therefore have less time for actual lesson preparation, are thus increasingly important.

Other hints when preparing information for teachers

- Bear in mind that teachers, like every other category you try to sell to, are short of time. Make your promotional information easy to read and use.
- Indicate the level at which the material is aimed clearly and consistently. In catalogues I feel the best way to achieve this is to have a series of 'running heads' along the top or perhaps down the side of the page so that the teacher can see at any one time the subject and age range of the material being looked at. Repeat the information, with any additional relevant details, under the individual title entry (eg header: 14–16; book entry: textbook for GCSE and similar courses).
- Highlight what is new. Teachers are interested in new materials for new needs. If they have been in teaching for a while and worked in several schools they probably know your backlist already; stress what they won't be familiar with.
- Mark series as such. When considering how to spend the budget, teachers are in general more interested in complete series that can cater for pupils over a number of years than one-off books that require a hunt for new materials once the final chapter has been reached. Even if the series you are promoting is new and you have only two or three proposed covers of the first few stages available, draw a diagram indicating where the

different stages will fit in; show planned materials by outlining covers. It will attract attention to a major new series.

- Illustrate as much as possible. Use covers, illustrations from the books and specimen pages. Make the specimen pages large enough to read: it is better to have one that can be read than half a dozen that require a free magnifying glass to be mailed with every catalogue.

- In catalogues include a contents list and an index; both make it easier to find information in a hurry. On the contents page it is also a good idea to list new titles and provide page references. Some publishers produce new book supplements which appear in the centrefold of the catalogue; copies of these can be usefully run on for use at exhibitions or insertion in mailings.

- Follow the principles of direct mail and include a letter with your catalogue. Some publishers put a letter from the subject editor (and occasionally a photograph) on the inside front cover of the catalogue, and research shows it gets read. Print it at an angle to attract attention and make sure you add a signature. This can be a very useful place to remind teachers that you are interested in *their* suggestions for publication, which always bonds your interests.

- Make it easy for recipients to reply. Include freepost inspection copy request cards. Put them on a separate sheet or an extension of the back cover of the catalogue rather than the back cover itself: teachers are reluctant to destroy books, even promotional ones. Perforate where the tear has to be made to detach them. Include a stock list/order form in case schools have difficulty in ordering and a card asking for a representative to visit the school.

- Make your information user-friendly. Include information on how particular schemes are working in certain schools, quotes from other teachers on the benefits of your materials, details on the progress of new materials under development. You are selling to a very specific market; write about what interests them.

Representation within schools

In the struggle to get your materials adopted in schools, the reps who visit them are immensely valuable. The feedback in terms of sales figures and cards returned from mailings is largely impersonal, it is the reps who get the eyeball-to-eyeball reactions to your pricing, subject coverage, durability of format and so on.

You may have a team of your own, or employ the services of external agency. The sales manager who organises the reps' activities won't want to set up a separate and time-consuming chain of command, whereby a host of additional people receive reports, but do make the most of your contact with them. You should get the chance to talk to them at sales conferences. If you can, arrange to go out visiting schools for a day with them. You *will* cramp their style: most reps value their independence and don't like being listened to. Make the most of the opportunity and learn from their swift delivery of sales benefits; there is not time to pass on all the background information you may consider relevant. It's a very useful lesson in copywriting.

After only a couple of calls you will find the reaction of teachers depressingly similar: they have no money; would like to order but can't; what's the point of looking? It can all be a very salutary lesson to budding educational marketing managers who spend most of their day thinking up bullet points on product benefits rather than understanding the practicalities of funding materials in schools.

Visits to secondary schools are usually made after appointments have been set up; display materials and sample copies are carried in for presentation during morning and lunchtime breaks, preferably in the staffroom. What the reps carry has become more complex in recent years. They travel in estate cars loaded with display boards, posters and boxes full of inspection copies.

After the lunch break reps will often call on a primary school, hoping for 15 minutes with the headteacher, or head for a teachers' centre to lay on an after-school meeting when products can be demonstrated in greater detail.

Many houses have used the difficult market as the justification for upping their sales effort; requiring reps to demonstrate products rather than just represent them, sometimes over a series of consecutive visits. The stakes between winning and losing adoptions in schools are so high that detailed explanations of products by the reps (often ex-teachers themselves) after hours are increasingly common. Teachers can be asked from a variety of different schools in an area, perhaps with an editor in attendance to explain the background to the new scheme. Similarly many schools have been involved in the development and piloting of new NC materials; the publishers not only demonstrate their commitment to practical and workable products but build up long term loyalty.

Reps are usually briefed by the editors and marketing team at regular sales conferences, held twice or three times a year in preparation for the major selling seasons ahead. More specific advice on presenting at sales conferences will be found in Chapter 10.

Telemarketing

In-bound

Although the names and addresses of the firm's schools reps usually appear in the catalogue, they are invariably out during the day when their contacts in schools would like instant answers on questions of availability, price, delivery and so on. Most reps have answerphones to take messages, but in addition several publishers offer a telephone help line for such information. And by doing this they get access to all the market feedback the telephone offers.

Out-bound

Bearing in mind the very limited times of the day that reps can talk to teachers (basically the lunch-hour and the short morning and afternoon breaks) some firms have found teleselling an effective means of making direct contact with specific subject teachers.

Inspection copies

Teachers need time to look at material they are considering for adoption in their schools, so most educational publishers offer a system of supplying books 'on inspection'. Freepost reply cards are included in mailings for teachers to request the titles they would like to see, and reps are encouraged either to hand out inspection copies or order them for the staff members they talk to.

The rules for getting them vary slightly from company to company but the principle is the same. A teacher may keep a book requested on inspection if multiple copies (usually 12–15) of the title are ordered for use in the school. In general a book available on inspection must be one capable of being adopted for class use. Other books are available 'on approval'; after the inspection period has elapsed they must be returned to the publisher in good condition or purchased. There is a grey area in between for some teacher-orientated titles that could be sold in multiple copies through colleges of education to student teachers. In such cases the lecturer recommending the book may qualify for a free inspection copy.

Send a form out with all sample copies asking for the recipient's comments – those that get returned will be an invaluable source of promotional quotations later on. It will not matter that the people commenting are not famous, first-hand feedback from practising teachers will be very convincing to the market.

Free copies to influential people

For similar reasons publishers sometimes mail new material free of charge to key people. The books are often sent in the expectation of a favourable recommendation that can then be published.

Exhibitions and conferences

Professional conferences for teachers tend to occur outside term time, and are another useful extension of the rep's activities. Some firms have mobile exhibition teams who mount large stands, others require the rep to do this as well. If you can, do get along to important meetings in your subject area. Not only do they provide a very useful opportunity for both editorial and marketing staff to meet school contacts made by the rep, and to explore current teaching trends, they also allow you to see at first hand what your competitors are up to!

Teachers' centres

Most local education authorities have a teachers' centre where staff can meet one another, attend training sessions, use the library and much more. The extent to which they are used varies; their budgets have been cut in recent years and some schools suppliers have stepped in to provide the show room service that they once offered. Nevertheless a well-organised teachers' centre can be a very useful means of disseminating information to the local teaching population, and provide an excellent location for a demonstration or seminar. With this in mind, many publishers offer significant discounts to teachers' centres. Keep the administrator/librarian of each centre on your mailing list.

School advisers

There is an established system of school advisers in this country. All are qualified and experienced teachers, the idea being that they can use that experience to the benefit of schools in the areas for which they are responsible: passing on information about how particular schemes work and trends in education, and helping with practical difficulties in the classroom. The extent to which they are listened to depends on the views of the headteacher or head of department (some regard them as spies, others as offering extremely valuable fresh viewpoints) and the disposition of the advisers themselves. Mailing lists are available by subject/age of children on which they advise. Keep them in touch with your publishing programme.

Space advertising

There are certain publications in which you will find all your competitors advertising and so should consider doing so yourself: for example *The Times Educational Supplement, Junior Education* and *Child Education*, and specific magazines for secondary subject teachers such as *History Today*. Even more valuable to you will be reviews or feature coverage in these papers.

The relationship between paying for advertising space and hence supporting an educational publication, and expecting coverage in return is a complicated one. Advertising pays for editorial yet advertisers are not rewarded with automatic coverage. You do however have the right to have your materials at least considered for review. See page 200.

Chapter 9 describes the organisation of space for advertising and promotions; increasingly linked areas of marketing activity today. Chapter 8 deals with securing free publicity.

Selling books overseas

British publishers used to export educational texts to Commonwealth countries virtually unchanged. As curricula were altered to reflect growing local nationalism and priorities, many UK publishers set up subsidiary houses in English-speaking Africa and the Caribbean. They used their experience to train local staff to edit and handle the production of texts specifically for the immediate market.

While some UK publishers still produce textbooks for export, in particular in science and mathematics (some funded by aid agencies), export sales have in general declined. But for the publishing industry as a whole, the decline has been more than offset by the dramatic rise in sales overseas of English language teaching materials. In contrast with the UK educational market where a stable population has ever-less money to spend, the expanding export market for English language teaching materials offers UK publishers significant potential for growth.

The group term for all the materials is ELT (English language teaching), and this can be further subdivided into EFL (English as a foreign language, eg teaching English to French nationals) and ESL (English as a second language taught in an English environment, eg teaching English to immigrants to Britain). The English that is taught may be British English (sometimes called TEFL or teaching English as a foreign language) or American English (sometimes called TESOL or Teaching English to Speakers of Other Languages). TOEFL is the qualification in English language to get into an American university; Cambridge Proficiency is the qualification for British universities.

British and American publishers compete to sell their wares and are successful depending on geographic location, old loyalties and hostilities, political trends, and the job/course aspirations of students. For example, in Latin America TESOL is mainly learnt (though Argentina uses TEFL and both systems compete in Chile), in Europe TEFL. The Gulf is mainly TEFL and both sectors compete for Japan. Sometimes different parts of the same international corporation compete with each other. For example, The Pearson Education Group includes the imprints of Longman (one of the largest UK publishers of ELT materials) and Longman Inc and Addison Wesley (two of the largest US publishers of American ELT materials). The newly merged Macmillan–Heinemann ELT combines the former company's strength in TESOL areas and the latter's in TEFL areas.

The main markets for ELT materials are: Western Europe, Middle East, North Africa, Far East and South East Asia, Pacific Basin and Latin America. Following the opening up of Eastern Europe there has been huge investment by West European countries in the developing former communist block. Now that so much industry is owned by other European countries there is virtually a requirement that if you want a reasonable job you must speak a second European language (usually English or German). There is also an international trend to start learning a second language at an earlier age, usually in primary school. This too has opened up marketing opportunities for relevant publishers.

Britain is also a centre for language summer courses and this brings a valuable influx of customers each year. Since the arrival of the single European market there has been a notable increase in the sale of self-study courses for beginners (many on CD ROM) and many general booksellers in this country and overseas are opening up special sections in the hope of cashing in. For booksellers, such adult learners (not students) are a good prospect as, being in full time work as well as studying, they have more disposable income to spend on materials. UK language courses and summer schools are also where new ideas on how to teach language are often developed.

The main ELT publishers are a few very large companies who can provide major courses supported by reference and dictionary material. Pearson Education, OUP and CUP between them have had 70 per cent of the UK market for the past five years. These big firms are consolidating their position through rationalisation and purchasing their competitors (Nelson is now part of Longman, the ELT part of Cassell and Prentice Hall were bought by Simon and Schuster which was in turn bought by Pearson). Other players in this market include Macmillan-Heinemann ELT, BBC Publications and Language Teaching Publications. Smaller publishers moving into this area need substantial backing; increasingly, few are tempted. Here are a few reasons why ELT publishing is now a sport only for large companies:

- The days when it was possible for a publisher to sell one edition of its English language teaching materials world-wide are largely over; today market specialisation is called for.
- There is increasing demand for courses to meet specific teaching needs. In the past young adults would make do with an adult ELT course, now increasingly teachers want one of their own. The same goes for primary materials; teachers want different courses for very young children and for the 10–12-year-old bracket, they do not want to have to make one course meet everyone's needs.
- There seems to be a low boredom threshold in this market: teachers quickly get tired of materials which need to be updated or changed every 3–4 years. Courses too have a short shelf life, which is getting shorter all the time. These days a course may last three years; 10 years ago it would last for five. Perhaps this has something to do with the self-esteem of the ELT teacher. In general they are often not highly respected, and hence motivated, and on summer courses getting to know the students can be particularly difficult.
- ELT Publishers need to adopt a very long-term view of publishing projects; they may need to give away very large amounts of *gratis* copies in order to tempt teachers into first using and then adopting their courses. This obviously needs substantial funding.

- With increased competition between publishers in this market, publishers are looking to increase their profitability and efficiency by improving the margin on sales. One example of this is the move by larger ELT publishers to open up companies themselves in suitable markets, rather than relying on the local book trade to handle distribution for them. So instead of exporting books from the UK to overseas markets at wholesale prices, and allowing booksellers there to mark up to and charge the full selling price, such organisations now supply local trade outlets from their own local warehouse giving the bookshops normal trade discounts. Obviously this leads to lower profits for local book trade, and tensions can result. For logistical reasons it is not possible in every overseas market.

- Again, due to the improved communications now possible, and to preserve as much margin as possible, there is less selling of rights and doing deals with overseas publishers, more attempts by British publishers to open a company there and 'do it yourself' in the local economy. Smaller publishers may continue to form co-publishing deals with European publishers to gain better access to overseas sales, others produce special editions for particular markets through deals with regional authorities or ministries of education. In the case of products where development and distribution can be difficult, such as CD ROMs, British publishers have tended to provide or sponsor the development capital needed to develop the product with a local software specialist, leaving distribution and marketing to the local publisher, who then pays a royalty on sales made.

- Smaller companies who do start ELT publishing often begin by concentrating on one particular market and then move on to exploit other opportunities as their efforts meet with success. For example Burlington, an Israeli-owned ELT publisher, began by targeting the Greek market and then moved on to the Spanish market.

Promotion opportunities for those with responsibility for ELT publications are many and varied. Most houses mail catalogues and leaflets to colleges and teachers. They also rely on extensive teams of reps who visit and provide them with promotional materials. Many firms organise free training sessions for ELT teachers using their own materials. The industry has spawned its own press both specific to certain examinations and general, and there is a very lively ELT publishers group that meets as an offshoot of the Publishers Association.

IV   Selling periodical and serial publications

This section considers the promotion of periodicals and serials; primarily research-based publications that offer a specific value for those working in a particular field to report and comment on recent developments.

Periodicals are generally published regularly on a subscription basis payable in advance, and are despatched directly by the publisher to the subscriber (even if the sale is made through a third party agent). A *serial* is usually published at irregular intervals (once a year or less frequently), is invoiced at the time of publication and is warehoused like a book by the supplier before sale. The term *journals* is commonly used to refer to both.

Periodicals and serials may be published in a variety of different formats besides the traditional printed version. For example, many are available on CD ROMs and through circulation on the Internet with the individual paying for information that is downloaded, or online via a computer link from the publisher. Many periodical publishers offer simultaneous publication in hard copy and alternative formats. Increasingly the hard copy may be dispensed with altogether. How long the printed version will continue to exist for is an interesting question.

Librarians claim they have no sentimental attachment to paper and are entirely used to managing non-print information, and academics appear to be very happy using computer terminals for delivery of the information they need; academic titles are one of the largest market sectors of books sold over the Internet.

Largely unproven for the future is the question of how durable (principally how incorruptible) CD ROMS will prove to be as a medium for long-term storage. Most agree that they are intermediate technology and that online journals are more likely in the future.

The advantages of working in this area

There are a number of reasons why promoting high level journals can be very satisfying.

1.   It can be a very profitable business

Most publishers ask for payment with order, before they have published or the customer received a single edition. Provided the publisher owns the journal,[11] the money received is available not only to finance the existing publishing programme but also for more speculative developments.

What is more, most journals subscriptions do not constitute a 'one-off' sale; individual subscribers tend to stay for at least a few years and libraries stay much longer. For the publisher, this means that securing new subscriptions and establishing sales for new journals are both very important and very time-consuming. But provided the information contained in the journal is of a consistently high quality and subscription prices do not rise to an unacceptable level, the initial income from a sale can be *anticipated in multiples, in advance, for several years to come.* There are several publishing houses whose wider publishing programme depends on highly successful periodicals.

Authors who contribute papers for publication are not usually paid for their efforts; sometimes they have to pay for the privilege of appearing in print. Journal editors usually receive only a small financial honorarium to supplement the prestige of office.

All this avoids the cash flow of the traditional two-year publishing cycle, from manuscript commissioning through to production and promotion, in which the publisher is constantly paying out before any revenue starts to come back.

2. A sense of continuity

When at a loss for ideas on how to promote a forthcoming title, the starting point is often: 'What is it like?', ie what have we already promoted from which we can glean pointers on how to market his product?

Of course, this can only be a starting point. Unless you are marketing a related title to an identical market, differences will emerge and plans diverge. Promoting journals offers you a rare sense of complete continuity in publishing. You have the chance to test your understanding of the market against its willingness to order, and to shape and refine your ideas with each marketing campaign.

3. A definable market

Selling high price journals to a limited market is the very best sort of 'niche marketing'. After some basic research, you should be able to define your market precisely. You will know who are your best prospects, who might also be interested, and be able to identify the no-hopers. If the field is specialised you will soon be able to identify a few key lists and associations through which to target your material.

Acquiring the basic information you need to draw up promotion plans

People identify themselves by the newspapers and magazines they read. Your basic task is to find out which groups of people identify with the publications you promote. You also need to be clear about whether they buy for themselves or rely on a third party (eg a librarian) to organise the information supply for them. This is crucial in enabling you to decide who makes the buying decision.

You should start by consulting the in-house editorial manager and team, and the department (in- or out-house) that looks after subscriptions. There are a number of questions that you should ask.

- What is the subscription level? What was it five years ago?
- What is the history of the journal? Was it started by your publishing house or acquired from another (moving a journal from publisher to publisher is fairly common)? How does it fit in with editorial plans for the future? Most journal editors have 'shopping lists' of titles they would like to acquire or start. Is this journal central or peripheral to these plans?
- How many institutions and how many individual subscribers are there? If your subscription department cannot tell you ask for a set of despatch labels and try working out the balance between libraries, individuals, institutions, press and in-house copies as well as any other categories that emerge. Most institutional subscriptions are prompted by an individual sending for a sample copy and then lobbying their library for a subscription.
- Is the journal the official title for a society or charity? This is a healthy position to be in as it guarantees a certain level of sales.
- Who is the editor and how long has he/she held the job? Have subscriptions increased during that time? What are the editor's current position, reputation and standing in the field? Can these be exploited in developing the subscriber list?
- What is the institutional and geographical spread of the editorial board? Selling a journal overseas is easier if the editorial board too is multinational. The same goes for the list of contributors.

- What are the competing titles on the market and how do they compare in content, readership, price and profile?
- Ask to see past promotion material and plans; this will help to show what markets have been targeted in the past. This is particularly revealing if the title has been acquired from another publisher.
- Ask if you can be added to the circulation list for future contents pages, for monthly journals usually available three to six months ahead of publication. Not only does this give you the chance to see the kind of paper being accepted, it offers you advance warning of any forthcoming topics which may arouse media interest.

Meet the subscribers

Profiling your readers is critical for market analysis; helping you plan where to market the journal and how.

If your journal is the official organ of a particular society a very good way to find out more about your readers is to attend their (usually annual) conference. Most of these meetings are held in university buildings during the vacations and you will find several other publishers in the field have also asked for tables on which to display their wares. There is usually space in the lobby leading to the lecture theatre or in the room where coffee breaks are taken. As the society's official publisher you may get (and should certainly ask for) a preferential rate.

Accommodation is provided in halls of residence. Arrange to stay there too: this will give you the perfect opportunity to establish current opinions on the content and availability of your titles.

For non-society journals, trying to profile the readership can be very problematic. Most library subscriptions will come via a subscription agent; those who do order direct seldom use the order form provided by the publisher asking for information on the kind of institution they are. What is more, the decision-making process on taking a new journal can take up to two years from the receipt of first information to final order, so tracking is very hard.

Asking those who order direct to classify themselves under one of several categories is one solution, but do beware of asking for so much information that the decision to complete the order form gets delayed – it's far better to send a questionnaire once the subscription is well established. As well as finding out who is subscribing, it's also interesting to find out how many readers have access to each copy (the 'pass-on factor'). The information you gather will be very useful both to you in deciding which markets to target in future, and to your advertising sales team in selling space (they will be delighted to claim that the readership is higher than the circulation).

Meet the editor

Journal publishing today is extremely competitive. In the setting up of a new journal or the negotiated move of a title from one publishing house to another, the role of the publication's editor, and the chemistry of their relationship with your firm's journals publisher (or commissioning editor), is crucial.

If your journals publisher is actively trying to poach or set up new journals, you may be required to come up with marketing plans and present marketing proposals to the journal's editor. In such circumstances the editor should be viewed as a client; a successful outcome is not only securing publication of the journal but subsequently managing editorial expectations. Editorial dissatisfaction with the publisher is often a key reason for wanting to jump ship.

Even for well-established journals owned by your publishing house, the opportunity to meet a journal's editor will help you understand more about who reads a particular publication and why. But do bear in mind that journal editors are very busy people and their reasons for taking on the job (in addition to their normal workload) will have much in common with those of their regular readers. They will not want to be responsible for your basic training.

Do your research before you go and make maximum use of the opportunity to clarify any areas of uncertainty, for example: the career stages at which individuals might consider personal subscriptions; the new advances in the field might widen potential readership; associations whose members should be interested; any forthcoming meetings to which information on the journal should be sent and so on. To make best use of the time it is often a good idea to send ahead of your visit a list of areas you would like to cover and questions you would like answered.

While you are visiting the editor, is there anyone else on the premises whom it would be useful for you to meet? Those running research programmes are particularly useful. Find out what they read and where they submit research articles; this will give you a sense of the closest competing journal. Specialist librarians can tell you of demand, and how new journals are vetted and approved. All this provides yet more market knowledge to fuel your future strategies.

Journals publishers and librarians

Libraries are immensely important to the serial and periodical publishers. Some journals with a wide appeal offer an institutional rate and a lower personal subscription rate, but it is still reckoned that *at least 80 per cent of the sales of an average high level journal (one that does not have a bookstall or newsagent sale) will go to libraries*.

Academic librarians see themselves as accountable to their institution and the academic community they serve for what they spend on books and journals and will provide interesting information on both the size of their budget and how it is divided. Discussions with specialist librarians too can provide useful information on the best way to target your material; what to send and when; how your message is received/perceived and so on.

How librarians view the serial publishing industry

Librarians feel increasingly that they are being held to ransom, caught between academics' desire to appear in print and publishers' desire to make money. Many subscriptions today are so expensive that very few individuals subscribe. Libraries are the sole and, they complain, captive market. They worry about a number of trends.

1. The proliferation of journal publishing

The 14th edition of *Ulrich's International Periodicals Directory* (1971–72) listed 50,000 different titles worldwide; the 28th (1989–90) 111,950 and the 37th edition (1997) 229,000. Each year at least 350 new titles come out. Some replace old ones, others are withdrawn, but the scale of publishing continues to grow.

As each new area of science or research develops the key figures involved are keen to launch a distinct and specific journal in which to publish their results (the jargon is 'twigging'). These increasingly specialised publications still require the back-up of secondary, and more general, publications to keep readers in touch with the wider subject area. With this huge flood of information, no library can cover a field comprehensively, and it is impossible for abstracting services to include all the relevant articles.

2. Publication for promotion

Librarians suspect that the vast majority of these titles are published for the benefit of contributors rather than readers. Journal publication has become central to the academic reward system: for promotion; for securing tenure; for gaining a grant. Board membership or editorial duties are undertaken for similar reasons.

In this process librarians suspect that the rigorous peer review system is breaking down. Too much is being accepted by journals for publication, and the effect is further complicated, particularly in the sciences, by the division of single research projects into a variety of different articles ('the salami effect'). This gives academics longer lists of published titles with which to impress their colleagues, but means that librarians have to stock more titles to cover the subject.

3. Price rises

Most libraries are spending at least 70 per cent of the books and journals budget on journals alone, and this is just to maintain those they already stock, without taking on new titles. Prices continue to rise, in part caused by subscription cancellations, then publishers seeking to compensate for further anticipated cancellations each year; a vicious circle. The effect of price rises has been made worse by a reduced central funding for academic libraries in both cash and real terms, and the need to fund and maintain computer equipment out of the same budget. It's worth pointing out that most library subscriptions come through subscription agents, and that they benefit too from publisher price rises.

Librarians don't like to maintain interrupted series but if they want to stock new periodicals it is usually a case of axing something else first. The result is a decline in the quality of their collections and slower access by academics to information they need for research.

In the US the suggestion of a 'National Periodicals Center' which would lend out copies, provoked the information industry to lobby for the swift passage of a copyright act, which greatly restricted library photocopying. In the UK libraries are increasingly forced to borrow from each other rather than update their own collections.

4. Monopolistic publishers

Most librarians feel that publishers are unsympathetic to their plight. Journal publishing is dominated by large multinational companies who face little direct competition (each journal is a unique product) and thus have small incentive to keep prices low. Elsevier, Academic Press and Springer Verlag dominate the industry; it has been estimated that for most libraries around 100 publishers out of 45,000–50,000 in existence are responsible for 70 per cent of their subscriptions.

Many suspect that the huge price differentials between subject areas are due not to publishers' costs but to excessive profit taking. Scientific journals are particularly expensive.

How librarians choose what they buy

How do librarians decide what to stock? To make the selection process as fair as possible, libraries have developed a range of monitoring procedures to establish what they need to stock to benefit the maximum number of users. Some libraries can provide you with printouts of which titles in a specific research area are most heavily used and which are often most requested for inter-library loan. Such information gives you a very useful guide to your competition and the relative performance of your title.

Librarians use citation indexes (references to previously published papers) as indicators of academic value. They make regular attempts to monitor which titles are used most heavily; special enquiries may be triggered by lists of journals that have extraordinary price increases or those for which the use appears to be low. Lists of titles held are circulated round departments for 'rating' by the academics working there, although sometimes the reliability of the figures produced is thwarted by library users equally aware of the vulnerability of subscriptions.

Most libraries hold regular meetings of a library committee two or three times a year to monitor information sources, at which decision about new titles are also taken. In between meetings, if information on an important new title arrives the librarian may request a sample, circulate it and secure an immediate decision on stocking. Interestingly, inter-library loans, often seen by publishers as a substitute for purchase, do not reduce the eventual sale of a subscription. If a title is frequently requested on inter-library loan a subscription may be bought as it is cheaper to stock rather than continually borrow.

It is worth remembering too that librarians see themselves as purveyors of information. Even if there is no money left in the budget and your new journal shockingly expensive, if the information you provide is relevant to the library's collection most librarians will circulate it. And on circulation you may attract potential authors and hence lobbyists for a subscription.

Subscription agents

Subscription agents look after library subscriptions to periodicals and serials. Instead of dealing with many different publishers a library need only deal with a single agent. The library provides details of all the titles it wishes to receive, the agent amalgamates their requirements with those of its other clients and orders from publishers. The agent also takes on the labour-intensive problems that go with the subscriptions: renewing on time; reporting on which titles are late or have changed their names; handling claims for issues that have not been received (Blackwells deal with over 100,000 such claims a year); arranging for specimen copies to be sent and so on.

In *The Work of a Periodicals Agent* (available free from Blackwells Periodicals Division) J B Merriman argues that most libraries with a substantial number of subscriptions probably order 70 per cent through agents. So if 80 per cent of any journal's print run goes to libraries, a very substantial number of subscriptions is being handled by agents.

In practice the agents are being squeezed on all sides: by publishers, libraries and the effects of new technology. Many publishers actively encourage direct orders, claiming that there is nothing the agents do for customers which they cannot do themselves. There is no fixed discount structure and discounts to agents are very low: the average worldwide is around 5 per cent, and falling by about 0.4 per cent every year. Most agents need a gross profit of around 10 per cent in order to survive in the face of financial pressure. Many resort to either charging customers for servicing their subscriptions, or trying to secure extra discount from the publishers in return for additional services such as promotion and catalogue production or supplying renewals in electronic format which saves the trouble of re-keying them.

Traditionally, learned societies have not offered any discount to agents at all and some publishers are wondering whether to adopt this practice too. Many publishers insist on payment with orders in around October–November for subscriptions that start in January, and yet not all libraries pre-pay agents.

But forcing agents to rely on librarians paying servicing charges presents agents with a very uncertain future. Libraries have suffered budgetary cuts and consequently are themselves looking to squeeze the margins agents are taking. Many libraries require several agents to tender each year for the job of securing subscriptions for the following 12 months and are required to take the lowest bid. Others spread their journals between two or more agents on the grounds that agents in competition are more likely to be efficient. In the long run both courses lead to a disrupted service for the library. Badly organised but cheap agents securing work on the basis of cost rather than service, and with the knowledge that the account may change hands the following year, have little incentive to improve.

Thirdly, agents are being being squeezed by the effects of new technology. The Internet has raised investment levels for subscription agents and introduced new competitors into the business. When it comes to securing online subscriptions, libraries are faced with the familiar problems of dealing with multiple suppliers, complicated by the need for a different password for access to each electronic delivery point. Subscription agents are all working on being facilitators in the provision of electronic access to libraries, but investment is hugely expensive. What is more, the agents' role as intermediary has been threatened by a process of 'reintermediarisation'; other organisations have offered to deliver material through co-operative network. For example, both agents and publishers offer libraries access to serials through the joint academic network (JANET) which connects all institutions of higher education in Britain and has links with similar electronic networks worldwide. Some publishers see the situation as an opportunity to sell direct, and there are other players in the wings such as library consortia.

Lastly, agents suffer from a very poor position in the 'value chain' between reader and writer. Their expertise involves taking orders from their customers (libraries) and putting them with a large number of monopolistic suppliers (publishers) and then, where appropriate, consolidating them. They do not do anything to the goods as they pass from one party to the other, have no warehouses or shops and do not carry stock.

With library budgets seldom rising in line with inflation, periodical prices usually rising well above it, and the general reduction of discounts, the result has been the demise of several agents. Many wonder whether there is room in the market for the four main players that survive (EBSCO, Swets and Zeitlinger, Dawson and Blackwell).

A visit to a subscription agent will provide a lot of useful information on the industry. Most of the larger agents belong to the

Association of Subscription Agents and would welcome a visit to explain their role in the subscription business.

Professional associations

A subscription to the UK Serials Group is a very good way of improving your understanding of periodicals and serials publishing. For a low annual subscription you receive circulars on important trends, the journal *Serials* plus information on courses and invitations to attend meetings. If you can, get to the annual conference which is held at a different university each Easter vacation. There you will find all involved; publishers; librarians; subscription agents and other secondary service providers.

There is a similar organisation for North America called NASIG which it may also be worth joining if you are promoting titles to that market.

Planning your promotional material

Whom to circulate

Try to find the decision makers. For most journal publishers this means contacting academic lobbyists who will fight for subscriptions in appropriate subject areas. Librarians are important too but remember that most library selection committees meet only about once every six months. Some US list brokers can provide very useful lists of library committee chairpeople (whether academic or librarian).

See Chapter 6 on direct marketing for advice on sourcing lists and the respective benefits of keeping your own as opposed to renting lists. Some career appointments or areas of research change with such speed it is not worth trying to maintain your own lists, for example newly qualified doctors, or PhD students taking on short-term research jobs in the hope of finding a permanent lecture-ship. Find out when departmental budgets are approved and mail at the time when decisions are likely to be made on how to spend them.

Other direct promotional methods besides the mail can be equally effective, for example using e-mail or circulating material in dele-gate information packs for forthcoming meetings.

What information to include in your promotion piece

The most important information to provide is journal *contents*. For new journals, the projected contents should be listed. For established titles, a list of samples from recent issues should be chosen by the editor. If you have room, these are easiest to read when shown laid out as actual contents pages.

The following will act as a checklist of what other information to include:

- A brief description of the journal, its aim and scope.
- Who is it for? If it is a new journal, why it is needed is an important area to cover.
- Who is the editor and what is the composition of the editorial board? List institutions and the relevant countries: promoting a journal overseas is easier if the members are geographically spread. Some institutions will buy a periodical if a member of their staff if on the board.
- An editorial statement; perhaps in the form of a signed letter.
- How often it is published.
- Are contributing papers welcome? New subscriptions to journals are often motivated by those who want to publish so either include a 'call for papers' in your brochure or give instructions to would-be contributors on a separate sheet.
- Is subscription by year or volume, or can you start a subscription when you like? If you order mid-way through the year, will you receive backdated issues for the past six months, and then new issues for the next six, or a year's editions, starting with the next due? Ninety per cent of publishers make periodicals available either by calendar or academic year. In general, libraries prefer to buy complete volumes by year, as this ensures a more complete and quantifiable collection.
- Is it the official journal of a society?
- What does a year's subscription cost? Is there any saving for ordering two years' (or more) worth at once? Some publishers offer a 5% discount for a second year, more for a third. Others offer no discount but stress that the recipient is insured against price increase during the lifetime of the subscription which is paid for now.
- Are there discounts for special categories of subscription (for example, an individual taking a personal copy working at an institution whose library already takes a copy at full price)?

- How about a special price for people who subscribe from the very first issue of a new journal ('founding subscribers')? Such special offers can be complicated to administer and will be unpopular with agents handling your titles, but may lead to more subscribers.
- Does the price include postage and packing? The general trend is for surface despatch to be included in the price, with an extra surcharge for airmail. Do make such information as clear as possible; unnecessary correspondence with confused subscribers eats into the profit margin.
- Is the journal centrally indexed, and if so in what, for example in *Index Medicus* and other online indexing systems?
- What is the ISSN (international standard serial number)?
- What is the publisher's name and address? Give telephone and fax numbers and an e-mail address for enquiries or credit card orders.
- How does the customer get hold of a sample copy? Many publishers now find their Web site is the best method of offering sample copies and get many requests this way.
- Include information on other journals or books published by your company in this and related fields. Not only does this establish your authority to publish in a particular area, it may lead to additional sales or attract new authors. At the very least it provides the librarian with a checklist of your publications. (Bear in mind that this may be unacceptable to certain societies who like to be promoted on an exclusive basis.)

The format of your promotion piece

Many publishers produce a journals catalogue listing all their titles once a year, with individual flyers or leaflets for each separate title.

A journals catalogue is useful as a checklist for librarians as well as serving your editorial team when you are trying to attract or bid for new titles. Again, including your related books shows publishing depth and expertise.

Individual leaflets for journals (which should still list related titles on the back) should be general in application to ensure they last as long as possible, preferably for at least a year. You can change the nature of individual promotions by altering the package you send. For example, if you are mailing researchers you could include a letter and a sheet with instructions to contributors, or perhaps a 'subscription recommendation form', for those impressed to sign and pass back to the librarian. If you are mailing librarians a circulation (or 'routing') slip could be added to encourage the package on its path around the institution.

If your individual title leaflets are light, not only will they fall within the first postage band and save mailing costs, they will also find a welcome home in lots of other useful places; in delegates' packs at related conferences; as loose inserts in society mailings or in journals (your own or those of other publishers); in the regular mailings sent out by subscription agencies to libraries they serve.

All the techniques spelled out in earlier chapters of this book on presenting information apply. Keep paragraphs short and make the information user-friendly and readable. Question and answer sections are a good way to vary pace and get across complex information, for example:

Why is a new journal needed?

Highly significant developments have taken place in this area of medicine in recent years. This fast developing field now falls outside the scope of any existing journal.

A new forum was badly needed for the publication of research and the exchange of ideas. This new journal provides just such a meeting place.

Don't make the appearance of your material too extravagant. If you are stressing a publication that must be purchased to keep abreast of a fast-changing field and your material is over-lavish, it may be assumed to be both overpriced and stale by the recipient.

Other promotional ideas

- Produce a range of 'filler' advertisements for your publications (books and journals) to go in the advertisement pages of your firm's related periodicals. Do change them regularly: you can bore as well as attract.
- Arrange list or advertisement swaps with other publishers with whom you have complementary but not competing interests. To maintain list security you should arrange for lists to be sent to and despatched by a third party mailing house.
- Arrange for promotional leaflets to be included in the announcements of forthcoming meetings; subsequent mailing of delegate information and then to be inserted in delegates' packs.

Alternatively, attend yourself and run a journal/book stall. There is prestige for attenders in being seen to buy expensive publications in front of their colleagues.

- Keep in touch with subscription agents. Let them know about delayed titles or name changes and they will in turn inform their (and your) customers free of charge. Many agents produce catalogues or promotion pieces in which you can advertise at favourable rates. Others will circulate information such as flyers on new journals in their regular mailings to libraries.

- With the consent of editorial, and for a journal for which the subscribers are mainly individuals rather than libraries, ask the members of your editorial board for suggestions of names to contact. Send each prospect a package of information on the journal in question with the option of a sample copy. Enclose a letter saying who recommended that they might be interested. E-mail promotions can work very well for this purpose too.

  Along similar lines, send out a letter to all subscribers with an edition of the journal asking for the names and addresses of colleagues/friends who might also like to subscribe (asking for the names of those who borrow their copies often works well). In return, offer those who reply entry into a sweepstake for something they want to win or some other incentive. Such offers usually work well with very academic/specialised markets as they receive so few of them.

- Try including your information in card deck mailings (see Chapter 6).

- Make up a few exhibition packs for quick despatch to relevant meetings. Include samples of your journals and copies of the leaflets that promote them.

- Liaise with the British Council on relevant meetings they are attending at which your material could be represented, perhaps in return for sponsorship from your company.

  Arrange for posters to be put up on notice boards. The publisher of one journal with a high individual subscriber base and a special rate for students, sends a driver off each autumn armed with a car full of posters and special discount subscription forms to be put up on the relevant notice boards of every university in the country.

- Keep in touch with appropriate societies, and find out how they are developing. Are any new newsletters circulated to members with particular interests? Can information on your titles be included or can you put a loose insert in the package in return for help with the postage costs? Just as new journals are founded to reflect changing research interests, so spin-off groups are formed from larger organisations. You may have the key mailing list within sight – or the genesis of yet another new journal!

Public relations

Sometimes newsworthy papers in a journal give cause for a press release and a bid for coverage in the mass media. To spot which papers are likely to be of interest you don't need to be a subject specialist – your own response to which papers out of all those on the forthcoming contents sound interesting is just as valid.

The launch of a new title can attract publicity in its own right as it often indicates the coming of age of a new field of research. Regular liaison with specific journalists can also provide useful opportunities for coverage; stories picked up by one paper may be spotted by Reuters and the Press Association and produce world-wide coverage for you; particularly valuable if you are hoping to sell more subscriptions internationally.

Sample copies

I have often heard the view from editors that the main aim of journal promotion is to get a sample copy into the hands of everyone likely to be interested. Follow this through logically and include a 'sample copy request card' in your mailings and you will most likely get a tremendous response. What matters much more is the conversion rate (of copy requesters to subscribers).

While seeing a sample *may* be essential in convincing a subscriber to sign up, it's equally possible for sample copies to delay the despatch of completed order forms (the reader starts reading – or means to start reading – and the order gets delayed). Instead of actively promoting samples, try stressing a guarantee of satisfaction or your money back if the journal fails to meet the subscriber's expectations. Alternatively, try limited duration or cheap rate 'trial subscriptions' (although these can be difficult to administer and are unpopular with agents). In the US, budget permitting, it is common practice to try a year's subscription of a new title rather than requesting a sample from the publisher.

Sending sample copies also costs a lot of money. While keeping a number in reserve in case a library claims not to have received a particular issue, most publishers sell unused back numbers to special agents who handle orders for complete past volumes. This is impossible if you have used up all the spares on free samples to those with only a marginal interest.

In conclusion, the availability of sample copies is well known and so does not need stressing. If you do offer the option of a sample copy put it after the option to order. Never send a sample unless it is requested. If one is asked for, be sure to enclose an order form for a subscription, and to follow up if it is not returned. The sample requesters have shown themselves to be interested in your publication – the jargon is 'qualified prospects' – and are therefore very well worth pursuing.

Use your Web site to display sample copies: present the papers from recent issues and projected contents lists for future editions. Include information on how to submit a paper.

Chasing renewals

This is very important: subscribers who fail to renew must not be ignored. Each year a certain percentage (ask your subscription department how many) will fail to renew. It is much harder to find completely new subscribers than to persuade former ones to rejoin. It is also much more expensive; one journal recently estimated that it costs six times as much to find a new subscriber as to persuade an existing one to renew.

If you are mailing subscribers direct (rather than informing them that renewals are due through an agent) look at your renewal forms. Are they sent out with the journal or separately? If the latter, can a slip be included with the last copy that has been paid for reminding the subscriber that it won't come again unless action is taken? Put the expiry date on the address label.

Look at the forms themselves. Are they encouraging? Do they suggest urgency? Are they patronising? Be aware of the impression you are creating. A renewal letter I received from a marketing journal pointed out that an annual subscription costs no more than a meal for two at a London restaurant. How would this go down in Edinburgh?

Most houses send several renewal reminders, of increasing urgency. Try varying the colours, perhaps blue for the first and red for the final one. The details of the subscription will almost certainly be a computer printout, so try putting a letter with a signature next to it to make the whole effect a little more personal. Even after the final reminder chase again or telephone; it is surprising how many lapsed subscriptions will still be renewed, even months later.

Telephoning can tell you most of all. I have carried out market research for journal publishers on the reasons for non-renewal. On several occasions I have been told that the library had forgotten to renew and, by the time they realised it was missing, they found no users had noticed the journal's absence. Not unreasonably it was concluded that it was not needed. What a pity the publisher had not reminded the library sooner.

Particular hints when promoting a journal overseas

Ask your subscription department for a geographical breakdown of subscribers. You will find the countries covered correspond to the developed – and fast developing – world. North America, Japan, Australia, Europe will provide the most subscribers, with representation from some newly emergent work tradings powers such as China, Brazil and South East Asia.

While some publishers still employ agents to sell subscriptions overseas for them, or sell rights to specific markets to similar publishers overseas, there is a general trend towards handling promotion to all customers from the UK; vastly improved world communications in recent years make this possible. Try to obtain copies of promotional brochures and mailshots from other parts of the world (from your reps, agents or other contacts). You won't be able to redesign your material for every single market, but for large potential sectors such as the US it will help your efforts if the layout of your mailshot is at least familiar to those receiving it. It makes sense to find out about the level of funding for research in the newly developing economies, and to follow it.

The largest English language market for UK journals outside the home one remains the US, and this can be mailed effectively from Britain. If you are responsible for promoting UK titles to the US, the following advice will be helpful.

1. The size of the market

Traditional assumptions need updating. The North American market has been seen as a gold mine for European journal publishers: libraries with lots of money; librarians with lots of clout.

Many publishers as a result offer dual rate subscriptions: a lower rate for Europe and a higher one for translatantic customers. These North American rates have continued to rise whatever the international currency movements on the assumption that customers there could afford to pay more.

But US publishers too have increased their prices. The result is that US librarians have grown tired of being exploited by a handful of what they see as monopolistic publishers from both sides of the Atlantic. They too have suffered budgetary cuts.

The US is still a huge market but do approach it with sensitivity. For example, if your company continues (as many do) to dual price, printing both rates on the journal information is asking for trouble. Print a special version of your leaflet with dollar prices only.

2.   The position of librarians in the US

Reports by the Association of American Publishers have emphasised the power of the librarian in making decisions on whether or not to stock a particular title. Americans are very conscious of the value of information and most commercial companies, even if too small to justify having their own librarian, will almost certainly have an individual whose responsibilities include that of 'information officer'.

3.   Direct mail

Direct mail is much more widely used in the US than the UK and mailing lists are correspondingly much more available: if a list exists it is likely to be rented out. For example, most key publications and professional associations rent their membership lists.

4.   Information from overseas

Most librarians are not concerned about ordering information from abroad; if a title looks necessary they will consider it. But do make it easy to order. The promotion material sent out to libraries by agencies in the US lays great stress on the help they can provide in procuring 'difficult' subscriptions from overseas.

US agencies offer similar promotional opportunities to their British counterparts: the chance to advertise in catalogues; distribute sample copies and circulate information on delayed issues and so on. Some firms have field representatives who can carry your titles when visiting libraries or display them on their exhibition stands.

5. Posting

There are many more bands of postage in the US than in the UK, but do take advice on which to choose. The ultra-cheap rate for bulk mailing would not be an economy if your material failed to arrive, which is not unknown! Arrange for contacts in various parts of the US to be on your mailing lists so you can check on when, if and in what shape your material arrives.

V *Marketing children's books*

Most general publishing houses have a children's division. Until comparatively recently their profile tended to be low. Very much a subsidiary activity to the development of the firm's main list, advances and royalties on children's titles were based on lower selling prices and so were worth less in cash terms to authors and illustrators. The books received smaller promotion budgets and share of company attention.

Today the area is much more active, a trend that is found in the book trade worldwide. The quality of children's books is better than ever and they are reaching the market through an increasing variety of outlets. Children are also buying books for themselves, often through school bookselling operations.

Why has there been such a change? In part it is the product of increased competition. The founding of Walker Books, by Sebastian Walker in 1978, as a company that would publish only for children, started a 'shake-up'. Larger advances were offered (dubbed 'cheque-book publishing' by his rivals) and titles were sold through new outlets such as Sainsbury's. Walker's fundamental legacy also lay in his insistence on the *importance* of producing excellent children's books; his company raised the profile of publishing for the young as an end in itself.

Since then two further developments have placed children's publishing in a very advantageous position: the growth of the mass market and the rise of character licensing:

'These two developments have enabled us to escape the constraints of an industry which regards children's books in the main as small fry and has lifted us into a retail environment where selling children's books is not viewed as a peripheral activity, but rated alongside toys, video and apparel as a volume business and a first-rate profit opportunity.' [12]

The size of the market

Each year around 8,000 new and new edition children's titles are published in Britain. The following figures show the number of titles bought and the money spent:

Table 12.7   Books bought for children (market size estimates)

	1996	1997	1998
Volume	110m	115m	120m
Value	£385m	£390m	£415m

Source: Books and the Consumer 1996–98 (BML 1999)

Non-fiction and reference accounted for around a half of the value of the books bought for children in both 1997 and 1998. The growth of this sector has come about both through the changes in the educational environment and consequent parental anxiety and through the activities of major publishers offering greater availability of non-fiction titles. Borrowings of children's books are holding up well too: nearly 20 per cent of the money paid by Public Lending Right to authors goes to children's books, mainly to fiction (16 per cent).

If you want to see the range of children's books published each year a very good place to start is Young Book Trust at Book House in south London. Established to influence government, education, parents and children of the importance of reading, a copy of every new children's title is sent here.

The Walker shake-up

Sebastian Walker's agreement with Sainsbury's in March 1985 shocked the traditional book trade; booksellers assumed that the number of titles sold through bookshops would reduce as a direct result. In fact, most people now accept that what Walker predicted has indeed occurred; that the new outlets introduced more people to quality children's books and the market as a result expanded.

The mass market

Ten years ago it was common to hear children's publishers complain that in most bookshops the children's department was all but invisible, often inaccessible (upstairs), low profile and staffed by the most junior members of staff. Booksellers responded that low discounts meant it was impossible to do more.

In the intervening period there has been a rapid expansion of new places to buy children's books alongside a range of other merchandise for children. Today most large centres of population are ringed by out-of-town supermarkets and superstores where people with small children are more likely to shop and, crucially, find it more convenient to buy books. Woolworth's *Kid's Store*, Mothercare World, *Toys R Us* and other children's superstores all offer books for sale to parents at the same time as toys and prams, and books can benefit from being displayed alongside non-book child related products.

A few statistics from the most recent *Books and the Consumer* survey confirm the mass market's importance as book buyers:

Social group	Percentage of population	Percentage of purchases for adults	Percentage of purchases for children
AB	17	33	28
C1	26	32	28
C2	24	16	22
DE	33	19	23

52% of purchases for children were bought by people aged 25–44.

77% were bought by females (mainly women, but some self-purchasing by girls).

63% were bought by households with children aged 15 and under.

43% were bought primarily on impulse (ie the thing that first made people consider buying was that they saw the book in the shop, or elsewhere, such as in a catalogue).

Source: Books and the Consumer 1998 (BML, 1999)

Many of these customers are probably not regular bookshop browsers, and in the superstores there is huge demand for high-profile media-related properties of the kind publishers can offer.

The new selling locations have necessitated a switch in marketing techniques. Instead of concentrating their energies on pursuing every possible opportunity for free coverage, publishers must become increasingly aggressive to maintain these opportunities, which are under threat both from adult books and a variety of other merchandise with potentially higher stock turns and profits. In doing so they must use techniques familiar to the rest of the retail world, such as:

- Price promotions (children's publishers experimented with price promotion long before the demise of the NBA).
- Limited period introductory offers to ensure titles are ranged by the retailer and sampled by the shopper.
- Multi-saves with books or related character merchandise.
- Voucher offers.
- Reciprocal offers with other manufacturers, eg cross merchandising books with toys (every effective with licensed properties).
- A variety of marketing formats, eg book and toy, book and cassette.
- Attractive display material.
- 'Value added packaging' (packaging that adds value to the product being sold). This is particularly important for certain retailers, for example for warehouse clubs, catalogues and cash and carries who are looking for a higher price and bulkier looking purchase (this is particularly important if the item is to be given as a present – customers want presents to look impressive!).
- Production of own brand items for supermarkets. This does not necessarily mean books alone, packages that consist of 'books plus' may bcome part of the store's gift or hobby range rather than book range.

Character licensing arrangements

Surely influenced by the wide availability of videos for children, and by the marketing efforts of Disney Corporation, there has been considerable growth in demand for 'character' images created for a book or film to adorn a wide variety of specially designed merchandise – from nightdresses and bedroom slippers to rucksacks and school lunch boxes. With their backlist of character titles, publishers were well placed to take advantage of this opportunity.

The superstore purchaser shops thematically, following the child's interests; they may not be looking for anything as specific as a book or cutlery set but a Power Rangers or Paddington item, and books can benefit enormously from being displayed in an accessible position alongside related merchandise. Some stores take this a stage further by launching specific boutiques within stores for certain characters that have a strong affinity with their own market. For example, BhS launched Thomas the Tank Engine boutiques in many of its stores in spring 1997.

Competition for books

How many of the books that are bought actually get read is debatable. It has become common practice to assume that the battle against television, computer games and other leisure attractions is already lost. But the children's market has remained buoyant and has managed at least to hold its own, during a period when demographic and economic factors have been against it and during which the competition for children's leisure time and the money available to spend on books has continually increased.

So for children how does reading compare with other pursuits?

Preferred activity

	4–7 Years		7–11 Years		11–14 Years		14–16 Years	
	Boys	*Girls*	*Boys*	*Girls*	*Boys*	*Girls*	*Boys*	*Girls*
	%	%	%	%	%	%	%	%
Reading fiction	33	43	46	62	32	47	24	38
Watching television	90	89	79	79	83	83	84	83
Using a computer	60	40	62	38	66	33	60	22

Source: Centre for Research in Children's Literature, 1996, Roehampton Institute.

In addition to the main survey, published in 1996, the Centre has carried out additional surveys of the reading habits of children, firstly of those from ethnic minority backgrounds and secondly of children with special educational needs (SEN). These have revealed further interesting facts about the market for children's books. For example, children from ethnic minority backgrounds are much keener on reading in general than the respondents in the 1996 survey, and use libraries (public and school) far more. Children with special educational needs buy and borrow significantly fewer books than their peers and parents are less likely to buy books for them.[13]

The importance of the backlist to children's publishers

Sales patterns for children's books are very different from those of adult books. The marketing manager will spend a good deal of time and money promoting the backlist, not just new highlights.

Whereas a new general hardback fiction title will have its heaviest sales period in the months following publication, with another boost when the paperback appears, children's titles can take a much longer time to get established and go on selling for much longer than adult titles.

The buyer is not usually the 'end user'

A marketing manager responsible for the promotion of a list of children's titles has to convince a middle market of the books' merits. Booksellers and wholesalers have to be persuaded to stock; and parents, relations, teachers and librarians to buy on behalf of the children they represent. Even those promotions which are sent straight to children (eg school book club leaflets) rely on teachers to organise and parents to pay.

About 85 to 90 per cent of books are paid for by adults, including the use by children of book tokens or vouchers. The spread of adults buying for children is also extremely wide, making the targeting of marketing very difficult. For example, 37 per cent of buyers for children are men, 46 per cent are not directly responsible for the children and 24 per cent are aged 55 or over.

Each year publishers produce catalogues and leaflets detailing their new and existing titles. In addition they prepare a range of promotional material for display in shops, schools and libraries: posters, leaflets, balloons and so on. This must be attractive both to the adult (so it gets put up) as well as to the children who will see it. Appealing to 'the child in us all' is not as easy as it sounds.

The following table shows the percentage of children surveyed who answered 'very often' or 'often' in response to the question 'What attracts you to a book in the first place?'

Table 12.8

	4–7 Years		7–11 Years		11–14 Years		14–16 Years	
	Boys	*Girls*	*Boys*	*Girls*	*Boys*	*Girls*	*Boys*	*Girls*
Look of cover	47	50	39	30	44	39	36	37
Title	33	45	44	45	49	50	40	52
Cover words	not asked		44	51	42	58	42	63
Illustrations	61	68	42	31	34	18	22	11
Recommended	22	27	36	43	31	46	33	51

Source: National Centre for Research in Children's Literature, 1996

All children seem to like books from a series. Over 80 per cent of those aged 4 to 11 say they like such books, as do 60 per cent of older children. They do so because of familiarity with characters, the story-lines and with the general style (source as before). Children from ethnic minorities in general do not like animal stories.[14]

Children's publishers must be very cost conscious

Children's publishing is probably the most price sensitive area of the book trade.

Economies of scale are vital where high development costs on mass-market novelty formats necessitate high print runs and hence volume deals. Mostly this is done using a schedule of discounts, rising according to the quantity bought. Costs at the same time must be kept as low as possible and most authors are remunerated on the basis of net receipts rather than published price.

At the same time children's books are highly price-responsive. There is a symbiotic relationship between retail price and volume in the mass market; adding an extra £1 to a title can ruin its chances of success. Egmont Children's Books have found that by reissuing selected character titles which were originally published at a trade price of £5.99 and giving them a mass market price point of £3.99, volume sales have improved by as much as 400 per cent. When pricing new materials they look not only at competing books but also at toys, stationery and gift items that jostle for the same leisure pound.

Money off can be a significant marketing gambit at certain times of year (eg Christmas) but in general low retail prices mean there is less margin to play with. The children's market also offers fewer high profile blockbusters of the Andy McNab, Delia Smith type. Far more important than money off are ingenious practices to ensure display and grab the consumer's attention.

Children's publishing and the traditional book trade

Where children's books are purchased
Children's titles have a very varied distribution structure, perhaps more so than adult books in general.

So how has the traditional book trade reacted to sales going through new locations?

Some major bookselling chains have experimented with dedicated children's shops (eg Young Waterstones and Heffers) but the

Volume bought for children, 1998   **Percentage**

	Percentage
Bookshop (including bargain)	29
Book/stationery (including W H Smith and Menzies)	18
Supermarket/chain store (including Woolworths)	17
Other retail (eg toy, gift, department store)	11
Total retail	75
Book club	10
Other direct (eg through workplace or school, party plan, off the page)	11
Total non retail	21
Other/not stated	4

Source: Books and the Consumer 1998 (BML, 1999)

combination of excessive rents for high street sites and low price products is a difficult one and casualties have occurred. Shops that have done particularly well are often those which have become local centres of advice and encouragement on reading, with welcoming premises and detailed knowledge of their stock. From their shop front they can organise displays for PTAs in schools and signing sessions in the store; advise children who visit in January with book tokens; arrange competitions and summer holiday reading schemes. For many of these activities they try to enlist the support of publishers.

Other booksellers have nurtured special markets. For example, Books for Students of Warwick services school bookshops (with a variety of well-thought-out recommended reading lists) as well as other junior markets, and is active in finding new ways to reach children. The organisation of school book fairs and school book clubs are two further areas of strong competition and activity.

The single-outlet independent bookshops continue to complain of low discounts and their exclusion from the large deals open to the superstores. In this context it is interesting to compare their situation with the toy trade. The independent toy trade has formed itself into buying groups to compete on terms and gain marketing muscle. They recognise the necessity of accepting a lower margin on stock lines that are heavily advertised on television ('keen lines') and make up margin through the rest of their range. Significantly, toy manu-facturers consider it their business to work with the independents to offer a wide spectrum of buying outlets for consumers, from small independents with advice on offer to large multiples which work like supermarkets.

In the book industry it is the wholesaler who acts as the buying group, negotiating offers and deals on their customers' behalf. Advice from them and from the BA over the demise of the NBA included stressing range and ordering facilities, the experience and advice on offer and the comfortable atmosphere in which to choose titles.

Generating free publicity

Children's publishers often complain of the paucity of review space devoted to their books. *The Guardian* does a regular feature on children's books which appears four times a year; The *Independent on Sunday* features such titles more regularly, but other papers make do with very patchy coverage. It is frustrating that the 'best-seller' lists featured in so many papers do not include children's titles.

However hotly editors protest their independence from advertising, it is true that children's publishers in general spend little on space in anything other than trade magazines, and that is usually concentrated in the run up to the Bologna Book Fair. It is hard to see the few editorial features on children's books as anything other than a direct result.

The result is that a great deal of the time of a children's marketing department is spent pursuing promotional initiatives that result in coverage. These may include the following.

- Organising promotional links with magazines and newspapers read by parents and children: for example features that 'review' new titles; articles on key authors; competitions; free branded material such as posters and height charts; all of which offer some element of magazine endorsement and thus more column inches and clout in return for the money spent.
- Arranging author tours, usually to a specific region for three to four days at a time: handling bookings from schools and libraries; liaising with the local press; arranging for copies of the relevant books to be there ready for signing sessions.
- Organising the firm's material for National Children's Book Week. Now in its 23rd year (1999) the week in October provides the stimulus to many schools and libraries to organise book-related events.
- Supporting specific local initiatives: perhaps supplying local booksellers with marketing material for a promotion they have organised or arranging for a character in costume to pay a special visit to a school.

- Sponsorship of events relevant to the market.
- Entry of titles for literary prizes. The resulting media coverage brings the winning titles to the attention of a wider public, as well as promoting reading and books in general. A list of the main prizes for children's books can be found in the guide produced by Book Trust.[15]

Book fairs, exhibitions and conferences

At the Bologna Book Fair all the major players in the trade gather for the sale of rights to overseas publishers and to display their wares. For a guide to the main companies in children's publishing read the Bologna edition of the *Bookseller* that comes out shortly before the fair in March each year.

In addition, many children's publishers exhibit at the London International Book Fair. The Edinburgh Book Fair in Charlotte Square (tied in with the Edinburgh Festival) offers good potential for exhibitors; many organise author- and book-related events. It is usually great fun and well attended by local children.

Many publishers have an exhibitions team that can be despatched to mount displays at teachers' and librarians' conferences, teachers' centres, schools, local fairs and other events.

Exporting children's books

Substantial numbers of UK children's titles are exported; in 1994 sales of physical books sourced from the UK were valued at about £88m and in addition, revenues from co-editions, rights and royalties overseas were around £70m.[16] Translations and overseas editions, often through co-edition deals with overseas publishers, have long been a profitable enterprise for British publishers. A co-edition deal secured at the right time can be the key to successful publishing of a children's book, allowing the publisher to extend the initial print run and keep the price down. This revenue is, however, threatened by the development of the indigenous publishing industries in many former traditional markets, for example Germany and France.

Secondly, UK publishers have exported the home editions to other English-speaking areas, eg Canada and Australia. The US has been an important source of such deals although there may have to be consequent editorial amendments across the run (no milk bottles, different uniforms).

The Children's Book Circle

This is a useful meeting place for those involved in any aspect of publishing for children – editing, marketing or production. Look in the jobs pages of the *Bookseller* for details of forthcoming meetings.

VI Selling information to professional and industrial markets

Selling books to people at their place of work can be very successful. Publishers for this market tend to be specialist divisions of larger companies (eg McGraw-Hill, Gower, Pearson Education, Jordans and Wiley) but many specialist companies have been formed more recently to meet market needs.

Main kinds of purchase

1. Statistical and historical information published in directories, yearbooks and annual publications
For example, information on industrial trends and market statistics and predictions for specific market sectors of industry.

Products tend to be expensive because of the high costs of maintaining and analysing data. They have to be marketed early and sold quickly as the information they contain is necessarily out of date before stock is released for sale.

It is worth pointing out that for publishers in this area the book is no longer the principal option. Business information can date very quickly and publishers have adapted to become packagers of information rather than producers of books. Information can be presented online, via the Internet, perhaps with regular online updates, and/or on CD ROM rather than via annual publication. Significantly however, even when marketing in new formats, there remains a role for the accompanying codex as an accessible and supporting back-up information source to the higher technologies.

Many publishers are producing both new and old formats side by side, and the new technology is not necessarily always preferred. For statistical information that changes relatively little from year to year (eg price tables, historical information, scientific/mathematical formulae or tables) the CD ROM or online may take longer to consult and may mean the user is unable to make marginal notes.

2. Professional information and standards

For example, guidance for lawyers and accountants on new legislation; interpretation of recent statutes.

Most professions have key reference texts that they need access to every day. Many are published in loose-leaf format, or on CD ROM or online and must be updated at regular intervals (annually, quarterly or even monthly). This is a prime market for the appropriate publishers; the professionals must be current and informed.

In many industries there is also a well-established 'bible' which sells to professionals and for which the announcement of a new edition is important news.

3. Managerial guidance and 'how to' books

This area includes information compiled and packaged to meet specific job/function needs. Examples could include a complete resource for personnel managers or managing directors' PAs, or titles that reveal the general principles of marketing or discuss specific problems such as how to handle difficult members of staff. Prices on the whole tend to be cheaper than for the former two categories – readers are often buying from their own pockets on impulse, and this is an area of strong price sensitivity.

The importance placed on development and training is particularly high in difficult economic times. When job security is threatened individuals become more motivated to try to improve their own performance. Of late there has been a significant increase in the perceived value for managerial expertise acquired through training rather than instinctive nous; the dramatically increased prestige and popularity of the MBA bears witness to this.

In addition to titles required for instant access on the desk top, the majority of larger companies have an information centre or library which buys books, or a training department which buys bulk copies to support courses they run.

4. Business blockbusters

I am here referring to socio-econo-political titles that sell well to the business and industry community. For example, Nick Leeson's account of the fall of Baring's Bank, *Rogue Trader*, Will Hutton's *The State We're In* and Jim Slater's personal finance titles are treated very much like new trade titles with heavy publicity, point of sale, advertising and so on.

5. Leisure titles

In recent years firms selling leisure books in the workplace have done very well. Large quantities can be shifted because those at work appreciate the chance to buy without having to visit shops. Perhaps the market also finds a little light browsing on cookery and gardening books a relief from high-level jobs! (see Chapter 1 for more on this trade.)

How big is the market?

The scope for selling information to the professional and industrial market is huge, the numbers involved very large. As the availability of mailing lists show, in the UK alone there are 19,000 firms of solicitors, 18,600 firms of accountants, 69,500 manufacturing companies, 7,800 estate agents, 10,000 bank branches. And all these addresses include individuals holding specific job functions who need information: managerial; marketing; statistical market analysis; technical and so on. The market for business information is expanding in key trading areas, for example there is a healthy demand for information on (former Communist) East European and South East Asian markets despite fluctuations in economies and sometimes unstable situations.

Other lists of interest to business publishers are compiled on the basis of previous items bought (not necessarily books); here again a healthy demand is revealed. Professional membership lists too are well worth pursuing – this is particularly important in very specialised markets such as engineering, surgery, environmental science and so on.

How the market views the purchase of business information

The professional and industrial community want access to publishers' products in the same way as any other commodity they require, from filing cabinets to coffee machines. Having decided on a particular product they want it delivered straight away, on credit, on approval and often at a discount. Publishers' products compete for the company purse with other business information sources such as online systems, training courses and seminars, videos and computer software.

Publisher and trade relations

Many professional and industrial book buyers are desk/factory bound or very busy and do not frequent bookshops. With exorbitant city rental values few bookshops can afford to position themselves in locations of prime convenience to possible business book buyers. Discounts offered by publishers in this area are lowish (usually around 10 per cent on reference books, rising to around 30 per cent on trade titles) and few bookshops can afford to tie up capital by stocking the wide range of high price titles available; particularly if they date very quickly (eg annual directories). Markets are often ill-defined (the same job functions receive a variety of different titles) and many booksellers cannot afford the high cost of mailing local and national markets to let potential customers know that particular titles are available.

Most business publishers therefore promote to their markets directly, perhaps spending as much as 15–20 per cent of the expected gross revenue from a title on promotion; vastly more than the average 5 per cent that is spent on the promotion of an academic monograph. The costs of a mailing campaign for a book can be anything up to £500 per thousand depending on the quality of the list chosen; a mailing may typically range from 5,000 to 60,000 addresses depend on the targetability of the market (as an example, see the mailing response chart in Chapter 6 for a typical business book).

How the book trade has reacted to this has varied. Some booksellers complain that publishers' direct marketing has robbed them of valuable business, to which publishers counter that they created the trade in the first place by promoting directly to the market. Many booksellers accept that publishers have expended the market through promotion and more sales for them have resulted. The Wyvern Business Library estimate that for every 100,000 books they sell themselves they generate an extra 60,000 sales through bookshops and that publishers with good distribution do particularly well.

Some booksellers have decided to specialise in the professional and industrial market themselves and have built up considerable expertise and local patronage. Such shops seek to build close links to local educational establishments (eg those offering MBAs) as well as large companies, advising on what is available and supplying what is required quickly and efficiently. Whereas traditional wisdom in selling business books held that the major accounts were the business libraries, many of which required standing orders for titles, they place far more emphasis on the wider market opportunities offered by industry: whole departments in which every employee needs a copy of a particular title on their desk; training departments that require multiple copies of a forthcoming speaker's book. They also undertake specific promotions to associations whose members are likely to purchase business books, for example the Institute of Directors or the Institute of Personnel and Development.

When dealing with shops of this kind, it is often worth providing versions of your direct mailshots overprinted with their order form and return address for them to use in their own mailings.

Online bookstores

Computing, business and many fields of science are some of the titles most commonly sold through the Internet, and many business booksellers and publishers now offer the opportunity to buy through a Web site. These sites have become increasingly popular for finding backlist and harder to find titles which bookshops don't always have in stock. This is also a useful way of drawing customers into learning more about your organisation and the other areas in which you publish.

How to reach the market for business and industrial titles

If a large proportion of business book buyers do not have access to a good business bookshop, title and availability information must be sent directly to them: through the mail, off-the-page advertising in Sunday supplements and specialist publications, telemarketing and so on. This means dealing with list brokers and other direct marketing specialists and developing expertise on likely sources of buyers: through analysis of previous campaigns and building up customer lists.

1. *Mailing lists*
When choosing mailing lists for a promotion campaign, the method of list compilation is very important: you would be more likely to get a good response from a list of previous book purchasers in accountancy than mailing accountancy firms in general. Your own lists of previous purchase should be the starting point. You should also consider arranging to swap your lists with those of other publishers, or renting business book buyer lists. Think laterally too.

What other purchases might be made by the market you want to reach (magazines, lifestyle, etc)?

Subscriber lists to publications relevant to your books should also be considered, and professional lists: individuals bearing specific job titles within the industrial sectors you seek to reach, for example personnel managers, export directors, senior partners and so on.

2. Loose inserts

In magazines, parcels you send out, membership information sent out by associations, lists of delegates from conferences and so on.

3. Space advertising

Taking space in a publication will probably restrict the amount of copy you have to explain your product, but may be the most effective means of reaching the market. For example, if you wish to reach the readership of a magazine whose sale is largely from newsstands you may not be able to include a loose insert and a mailing list will not exist. Space advertising may be the only option, but try to tie this to some guaranteed editorial coverage in the same publication.

Given that you have less space to explain your product's benefits, concentrate on the main selling points, the currency of the information and the guarantee. Alternatively, would your material best be presented as an 'advertorial' (a mock editorial feature)?

4. Book clubs (see Chapter 1).

5. Card deck mailings (see Chapter 6).

6. Other direct sales methods

Try telemarketing (see Chapter 6), e-mail (see Chapter 7), business-to-business leaflet distribution, view data and interactive cable. One highly targeted direct sales technique gaining in popularity is 'upselling'. This means using information available at the time of the order to increase the amount purchased. For example, when a customer rings to order by credit card, the person handling the order, using the customer service screen, can be prompted to offer other titles by the same author/related titles in the same subject area.

7. Shared marketing
The business book trade is still heavily larger-city dominated but shops are opening up or developing special business operations in other towns: ask your reps to keep you in touch with important accounts.

Provide leaflets overprinted with the bookseller's address and ordering details (enough stock for both their mailing list and to hand out in the shop); advertise in their catalogues; share the costs of mailing their customer list; agree to higher discounts in return for inclusion in their promotions. (For specific examples of booksellers who promote in this way see Chapter 6 on direct mail.)

8. Review, feature and other free coverage
See Chapter 8.

9. Displays at exhibitions
Don't forget the prestige available to delegates who buy your expensive publications in front of their colleagues. Such business purchases are usually tax deductible.

What to say in promotional copy for business and professional books

Your material should provide all the information that the customer would have available were they standing in a bookshop leafing through a copy of your title prior to making a decision on whether or not to buy. All the details you provide should be fully supported by facts, and they should include the following.

1. Who is the title for? List all the job functions; in what types of company.
2. How will the users benefit from it? Provide examples of actual usage.
3. How current is the information included? How was it compiled; how up to date is it; what is new about the title; what specific needs it meets which were not covered before.
4. What is included? Contents are essential, and should be as detailed as the space allows.
5. Sample pages (use arrows to indicate major benefits such as information type and layout; ease of access).
6. Who are the compilers or authors? Include information on their relevant credentials.

7. How is it available? Telephone/fax lines and e-mail for urgent orders.

8. What guarantee of satisfaction is available? The inclusion of a guarantee is absolutely essential. You must make it completely clear that if a customer is dissatisfied with what they receive, a full refund will be available; this creates the security for ordering. In practice few purchasers will return a title they have bought: the inertia factor will be supported by an awareness that it is company money they are spending rather than their own. But all need the professional reassurance (at the moment of decision) of knowing they are not spending money unwisely.

9. What's the incentive to encourage the customer to order straight away? There may be an offer and perhaps a further discount, or free carriage for a standing order or swift response. Offering a discount for purchases over a certain value works very well in certain markets if you allow customers to club together with colleagues and send a joint order. The result is often that the customers order more titles to benefit from the discount, while you save on the administrative and despatch costs of sending small orders to individuals at different addresses.

Notes

1. Young People's Reading at the End of the Century. Focus on Ethnic Minority Pupils, British National Bibliography Research Fund, Report 94.
2. Paper from the Department of National Heritage, 1995 *The Public Library Services in the 1990s: Guidance for local authorities from the DNH.*
3. Hampshire.
4. Source: PLR.
5. National Committee of Inquiry into Higher Education, published on 23rd July 1997, see it on the Internet at http://wwwd2.leeds.ac.uk/niche/
6. Higher Education Funding Council for England.
7. Surveys by IBIS Information Service of 1976 and 1986, surveys by the author of academics at Exeter University 1990 and 1996.
8. Ibid.
9. Source: Book Trade Yearbook 1995, The Publishers Association.
10. John Davies, Director of the Educational Publishers Council in an article in the *Bookseller, Reading maketh a full man,* 23.8.96.
11. Many journals are published on behalf of societies by professional publishers.
12. Clare Somerville, Marketing and Sales Director of Reed Books in a paper *Adapt to survive: the pursuit of alternative markets and products,* April 1996.
13. British National Bibliography Research Fund Reports 93 and 94, both, available from the National Centre for Research in Children's Literature, address in Appendix.
14. Ibid.
15. *Guide to Literary Prizes, Grants and Awards* published by Book Trust.
16. Source: BML estimates based on PA/ONS data.

Appendix 1

Glossary

above and below the line   The traditional distinction between different sorts of advertising. 'Above the line' is paid for (eg space advertisements taken in newspapers). 'Below the line' marketing involves no invoice; it is normally negotiated in a mutually beneficial arrangement between two or more organisations. The usual result is an augmented offer to the consumer (more than just the product being sold), often with a time limit. The distinction between 'above' and 'below the line' is blurring as techniques get used in combination; some marketing agencies are now offering 'through the line' services.

advance notice (or advance information sheet; AI)   A single sheet giving brief advance details of a forthcoming publication. Usually circulated six to nine months before publication, it is sent to anyone who needs the information – bookshops, reps etc.

advertorial   Advertising copy that masquerades as an editorial item.

answers   Shorthand used on a publisher's or distributor's invoice to show the status of particular titles ordered by a bookseller and not immediately available. The most common abbreviations are:

nyp	not yet published
nk	not known
oo	on order
op	out of print; no plans to reprint
os	out of stock (reprint under consideration)
rp Jan	reprinting, will be available again in January

artwork   Typesetting and illustrations were conventionally pasted on to board to form artwork which could then be photographed to make printing plates. Today most artwork is produced on computer and provided on disc.

backlist   Older titles on a publisher's list that are still in print.

bar code   A machine-readable unique product code. The bar code usually appears on the back cover of a book and is used for stock control and sales.

blad   Originally this meant a section of a book printed early to help in the promotion, and be shown as a sample. Today blads can consist of marketing information about, a random assortment of pages from, or a synopsis of a forthcoming publication, and do not necessarily constititute a distinct section.

bleed   Printed matter that extends over the trimmed edge of the paper; it 'bleeds' off the edge.

blurb   A short sales message for use in leaflets or jackets.

body copy   The bulk of the advertising text; usually follows the headline.

bottom line   Financial slang referring to the figure at the foot of a balance sheet indicating net profit or loss. Has come to mean the overall profitability, for example: 'How does that affect the bottom line?'

brand   A product (or service) with a set of distinct characteristics that make if different from other products on the market.

break-even   The point at which sufficient copies of a publication have been sold to recover the origination costs. The break-even point in a mailing is reached when enough copies have been sold to recoup the costs of the promotion. (See Chapter 11.)

bromide   A type of photographic paper. Producing a bromide is a one-stage photographic process on to sensitised paper or film which is then developed. *PMTs* are routinely produced on bromide paper but alternatives now include acetate or self-adhesive paper.

budget   A plan of activities expressed in monetary terms.

bullet point   A heavy dot or other eye catching feature to attract attention to a short sales point. A series of bullet points are often used in advertisement copy both to vary pace and to engage the reader's attention:

- good for attracting attention
- uneven sentences and surrounding spaces draw in the reader
- allows you to restate the main selling points without appearing over-repetitious.

buyer   The job title within a retail or wholesaling firm responsible for selecting/ordering stock. Large shops will have a different buyer for each department.

b/w   Abbreviation for black and white.

camera-ready copy   Frequently abbreviated to crc. *Artwork* that is ready for photography, reproduction and printing without further alteration.

card deck (also called business reply card mailing or cardex mailing) A collection of business reply cards each offering a separate sales message to which the recipient can respond by returning the card concerned. Often used for selling business and professional books.

cased edition A book with a hard cover, as opposed to limp or paperback.

CD ROM Short for compact disc, read only memory. A high density storage device that can be accessed but not altered by those consulting it.

centred type A line or lines of type individually centred on the width of the text below. Type on a blank title page can also be centred on the page width.

character A individual letter, space, symbol or punctuation mark.

Cheshire labels Mailing lists required on labels are available either on Cheshire or self-adhesive stationery. Cheshire labels are presented as a continuous roll of paper which is cut up and pasted on to envelopes by a Cheshire machine.

closed market Closed markets are created when local selling rights are sold to a particular agent. Booksellers in an area that is part of a closed market must obtain stock of titles from the local agent rather than direct from the original publisher. This arrangement is under threat from the Internet which knows no geographical boundaries.

coated paper Paper that has received a coating on one or both sides, eg art paper.

colour separations The process of separating the colours of a full colour picture into four printing colours, done either with a camera or electronic scanning machine. The separated film may then be used to make printing plates.

competitive differentials What a company is good or bad at; the things that set it apart from its competitors.

controlled circulation A publication circulated free or mainly free to individuals within a particular industry; advertising sales paying for circulation and production costs. Much used in medicine and business.

co-operative mailing A mailing to a specialised market containing material from several advertisers who share the costs between them.

copy Words that make up the message, often used of material prepared for advertising or newspaper features.

cut-out An irregularly shaped illustration which will require handwork at the *repro* stage of printing.

database marketing Building up increasingly complex information about your customers in order to serve their needs more precisely and sell more to them in the future. The long-term aim of direct marketing.

database publishing Publishing from information stored on a database. Can be a fast method of producing complex material or material which will date very quickly, information existing on the database does not need to be re-keyed by typesetters with the resulting delays and possibility of errors.

desktop publishing Producing camera-ready copy and artwork on computer screen (rather than the old method of pasting down on to board). This allows easy experimentation with different layouts and formats.

die-cutting A specialised cutting process used whenever the requirement for a cut is other than a straight line or right angle (ie when a guillotine cannot be used). A metal knife held in wood is punched down on to the item to be cut. Many old letterpress machines have been adapted to form die-cutting equipment.

direct costs Costs attributable to a specific project, as opposed to general overheads or indirect costs. For example, the printing bill for producing a particular title is a direct cost.

direct marketing The selling of services directly to the end consumer – including direct mail, telemarketing, house-to-house calling.

direct response advertising Advertising designed to produce a measurable response, whether through the mail, telemarketing, space advertisements etc. This compares with direct promotion, whereby material is sent directly to the market which may, or may not, produce a direct response back.

display type Large type for headlines, usually 14 points or more.

dues (also called arrears) Orders for a new (or reprinting) publication before it is released. Publishers record the dues and fulfil orders as soon as stock is available. Checking the dues of forthcoming titles is a good way of finding out how well the reps are subscribing particular titles in bookshops and hence estimating sales.

dumpbin Container to hold display and stock in retail outlets; usually supplied by the manufacturer to encourage the retailer to take more stock than might otherwise be the case. Most are made from cardboard, to be assembled in the shop.

duotone A half-tone shot printed in two colours. This is a more expensive way of printing a photograph than simply using a single printing colour, but can add depth and quality to the image presented. It is usually printed in black plus a chosen second colour. An alternative effect can be produced by using a tint of the second colour behind a black and white half-tone.

ELT English language teaching (see Chapter 12, page 280).

embargo A date before which information may not be released; often used on press releases to ensure that no one paper scoops the rest. Sometimes ignored by the media to secure just such a competitive advantage.

EPOS Electronic point of sale. Machine readable code that can be read by a terminal at a shop checkout to establish price, register any appropriate discounts and reorder stock.

extent Book or leaflet length. For example, for a book, extent: 192pp (192 pages); for a leaflet, extent: 4pp A4 (four sides of A4 paper).

FE Further education Education that is beyond school but not within university (those still at school under the age of 19 receive secondary education). FE can be academic (eg GCSEs and A levels) or vocational (eg GNVQs), carried out in the student's own time or supported by an employer.

firm sale The orders placed by a bookseller from which the publishers expect no returns. In practice most publishers have to be flexible and allow at least a credit for unsold titles, to ensure goodwill and the stocking of their titles in the future.

flush left (or justified left) Type set so that the left-hand margin is vertically aligned, the right-hand margin finishing raggedly wherever the last word ends.

flush right (or justified right) Type set so that the right-hand margin only is aligned vertically.

flyer A cheaply produced leaflet, normally a single sheet for use as a hand-out.

font The range of characters for one size and style of type.

format The size of a book or page. In the UK this is usually expressed as height × width, in the US and most of Europe as width × height.

gsm (or g/m^2) The measure by which paper is sold: grams per square metre.

half-life   The point at which the eventual outcome of an experiment can be predicted.

half-tone   An illustration that reproduces the continuous tone of a photograph. This is achieved by screening the image to break it up into dots. Light areas of the resulting illustration have smaller dots and more surrounding white space to simulate the effect of the original. A squared-up half-tone is an image in the form of a box (any shape), as opposed to a *cut-out* image.

hard copy   Copy on printed paper as opposed to copy on disk or other retrieval system (which is soft copy).

HE   Higher education. Study at university level and above.

headline   The eye-catching message at the top of an advertisement or leaflet, usually followed by the *body copy*.

house ad   An advertisement which appears in one of the advertiser's own publications or promotions.

house style   The typographic and linguistic standards of a particular publishing house. For example, there may be a standard way of laying out advertisements, standard typefaces that are always used and standard rules for spelling and the use of capital letters. Most publishing houses provide their authors with a sheet of instructions on the house style. See Chapter 5 for advice on the use of a house style in advertisements.

hype   Short for hyperbole, it literally means exaggerated copy not to be taken seriously. It has come to mean over-praising, and is part of the generation of interest in titles that appeal to the mass media.

impression   All copies of a publication printed at one time without changing the printing plates. Several impressions may go into the making of a single edition.

imprint   The name of the publisher or the advertiser which appears on the title page of a book, or at the foot of an advertisement. One publishing house may have several imprints, eg Grafton is an imprint of HarperCollins, Puffin of Penguin.

indent   1. To leave space at the beginning of a line or paragraph; often used for subheadings and quotations. 2. To order on account; to 'indent for'.

in-house and out-of-house work   Jobs that are carried out using either the staff and resources within the firm or those of external companies or freelances.

in print   Currently available. Telephone enquirers will often ask if a particular title is still 'in print'.

insert   Paper or card inserted loose in a book, journal or brochure; not secured in any way.

inspection copy   Copy of a particular title (usually a school text or other educational book) supplied for full examination by a teacher in the hope that a class set will be bought or the title will be recommended on a key reading list. If the title is adopted and a certain number purchased, the recipient may usually keep the inspection copy. Books for which a multiple sale is unlikely are generally available 'on approval'; after inspection they must either be returned or paid for.

ISBN   International standard book number, a system of providing each edition of a book with an individual identifying number. The first digit identifies the nationality of the publisher, the next group the individual publisher, the next five form the unique identifying number and the final one is a check to ensure the previous digits are correct. For example:

English language publisher	Firm Kogan Page	Unique number	Check digit
0	7494	1678	5

The appropriate ISBN should appear on any piece of information to do with the book: it is essential for bookshop and library ordering; stock control; despatch and more.

ISDN   International standard data number, use of a telephone line for the exchange of data between computers.

ISSN   International standard serial number, a similar system to *ISBN* for identifying serial publications. The number allocated refers to the serial in question for as long as it remains in publication. It should appear on the cover of any periodical and in any promotion material. Libraries catalogue and order by ISSNs.

jacket rough   A design for a book jacket prepared for the approval of author, editor and marketing department.

justified type   Type set so that both left-and right hand margins are aligned vertically – as in newspaper columns.

lamination A thin film available in matt or gloss applied to a printed surface; often used for book jackets, glossy brochures or the covers of catalogues which can expect a lot of use. Varnishing has a similar effect and is becoming less expensive; it adds less to the bulk than lamination.

landscape A horizontal oblong format, ie wider than it is deep (as opposed to *portrait*).

letterpress A printing process whereby ink is transferred from raised metal type or plates directly on to paper. All newspapers used to be printed by this method.

limp (or C format) A format midway between hardback and perfect bound paperback; the spine is usually sewn but encased in card covers rather than boards.

line work Illustrations such as drawings that consist of line only rather than the graduated tones of photographs. The cheapest kind of illustration to reproduce.

list All the publications a particular publisher has for sale. Also used for a group of new publications, eg spring list.

litho Short for lithographic. A printing process which works on the principle of greasy ink not sticking to those parts of the wet plate which are not to be printed. Most usually ink is transferred (off-set) from a printing plate on to an intermediary surface ('blanket') and then on to the paper. (See Chapter 5). How most marketing material is now printed.

logo Short for logotype. An identifying symbol or trademark.

mark up 1. To prepare a typescript for the typesetter by writing on the instructions needed such as type specification, width of setting, indentations, space between paragraphs and so on. 2. To increase the price of a particular title above that shown in the list price. Examples of use include when individual copies – rather than class sets – of school books are ordered, (this is also called double pricing) or when selling expenses are likely to be high, perhaps due to exporting.

measure The width of text setting, usually measured in pica 'ems' (the m is chosen because it is the widest letter for setting).

merchandise Branded goods.

merchandising In a publishing context, this means persuading retail outlets and those who supply them to stock branded goods related to a key title, for example a stationery range that relates to a key children's title. Merchandising is a key function of the reps in bookshops, now that so much buying is done centrally.

monograph A single subject study by an author or group of authors, usually of a scholarly nature.

negative option A practice often used by book clubs whereby, unless a member responds to say a particular title is *not* required, it will be sent – eg the 'book of the month' is often a negative option.
net The final price or sum to be paid, no further discount or allowances to be made. For example, net profit is the surplus remaining after all costs, direct and indirect have been deducted, as opposed to gross profit which is the total receipts, only allowing for the deduction of direct costs.
nix (-ies) Addresses on a mailing list which are undeliverable by the carrier. If these amount to more than a certain percentage of the total list supplied, a reputable list owner or broker will provide a refund or credit.

online Connected to a telecommunications system. Journal publishers frequently offer an online back-up service to printed copies, with access through a telecommunications link to the publishing information database. This can be tapped to answer queries as they arise, eg to obtain instant copies of papers that have appeared in past issues, or details of whether a particular topic has ever been covered in the journal. Information that dates very quickly is already sold principally online.
over-run 1. Type matter which does not fit the design and must either be cut or the letter and word spacing reduced in size until it fits. 2. Extra copies printed, over and above the quantity ordered from the printer (see *overs*).
overs Short for *over-run*. The practice of printing a slightly larger quantity than ordered to make up for copies spoilt either during printing or binding. It is commercially acceptable for the printer to allow 5 per cent over or under the quantity ordered unless otherwise specified. You will be charged for the overs.
ozalid A contact paper proof made from the film and usually used as a last minute check on positioning on more complex jobs. A final check before printing, unless a printed proof is requested.

perfect binding The most common binding for paperbacks. The different sections of the book are trimmed flush and the pages glued to the inside of the cover. This is more expensive than saddle stitching but cheaper than sewing.

PMT   Short for photo mechanical transfer. The production of a PMT is a two-stage process: the creation of a photosensitive negative which is then developed with a chemically sensitive carrier. The line image produced provides *artwork*.

point of sale   Eye-catching promotional material to be displayed with the product where purchases are made. For example publishers produce showcards, posters, bookmarks, balloons, single copy holders, dump bins and counter packs for display by the till.

point system   A typographic standard measure based on the pica, eg 12 pt.

portrait   An upright oblong format, ie taller than it is wide (see *landscape*).

pos   Abbreviation for positive eg pos film; or *point of sale.*

print on demand   As printing technology becomes cheaper and specialist publishers increasingly target highly niche markets, it may be cost-effective to print only the number of copies you have actual orders for. This can work particularly well for a high-price product relevant to a very small market, for example a market research report. Don't forget, however, that before any printing on demand can begin the origination costs must be covered. It follows that this is not as cheap an alternative to conventional production as is often imagined!

print run   Number of copies ordered from a printer (see *overs*).

pro forma invoice   One that must be settled before goods are despatched, often used for export orders or where no account exists.

progressive proofs   A set of printed proofs showing each colour individually and then in combination.

proof-reading   Reading typeset copy for errors. There is a standard series of proof-reader's marks which should be made both by the mistake and in the margin. Typesetter's mistakes should be noted in red, and author's and publisher's in black or blue.

publication date   Date before which stock may not be sold, to ensure no one seller saturates the market before all have the same opportunity. Sometimes ignored to secure a competitive advantage. (See *release date.*)

reading copies   Copies of a forthcoming title distributed before publication date to key people in the trade (notably booksellers and wholesalers) to create enthusiasm and promote word of mouth. Done on the grounds that those who sell books are more likely to enthuse to customers about titles they have themselves read and enjoyed.

recto The right-hand page of a double page spread (with an odd page number). The opposite of *verso*.

register *Trim* marks that appear on the artwork supplied to a printer, should reappear on the plates made, and need to be matched up when printing to ensure the whole job will be in focus or register. If the plates have not been aligned according to the register marks or the marks placed incorrectly the job is said to be 'out of register'.

release date Date on which stock is released from the publisher's warehouse for delivery to booksellers in anticipation of the publication date. Some booksellers complain release dates are far too early and they end up warehousing the books instead of the publisher. This can fuel the temptation to sell early.

remainder To sell off unsold stock at a cheaper price, often to 'remainder shops' such as discount book stores.

repro Short for reproduction; the conversion of typeset copy and photographs into final film and printing plates.

response device How the order or response comes back to the mailer, for example reply card or envelope.

retouching Adapting artwork or film to make corrections or alter tonal values.

returns Unsold stock of particular titles that may be returned to the publisher by the bookseller with prior agreement. Reps often use the authorisation of returns as a bargaining point in persuading booksellers to take new titles.

reverse out To produce text as white or a pale colour 'reversed out' of a darker background colour, as opposed to the more usual practice of printing in dark ink on a pale background. This technique can be very effective in small doses, but for lengthy passages of text can be very hard to read.

review slip The enclosure in a book when it is sent out for review by a publisher. It should include details of title, author, *ISBN*, price and publication date, as well as a request for a copy of any review that appears.

rights The legal entitlement to publish a particular work. Permission is given by the copyright holder (usually the author of editor) to reproduce the work in a particular format – most frequently a book.

Subsidiary rights (for film, paperback, merchandising deals and so on) are then sold by either the firm's rights manager, or the author's agent. The major occasion for selling rights is the annual Frankfurt Book Fair.

roman Upright type (not bold), as opposed to *italic*.

royalty The percentage of list price or net receipt paid on each copy sold to the copyright holder, usually the author. Royalties are paid to the author's estate for 70 years after his or her death; the manuscript is then deemed to be out of copyright and may be reproduced by anyone without paying royalties.

rrp Short for recommended retail price. Usually set by the manufacturer, this is the basis for calculating the discount given to the retailer. Since the demise of the Net Book Agreement, the actual selling price is decided by the retailer, who may choose to lower prices and take a reduced profit margin in the hope of selling a greater quantity.

run of paper Refers to the position of an advertisement that will appear in a particular journal or paper wherever there is room, at the editor's or designer's discretion. This is usually cheaper than specifying a particular (or preferred) position.

saddle stitching A method of binding pamphlets or small books (48–64 pages is probably the limit for saddle stitching successfully). Wire staples or thread are used to stitch along the line of the fold. Also called *wire stitching*.

sale or return Booksellers or wholesalers take books 'on sale or return' on the understanding that if they have not been sold after a specified period (usually 6–12 months after ordering), and provided the titles are still in print, they may be returned for a credit. This leaves the long-term financial risk with the publisher. The opposite of *firm sale*.

school supplier (also called educational contractor) A firm which seeks to supply both schools and local education authorities with books and other educational products.

screen 1. The process used to convert continuous tone photographs into patterns of dots, in order to reproduce the effect of the original when printed (see *half-tone*). A coarse screen is used in the preparation of illustrations for newsprint and other less demanding jobs. 2. Short for silk screen printing.

see safe Booksellers or *wholesalers* usually take books on a 'see safe' basis. They are invoiced immediately for the total taken; those they do not sell may be returned for a credit or exchange. While the immediate financial outlay is thus with the shop, they are protected by the practice of *sale or return*.

self mailer   A direct mail piece without an envelope or outer wrapping. Often used to refer to all-in-one leaflets, which combine sales message and response device. Space for copy is limited so this format works best when the recipient already knows of the product being advertised.

serif; sans serif   A 'serif' typeface has 'handles' on the letters, like the typeface used in this book; sans serif is the opposite.

showthrough   How much ink on one side of a printed sheet of paper can be seen through on the other side.

specs   1. Short for type specifications. Designers may refer to 'doing the spec' by which they mean laying down the parameters of text design – choosing a typeface and size. 2. The specifications for printing a job are all the production details (*format, extent,* illustrations, *print run* etc) sent to printers for a quote.

subscribe   To secure orders from bookshops and *wholesalers* before publication date, either by phone or through a rep visiting. The results are recorded by the publishing house as *dues*.

tag line (or strap line)   A line of copy that sums up the product or the general philosophy of the company. Often displayed on the front cover of books.

telemarketing; teleselling   Using the telephone to sell.

terms   The discount and credit conditions on which a publisher supplies stock to a bookseller or *wholesaler*. Terms will vary according to the amount of stock taken and the status under which it is accepted. (See *see safe, firm sale* and *sale or return*.)

tint   A pattern of dots that when printed reproduces as a tone. Using tints is a good way to get value from your printing inks. For example, even if your have only one printing colour, try putting the text in solid, and using a 10 per cent tint of the same colour to fill in and highlight certain boxes around copy. Further variations can be achieved if you are using more printed colours.

trade counter   A collection point from which books can be picked up by booksellers, usually located at a more central spot than the warehouse. For example, some publishers with offices in Central London and warehouses in the provinces maintain a trade counter in London. As publishers invest in speedy distribution, the need for a trade counter becomes less.

trade discount   The discount given by publishers to booksellers and *wholesalers* on the price at which they will subsequently sell. The amount of discount given usually varies according to the amount of stock taken or the amount of promotion promised. 'Short discounts' are low scale discounts on products that are either very expensive (often those that are extensively promoted by the publisher directly to the end user) or those that are sold in sets (eg school books).

trim Short for 'trimmed size' of a printed piece of paper, ie its final or guillotined size.

turnover The total of invoice value over a specified period for a particular company's sales.

type area The area of the final page size that will be occupied by type and illustrations, allowing for the blank border that will normally surround text.

type face The style of type, eg Garamond, Helvetica.

type script The *hard copy* (usually typed or a printout) of the manuscript or copy to be reproduced and printed.

typo Short for typographical error; a mistake in the setting introduced by the typesetter.

unjustified type Lines of type set so that the right-hand margin does not align vertically and thus appears ragged. this can also be described as 'ranged left' or 'ragged right'.

upper and lower case Upper case characters are CAPITALS, as opposed to lower case.

verso The left-hand side of a double page spread (even page numbers). The opposite of *recto*.

visual, mock up or rough layout A layout of planned printed work showing the position of all the key elements: headlines; illustrations; bullet points; *body copy* and so on. Blank 'dummy' books are often created before finished copies are available for promotional photographs.

weight of paper Paper is sold in varying weights defined in *gsm* or *g/m²*: grams per square metre. Printers can offer you samples of various papers in different weights.

wholesaler An organisation that buys books in bulk from publishers in order to supply bookshops and other retail outlets; often securing higher than usual discounts in return for the large quantities taken.

The national bookshop chains, and outlets with large designated markets (eg library suppliers and school suppliers) will similarly demand substantial discounts from the publisher for large quantities of stock taken.

Appendix 2

Author's Questionnaire

We ask all our authors to complete this form (typewritten if possible), as the information we seek will help us considerably to market your book successfully.

Because of the wide range of our list and our publishing activities the form has to be comprehensive in its scope but, naturally, we do not expect every author to answer every question. We do ask, however, that you answer as fully as possible all those sections relevant to your book.

Please do not be over-modest about yourself or your work, or reluctant to 'run on', and answer on a separate sheet if necessary. Effective promotion and sales result only from full and accurate information. We shall be most grateful for your help.

The manuscript
Please give a brief description of your book/series. This should indicate the importance or topicality of the subject and aims of the book/series. Please add a summary of its contents, emphasising salient features.

Specialist origins
Does this work aim to follow the recommendations of any particular committee report or research project? If so, which?

Competition
Please indicate the chief features which differentiate your book from its main competitors, which should be listed with the names of their publishers.

The market

(a) What is the main market of the book/series? In the case of a school/technical book indicate the type of school, college, university, age group and ability level for which it is suitable, mentioning any examination for which it is specifically designed, or for which it might be useful.

1. United Kingdom
2. Commonwealth
3. Elsewhere

(b) What subsidiary markets might also be interested?
1. United Kingdom
2. Commonwealth
3. Elsewhere

(c) Suggested review list. Please list separately any newspapers or periodicals which you think might be interested in reviewing your book.

Sales promotion, publicity and reviews

(a) Please list any contacts among professional bodies, the press, radio and television, booksellers, reviewers, or other individuals of influence to whom a copy of the book could be usefully sent.

(b) Can you, or any of your contacts, provide us with membership lists of organisations which we might circularise?

Yourself

(a) We should appreciate any biographical details which you think might be useful.

(b) Please list your other published works (books, articles etc), works in preparation and contribution to television, radio, lecturing etc.

Signature   Date

NB: This is a condensed version of the Kogan Page form. The original allows ample space for writing.

Appendix 3

Proof-reader's Marks

It is important when marking up copy for setting or checking proofs that the standard correction symbols are used. The following are reproduced with the permission of BSI. Complete copies of their leaflets (BS 5261) can be obtained by post from:

BSI Sales
Linford Wood
Milton Keynes
MK14 6LE

Classified list of marks (Table 1 from BS 5261: Part 2)
NOTE: The letters M and P in the notes column indicate marks for marking-up copy and for correcting proofs respectively.

Instruction	Textual mark	Marginal mark	Notes
Correction is concluded	None	/	P Make after each correction
Leave unchanged	- - - - - - under characters to remain	(√)	M P
Remove extraneous marks	Encircle marks to be removed	X	P e.g film or paper edges visible between lines on bromide or diazo proofs
Insert in text the matter indicated in the margin	⋏	New matter followed by ⋏	M P
Delete	/ through character(s) or ⊢——————⊣ through words to be deleted	⌀	M P

Instruction	Textual mark	Marginal mark	Notes
Delete and close up	⌒ through character or ⊢———⊣ through character e g chara ̸cter chara ̶d̶cter	⌒	M P
Wrong fount Replace by character(s) of correct fount	Encircle character(s) to be changed	⊗	P
Set in or change to italic	——— under character(s) to be set or changed	⊔	M P Where space does not permit textual marks encircle the affected area instead
Set in or change to capital letters	≡ under character(s) to be set or changed	≡	
Set in or change to bold type	∼∼∼∼ under character(s) to be set or changed	∼	
Change capital letters to lower case letters	Encircle character(s) to be changed	≠	P
Substitute or insert character in 'superior' position	/ through character or ∧ where required	� under character e.g ⅔	P
Substitute or insert full stop or decimal point	/ through character or ∧ where required	⊙	M P
Substitute or insert semi-colon	/ through character or ∧ where required	;	M P

338

Instruction	Textual mark	Marginal mark	Notes
Substitute or insert comma	/ through character or ⋏ where required	,	M P
Substitute or insert ellipsis	/ through character or ⋏ where required	⋯	M P
Start new paragraph			M P
Run on (no new paragraph)			M P
Transpose characters or words	between characters or words, numbered when necessary		M P
Centre	⌐enclosing matter to be centred⌐	[ ]	M P
Indent			P Give the amount of the indent in the marginal mark
Cancel indent			P
Move matter specified distance to the right	enclosing matter to be moved to the right →		P Give the exact dimensions when necessary
Raise matter	↑ over matter to be raised under matter to be raised		P Give the exact dimensions when necessary

Instruction	Textual mark	Marginal mark	Notes
Lower matter	over matter to be lowered / under matter to be lowered		P Give the exact dimensions when necessary
Close up. Delete space between characters or words	linking characters		M P

Appendix 4

Useful Addresses and Telephone Numbers

Publishing in general

Book Trust
Book House
45 East Hill
London SW18 2QZ
Tel: (020) 8516 2977
Fax: (020) 8516 2978
http://dspace.dial.pipex.com/booktrust

Book Trust Scotland
The Scottish Book Centre
Fountainbridge Library
137 Dundee Street
Edinburgh EH11 1BG
Tel: (0131) 229 3663
Fax: (0131) 228 4293
Executive Director: Lindsey Fraser

Book Trust (formed 1986) is the continuation of the National Book League, originally founded in the mid 1920s. Book Trust continues the League's aims of promoting books and reading to people from all ages and cultures, now under siege from a variety of other more technological entertainments. To this end it provides an extensive book information service, administers nine literary prizes (including the Booker Prize), prepares book guides and exhibitions, carries out research on aspects of reading, and plays an important role as a pressure group for the publishing industry.

Also run from Book Trust is Young Book Trust, established to emphasise the importance of reading to government, education, parents and children. It administers National Children's Book Week (1999 is its 23rd year), a reference library, a database on children's books and an information centre on all aspects of children's reading.

The Publishers Association
1 Kingsway
London WC2B 6XF
Tel: (020) 7565 7474
Fax: (020) 7836 4543
http://www.publisher.org.uk
The trade association of UK publishers.

International Publishers Association
Avenue de Miremont 3
CH 1206
Geneva
Switzerland
Tel: (00 41) 22 463018
Fax: (00 41) 22 475717

The Booksellers Association of Great Britain and Ireland
Minster House
272–74 Vauxhall Bridge Road
London SW1V 1BA
Tel: (020) 7834 5477
Fax: (020) 7834 8812
www.booksellers.org.uk
The trade association for over 3,300 member bookshops selling new books.

International Booksellers Federation and European Booksellers Federation
34a rue du Grande Hospice B-1000 Bruxelles, Belgium
Tel: (00 32) 2 223 49 40
Fax: (00 32) 2 223 49 41
e-mail: eurobooks@skynet.be
www.ebf-eu.org

J Whitaker and Sons Ltd
12 Dyott Street London WC1A 2DF
Tel: (020) 7420 6000
Fax: (020) 7420 6191
www.thebookseller.com

As well as producing the *Bookseller*, Whitaker's editorial department produces a complete list of all titles published in the UK. Publishers are supplied with standard forms and these are returned free of charge; booksellers and libraries pay to access the system in a variety of different formats:

1. Five-volume directory: *Whitaker's Books in Print* produced annually.
2. Monthly list available on CD ROM.
3. Monthly and annual list available on microfiche.
4. Weekly list on microfiche: *New and Forthcoming Books*.
5. Weekly list in the back pages of the *Bookseller*: Publications of the Week.

Whitaker Book Track provides market research on the book business.

British Council: Publishing Promotion Unit
Bridgewater House
58 Whitworth Street
Manchester M1 6BB
Tel: (0161) 957 7182
Fax: (0161) 957 7168
www.britishcouncil.org
Head of Unit: Valerie Teague

One of the many activities of the British Council is to promote British books abroad. Each year the Council takes exhibition space at over 100 events; they display sample copies of books sent to them by publishers. The Council makes the selection of what to take but there is no charge to publishers for this service.

The 200 British Council offices worldwide also function as a very useful first port of call for publishers' representatives seeking to establish relations in a country. They can provide invaluable local information on the market, bookshops, important considerations, interests and much more.

British Trade International
Export Services Directorate
Kingsgate House
66–74 Victoria Street
London SW1E 6SW
General Information Point: (020) 7215 2400
Fax: (020) 7215 2424
www.dti.gov.uk/ots/tfairdatabase

Provide financial support for companies wishing to participate in overseas events such as exhibitions and seminars as part of the British Trade International representation. For more information ring the general telephone number above and ask for the person dealing with the country you are interested in.

Book Marketing Limited
7a Bedford Square
London WC1B 3RA
Tel: (020) 7580 7282
Fax: (020) 7580 7236
e-mail: bml@bookmarketing.co.uk
Managing Director: Jo Henry

Originally the Book Marketing Council of the Publishers Association, BML began operating as a private company in 1990, providing research and information on and to the book trade and other interested parties.

Besides running the unique, continuous survey into consumer buying, *Books and the Consumer*, and conducting a whole range of *ad hoc* research projects on all aspects of book publishing and selling, BML also publish market reports, including the annual compendium of book trade data, *Book Facts*.

Book Watch
15-up East Street
Lewin's Yard
Chesham
Bucks HP5 1HQ
Tel: (01494) 792269
Fax: (01494) 784850

Book Data
Northumberland House
2 King Street
Twickenham
TW1 3RZ
Tel: (020) 8843 8600

Independent Publishers' Guild
Sheila Bounford
4 Middle Street
Great Gransden
Sandy
Beds
SG19 3AD
Tel: (01767) 677753
www.ipg.uk.com

Started in 1962 for mutual help between independently owned
publishers. Organises regular meetings and attends trade fairs with
members' books.

The Society of Young Publishers (SYP)
c/o J Whitaker and Sons Ltd
(as above)

Organises monthly meetings for members of the book trade under
35, and now includes printers, librarians, booksellers and members
of other related organisations as well as publishers. Publishes a
monthly newsletter *Imprint*, holds an annual conference and study
visits.

Women in Publishing
c/o J Whitaker and Sons Ltd
(as above)

Regular meetings for women working in the publishing industry:
the second Wednesday of each month; 6.30 for 7.00 at the
Publishers Association.

Training for publishers

The Publishing Training Centre at Book House
45 East Hill
Wandsworth
London SW18 2QZ
Tel: (020) 8874 2718/4608
Fax: (020) 8870 8985
http://train4publishing.co.uk
Chief Executive: Dag Smith

A variety of courses for publishers lasting between one and five days.
    A complete list of publishing courses in Higher Education is also available free of charge from this address.

Courses are also run by Women in Publishing, Oxford Women in Publishing and the NUJ; details are circulated to members or see the jobs section of the *Bookseller*.

Advertising

Advertising Standards Authority and Committee of Advertising Practice
Brook House 2-6 Torrington Place
London WC1E 7HN
Tel: (020) 7580 5555
Fax: (020) 7631 3051
www.asa@org.uk

This organisation should approve all campaigns before they appear. They administer the British Code of Advertising Practice and are the people you complain to about advertisements you don't consider legal, decent, honest and truthful.

Institute of Sales Promotion
Arena House
66–68 Pentonville Road
London N1 9HS
Tel: (020) 7837 5340
Fax: (020) 7837 5326
www.isp.org.uk

Trade magazines

Books for Keeps
6 Brightfield Road
Lee
London
SE12 8QF
Tel: (020) 8852 4953
Fax: (020) 8318 7580
Editor: Rosemary Stones

Carousel, The Guide to Children's Books
7 Carrs Lane
Birmingham B4 7TQ
Tel: (0121) 643 6411
Fax: (0121) 643 3152
Editor: Jenny Blanch

Books in the Media
Book Watch Ltd
(see above)
Editor: Peter Harland

Books Magazine
39 Store Street
London WC1E 3DB
Tel: (020) 7692 2900
Fax: (020) 7491 2111
Editor: Liz Thomson

The Bookseller
see page 343
Editor: Nicholas Clee

Grocer Magazine (CTN section)
William Reed Publications Ltd
Broadfield Park
Crawley
West Sussex RH11 9RT
Tel: (01293) 613400
Fax: (01293) 610333
Editor: Clive Beddall

Publishing News
Same address as *Books Magazine*
Tel: (020) 7692 2900
Fax: (020) 7491 2111
Editor: Rodney Burbeck
www.publishingnews.co.uk

The School Librarian
The School Library Association
Liden Library
Barrington Close
Liden
Swindon SN3 6HP
Tel: (01793) 617838
Fax: (01793) 537374
Editor: Ray Lonsdale

Signal (in-depth look at children's books in a literary, educational and historical context)
Thimble Press
Station Road
South Woodchester
Stroud, Gloucestershire
GS5 5EQ
Tel: (01453) 873716
Fax: (01453) 878599
Editor: Nancy Chambers

Chapter 2: Marketing in Publishing: Planning for Effective Promotion

Romeike & Curtice
Hale House, Palmers Green
290–296 Green Lanes
London N13 5TP
Tel: (020) 8882 0155
Fax: (020) 8882 6716

Chapter 5: The Design and Print of Promotional Material

The Society of Freelance Editors and Proof-readers
Mermaid House
Mermaid Court
London
SE7 1HR
Tel: (020) 7403 5141
Fax: (020) 7407 1193
e-mail: admin@sfep.demon.co.uk

The SFEP promotes high editorial standards and the professional status of its members. The benefits of membership include a monthly newsletter, reduced rates for SFEP training courses, an annual conference and the opportunity to take an entry in the annual *Directory of Members' Services*. For more information send a stamped addressed envelope to the above address.

Association of Print and Packaging Buyers
311 Blackfriars Foundry
156 Blackfriars Road
London SE1 8EN
Tel: (020) 7721 8530
Fax: (020) 7721 7347

An association of buyers providing technical advice, help with finding printers and general industry know how.

British Printing Industries Federation
11 Bedford Row
London WC1R 4DX
Tel: (020) 7242 6904
Fax: (020) 7405 7784
www.bpif.org.uk

Membership is by company; benefits on offer include advice to print buyers on sourcing printers and on specific jobs. Produce a regular guide to suppliers, the *Print Buyer's Directory*.

British Promotional Merchandise Association
Suite 12, 4th Floor
Parkway House
Sheen Lane
London SW14 8LS
Tel: (020) 8878 0738
Fax: (020) 8878 1053

Help with sourcing printers who can handle specialised jobs.

Pira International
Randalls Road
Leatherhead
Surrey KT22 7RU
Tel: (01372) 802000
Fax: (01372) 802238

An independent research and consultancy service to the printing,
packaging, paper and publishing industries.

Chapter 6: Direct Marketing

The Direct Marketing Association UK (DMA UK)
Haymarket House
1 Oxenden Street
London SW1Y 4EE
Tel: (020) 7321 2525
Fax: (020) 7321 0191
hwww.dma.org.uk

Formed in April 1992 by the amalgamation of the Association of
Mail Order Publishers, The British Direct Marketing Association,
the British List Brokers Association and the Direct Mail Producers
Association. The intention was to provide a single voice to represent
and promote the needs of the UK's direct marketers.

European Direct Marketing Association (EDMA)
Rue du gouvernement provisoire, 36
1,000 Brussels
Tel: (00 32) 2 217 6309
Fax: (00 32) 2 217 6985

The Institute of Direct Marketing
1 Park Road
Teddington
Middlesex TW11 OAR
Tel: (020) 8977 5705
Fax: (020) 8943 2535
www.theidm.com
A professional body solely for individual direct marketing practitioners.

The Direct Mail Information Service
5 Carlisle Street
London W1V 5RG
Tel: (020) 7494 0483
Fax: (020) 7494 0455
www.dmis.co.uk
e-mail: jo.howard-brown@virgin.net

The source of official statistics on direct mail. It also provides the advertising industry, trade and national press with regular reports and updates on major trends and relevant issues within the direct mail industry. Now run for the Royal Mail by the HBH Partnership who also offer direct marketing consultancy.

Mailing Preference Service
Freepost 22
London W1E 7EZ

Mail Order Traders Association
40 Waterloo Road
Birkdale
Southport PR8 2NG
Tel: (01704) 563787
Fax: (01704) 563787

Data Protection Registrar
Wycliffe House
Water Lane
Wilmslow
Cheshire SK9 5AX
Tel: (01625) 545745
Fax: (01625) 524510

Royal Mail Customer Service Centre
(0345) 950950

This central number covers 9 regional centres and you will be connected to the one nearest you. All calls to this number are charged at local rate.

IBIS Worldwide Academic and Library File
Mardev Ltd
Quadrant House
The Quadrant
Sutton
Surrey
SM2 5AS
Tel: (020) 8643 0955
Fax: (020) 8652 4580
e-mail: mardevlists@rbi.co.uk

KPA Business Lists Ltd
Unit 8
Rainbow Estate
Trout Road
West Drayton
Middlesex UB7 7XE
Tel: (01895) 444200
Fax: (01895) 447493

The Wyvern Business Library Ltd
Wyvern House
6 The Business Park
Angel Drove, Ely
Cambs CB7 4JW
Tel: (01353) 665522
Fax: (01353) 667666
www.wyvern.co.uk
e-mail: wyvern@wyvern.co.uk

Chapter 8: 'Free' Advertising

BBC World Service
Bush House
Strand London WC2
Tel: (020) 7240 3456
Fax: (020) 7240 4634 (general news)

The Press Complaints Commission
1 Salisbury Square
London EC4Y 8AE
Tel: (020) 7353 1248
Fax: (020) 7353 8355

PIMS (UK) Ltd
PIMS House
Mildmay Avenue
London N1 4RS
Tel: (020) 7226 1000
Fax: (020) 7704 1360

The Press Association
292 Vauxhall Bridge Road
London SW1V 1AE
Tel: (020) 7963 7000
Fax: (020) 7963 7594
http://pa.pres.net

An extensive domestic news agency. Send a copy of a press release on a big story to the news desk and it may end up being circulated to regional papers all over the country. There is no fee but no guarantee the material sent will be used (same applies to Reuters).

Reuters
85 Fleet Street
London
EC4P 4AJ
Tel: (020) 7250 1122
Fax: (020) 7542 7921

Reuters are an international news agency; the London office receives overseas stories for distribution in this country.

PR Newswide Europe
210 Old Street
London EC1V 9BR
Tel: (020) 7490 8111
Fax: (020) 7490 1255

This is the commercial arm of the Press Association (formerly Universal News Services). Send them a copy of your press release and they will (for a fee) circulate to news rooms in Britain (you specify where) and overseas (due to affiliations with other news associations). The client retains control of how the story is presented in the release.

For further details of press cuttings agencies, newspapers and other related services consult the latest edition of the *Writers and Artists Yearbook* (A&C Black).

Chapter 9: Paid Advertisements and Organising Promotions

Mail Order Protection Scheme
Newspaper Publishers Association Ltd
16 Took's Court
London EC4A 1LB

Display advertisements in national newspapers that ask for money in advance must conform to the scheme. For full details send a stamped addressed envelope to the above address.

Chapter 10: Organising Events

Arts and Business (formerly The Association for Business Sponsorship of the Arts)
Nutmeg House
60 Gainsford Street
Butler's Wharf
London SE1 2NY
Tel: (020) 7378 8143
Fax: (020) 7407 7527

Chapter 12: Approaching Specific Interest Markets

Selling books to public libraries

Department of Culture, Media and Sport
2 Cockspur Street
London SW1Y 5DH
Tel: (020) 7211 6387/6497/6200
Fax: (020) 7211 6210
www.culture.gov.uk

The Library Association
7 Ridgemount Street
London WC1E 7AE
Tel: (020) 7636 7543
Fax: (020) 7436 7218
www.la_hq.org.uk

The professional association for librarians, the LA holds professional
examinations, meetings and promotes information on librarianship.

National Acquisitions Group (NAG)
Lime House
Poolside
Madeley
Crewe
Cheshire CW3 9DX
Tel: (01782) 750462

Public Lending Right
Bayheath House
Prince Regent Street
Stockton on Tees,
Cleveland TS18 1DF
Tel: (01642) 604699
Fax: (01642) 615641
www.earl.org.uk/partners/plr/index.html
e-mail: registrar@plr.octagon.co.uk
Registrar: James Parker

Selling to educational markets

Chartered Institute of Public Finance and Accountancy (CIPFA)
3 Robert Street
London WC2N 6BH
Tel: (020) 7543 5600
Fax: (020) 7543 5700

Selling periodical and serial publications

Association of Subscription Agents
Honorary Secretary: John Merriman
Thames Gardens
Charlbury
Oxford OX7 3QH

UK Serials Group
114 Woodstock Road
Witney
Oxon
Tel: (01993) 703466
Fax: (01993) 778879
Business Manager: Mrs Jill Tolson

North American Serials Interest Group Inc (NASIG)
2103 North Dacatur Road, 24
Dacatur
GA-30033
USA
www.nasig.org

Marketing children's books

National Centre for Research in Children's Literature
Roehampton Institute
Digby Stuart College
Roehampton Lane
London SW15 5PH
Tel: (020) 8392 3000
Fax: (020) 8392 3031
e-mail: NCRCL@roehampton.ac.uk
Director: Dr Kimberley Reynolds

The Children's Book Circle

An informal group of interest to anyone who works in children's book publishing, in whatever job capacity. For details of the current Membership Secretary please contact Young Book Trust.

Appendix 5

Bibliography

A complete list of books relating to the publishing industry is available, free of charge, from Book Publishing Books, The Publishing Training Centre at Book House, 45 East Hill, Wandsworth, London SW18 2QZ (tel: 0181 874 2718; fax: 0181 870 8985).

The following references from the text will also be useful:

Are Books Different?, Alison Baverstock (Kogan Page, London, 1993)
The Craft of Copywriting, Alastair Crompton (Arrow, London, 2nd edition, 1993)
Ogilvy on Advertising, David Ogilvy (Prion, London, 1983)

On the media

Benn's Press Directory Volume 1 is UK, Volume 2 is overseas.
Blue Book of British Broadcasting
PR Planner Produced by Media Information Lrd (part of Romeike and Curtice).
   A subscription service for up-to-date media information. Loose-leaf ring binder
   is supplied with regular updates; labels are available for press release mailings.
Willings Press Guide lists all periodicals in the UK.

Directories

Booksellers' Association Members Directory. Annual.
Cassell and the Publishers Association *Directory of Publishing*. Annual; Cassell.
Directory of Book Publishers and Wholesalers. Annual; Booksellers Association.
Print Buyer's Directory. Annual; The British Printing Industries Federation.
Publishers in UK and their Addresses. Annual; Whitaker.
Ulrich's International Periodicals Directory; available from Bowker-Saur Ltd.
Writers' and Artists' Yearbook. Annual; A&C Black.
Writer's Handbook. Annual; Macmillan.

Index

NB: numbers in *italics* indicate figures, tables or illustrations